THE JESUS CONSPIRACY

THE JESUS CONSPIRACY

AN INVESTIGATIVE REPORTER'S LOOK AT AN EXTRAORDINARY LIFE AND DEATH

GORDON THOMAS

BakerBooks
Grand Rapids, Michigan

Published by Baker Books
a division of Baker Publishing Group
P.O. Box 6287, Grand Rapids, MI 49516-6287
www.bakerbooks.com

Paperback edition published 2005
ISBN 0-8010-6532-1

Second printing, February 2005

Printed in the United States of America

The Library of Congress has cataloged the original hardcover edition as follows:
Thomas, Gordon.
[Trial]
The Jesus conspiracy : an investigative reporter's look at an extraordinary life and death / Gordon Thomas.
p. cm.
Originally published: The trial. London : Bantam Press, 1987.
Includes bibliographical references.
ISBN 0-8010-1194-9 (cloth)
1. Jesus Christ—Trial. 2. Jesus Christ—Passion. I. Title.
BT440.T46 2000
232.96'2—dc21 99-048307

To Joachim Kraner
A friend who became a father-in-law
yet remained a friend

Many years ago we spoke, among other things, of books. In your forthright way you said none could equal the Bible. In some embarrassment I admitted to having hardly looked at a copy since my school days. You urged me to correct the situation, adding that one of the unspoken tragedies of our times is that Bible reading is largely a pleasure of the past. The next day I purchased a Bible.

Though you are physically no longer with us, the Bible remains a reminder of you as well as being a continuous reading experience. Itself unsurpassed literature, my Bible has led me into many scriptural byways—which finally brought me to tell the story in these pages. It deals with the most momentous event in history, one which you also said is the greatest challenge any writer can face: to understand the form of his life insomuch as it shows us all how to live, not for a few years, but forever.

In recounting it faithfully and reverently, I have the support of the one person you surely would have approved of as a collaborator—your daughter, Edith. Like you, she has a questing mind coupled to the faith of true belief but is concerned with neither clever explanation for the inexplicable nor attempting to interpret what defies interpretation.

The trial of Jesus is the most interesting isolated problem which historical jurisprudence can present.

—A. T. Innes
The Trial of Jesus Christ:
A Legal Monograph

You may object that it is not a trial at all; you are quite right, for it is only a trial if I recognize it as such.

—Franz Kafka
The Trial, 11, "First Interrogation"

The historical question about the responsibility for Jesus' death is still wide open. There is in any case very wide agreement that there existed a religious issue between Jesus and his own people which went far deeper than an attack on the collaborating priestly aristocracy; that he brought a theological challenge of the most fundamental kind, making claims for himself, whether directly or indirectly, which were either true or false, and if false demanded his condemnation and death.

—J. P. M. Sweet
Jesus and the Politics of His Day
(edited by Ernest Mabbek and C. F. D. Moule)

CONTENTS

IN SEARCH OF CHRIST

I am the pause between two notes that fall,
Into a real accordance scarce at all:
For Death's note tends to dominate—
Both, though, are reconciled in the dark interval tremblingly.
And the son remains immaculate.

R. M. Rilke, *The Book of Hours,* 1

INTRODUCTION
Towards Understanding

What is truth? Said jesting Pilate; and would not stay for an answer.

Francis Bacon, *Of Truth*

Jesus once asked his disciples: "Whom do men say that I am?" According to the Gospel of Matthew, their responses were varied: "Some say John the Baptist, others Elijah . . . or one of the prophets." Even among those who had known him firsthand, there was little consensus over the identity of the enigmatic preacher from Galilee.

Almost twenty-five years since I first began to research this book, the controversy continues. When it was first published under the title of *The Trial*, I was gratified for the general consensus that the book, though in some ways profoundly controversial in its conclusions, was a genuine attempt at clarification by someone who had developed an early interest in the mysteries of faith, and who found the origins of Christianity of abiding fascination.

There were, I suppose inevitably, some who challenged my right to join the debate. There was the morning I sat in a Dublin national radio studio listening to the ire of a Catholic priest, who kept insisting "the question of Jesus is not one for a layperson."

Views like that, I gently suggested, may well be contributing to a decline in church attendance. That priest saw it as a "failure" that I came to my study of Jesus without a presupposed theological position. He had no interest that I was writing from within the Christian tradition, or that I was driven to write what I have because of an inward necessity. Yet trying to debate with him was not entirely a waste of time: it expanded my horizons, sharpened my vision, and made me realize I must continue to monitor the debate about Jesus that centers on the question: "Whom do men say that I am?"

The controversy surrounding Jesus' life on earth continues with ferocious vigor, and has now prompted me to revise the original text and to republish it under a new title. *The Jesus Conspiracy* is, I believe, in accordance with the temper of our times. In biblical research there is no greater truth than there is nothing permanent except change itself.

Today one of the many questions about the earthly life of Jesus focuses on how deeply Jesus was involved in his nation's cause against Rome: was he a revolutionary, even a fanatic? Certainly, both Judas Iscariot and Simon the Zealot come from that background. When they answered Jesus' call—"Come, follow me"—did they also abandon their old lifestyle? On balance, probably not. Their special talents as guerrilla fighters would certainly have been useful at a time of ruthless oppression by Roman occupiers of Judea.

Again there can be no disagreement that Jesus, from the very outset of his ministry, began to prepare people for the coming of great events. Instead of being like any other rabbi ministering only to a local community, he quickly became a figure attracting considerable crowds, first throughout Galilee and then nationally, when he went to Jerusalem in the closing days of his career. From that it is not unreasonable to deduce Jesus saw his role as someone with a mission to the Jewish nation as a whole. Why else would he constantly travel, exhorting people to be aware that "the time is fulfilled, and the kingdom of God is at hand: repent ye and believe in the gospel."

Again, in his deliberate decision to form a small commune—his immediate disciples—he was following the long-established pattern of such prophets as Elijah and Elisha. They were political figures. Was Jesus cast in the same mold? Is that why in parable after parable he drives home the same points with what can justifiably be called apocalyptic fervor: that the coming of the kingdom of God will be sudden and that only those who have prepared themselves to receive it will not perish? Is this not the preaching of a man whose message is urgent? Can it be said to be only doctrinal, only the words of someone who is trying to found a new religion, who is only concerned with advocating new moral attitudes and spiritual insights?

All we can say without contradiction is that, for a short period in Jewish history, Jesus was the sole hope of a great number, perhaps even the majority, of the Jewish people. How many of them were attracted by the daring of Jesus' claims, by the sheer charisma of his personality, by the power of his miracles—and by the prospect that here was someone who could lead them to lift the yoke of Roman occupation? How many were deeply disappointed when he failed to launch violent rebellion? How many turned against him for that very reason?

The question of how Jesus saw himself is one of the most disputed of all New Testament controversies. The great difficulty is that Jesus left no firsthand record: he wrote nothing down. Those who subsequently did set down his words appeared to have been primarily concerned to make him out to be a religious reformer rejected by his own race. But supposing Jesus had been a high-minded revolutionary in the way that term can be applied to George Washington? Ultimately what difference should that make in our assessment of him? He lived at a time of religious fanaticism and his people remain fervent in their religious beliefs; even the creeping secularism that confronts Israel today has not loosened its people's ties with faith.

Nor should we forget that Jesus was born, raised and died a Jew. It is one of many ironies that the Jesus on the cross, who is the most potent symbol of Christian faith, wears a cloth that covers his loins. It is not propriety but theology that is responsible for modesty. The loincloth hides the essential Jewishness of Jesus, the knife mark in the flesh of his circumcision.

From this other questions, uncomfortable questions, must still be asked, and have still to be answered. If Jesus on the cross had been a visible constant reminder that he was a Jew, would Christians down the centuries have carried out all those pogroms against his fellow Jews? Did Hitler, even for a moment, hesitate when he wrote of Jesus in *Mein Kampf* as, "the Great Founder of this new creed"? Did he stop thinking that Jesus was also a Jew? Why did Hitler, when he decreed every Jew over the age of six in the Third Reich must, under penalty of death, wear the yellow Star of David, not also insist a similar mark of shame should be pinned on the loincloth of every crucified Christ on display on effigies in the churches of Nazi Germany? And suppose Jesus had appeared as he really had died on the cross—naked, like all the other thousands who met such a fate under the Roman occupation—would the German bishops and Pope Pius XII have remained mute? Indifferent? It is a matter of interpretation—if they were constantly reminded of the antecedent of their crucified Son of God.

It would be fifteen long years after the Holocaust before a pope, the compassionate and enlightened John XXIII, would compose one of the most moving prayers since the words of the Lord's Prayer.

> The mark of Cain is stamped upon our foreheads. Across the centuries, our brother, Abel, has lain in blood which we drew, and shed tears we caused by forgetting thy love. Forgive us, Lord, for the curse we falsely attributed to their name as Jews. Forgive us for crucifying thee a second time in their flesh. For we knew not what we did.

In those words of the Supreme Pontiff we can discern more than atonement. We can sense the need to judge Jesus only by reference to his time and place in earth. The Jews of his time were primarily concerned with winning their freedom. There is nothing written that presents Jesus as other than a normal Jew: a man completely in tune with the religious and nationalistic aspirations of his own people.

And, whatever else remains under challenge about Jesus, there is one inescapable truth. His essential teaching remains.

There are those who say that Jesus taught nothing that was new; that his ideas were drawn from contemporary Jewish thought, from the very literature and traditions of his own people. There is truth in that. Jesus' admonition, "Do unto others as you would they should do unto you," is remarkably similar to the Golden Rule pronounced by the great Jewish scholar, Rabbi Hillel, who taught: "That which is to thee hateful, do not to thy neighbor." Again the ancient Jewish proverb—"whenever thou are merciful, God is merciful to thee," is repeated by Jesus as "Blessed are the merciful for they shall attain mercy." Again, Judaism's "God loves him who is pure in heart," is offered by Jesus as "Blessed are the pure in heart for they shall see God."

Jesus may indeed not have said anything new. He only said it better.

But was Jesus a revolutionary as we know the word? The question can best be answered by saying he was certainly charged, prosecuted and condemned as one. The accident of his being born in Galilee at a time when that province was regarded by Rome as the very center of the Jewish resistance, was a powerful contributing factor. Automatically Jesus came to the notice of the authorities by his radical preaching, a political suspect and, when he began to preach more widely, also a religious one.

While believers down the ages continue to echo Peter's faith-filled declaration—"you are the Christ, the son of the living God"—the quest for the so-called "historical" Jesus today roils the consciences of academics in a way not seen since the American Protestant schisms of the 1920s. As we approach the uncertainty of a new millennium, we can be certain that the iconoclastic and liberal biblical scholars will continue to find more radical ways to promote their views.

Typical was the controversy ignited during Easter 1996, by those who were once seen by many as bastions of the English establishment. The BBC and *The Sunday Times* announced that ossuaries bearing the names of Joseph, Mary and Jesus had been found in a family tomb in Jerusalem in 1980. Quite why it had taken so long for the news to surface was lost in what was trumpeted as a truly faith-shattering "discovery." The initial broadside of publicity implied Jesus was not only the son of man, but a father himself.

The Sunday Times wanted its readers to be quite certain of the implication: "if the burial caskets, known as ossuaries, contain the remains of Christ and his family, they would cast doubt on the Christian belief central to Easter: the Resurrection." The newspaper quoted Keith Ward, professor of divinity at Oxford, who said that if the report was validated, he would cease to be a Christian, "because to me that would invalidate the testimony of the apostles, and without that I wouldn't believe Jesus was of any particular importance."

By Easter Monday the BBC's account of the "discovery" had been dismissed as "absurd." The archaeologist, L. Y. Rahmani, who has catalogued almost all the one thousand ossuaries found in Israel, noted that the names Joseph, Mary and Jesus were common in antiquity and that some ten ossuaries bearing the name of Jesus, whether of Hebrew or Greek variations, have been found over the years. Variations of Miriam, from which Mary is derived, and Joseph are even more plentiful. Rahmani reassured Christians that, despite the BBC, they had no reason not to remain firm in their faith that the burial of Jesus was of limited duration.

Christological chatter continued to attack the Bible's traditional authority—insisting this is the only way for "a more rational basis for belief and a clearer essence of Jesus' teachings." At the core of the claim is the assumption it is possible to improve upon the words and images of Jesus in the Gospels. The issue has now achieved a kind of religious critical-mass that pervades even the Internet.

The revisionists are driven by the need, in the words of one, "to set Jesus free from the scriptural and creedal prisons in which we have entombed him. It is time to reinvent Christianity, complete with new symbols, new stories and a new understanding of Jesus." The words are those of Robert Funk who taught Biblical Studies at, among other places, Harvard. He claims that no more than twenty percent of the sayings, and even fewer of the deeds, attributed to Jesus are authentic. The Lord's Prayer, Jesus' words on the cross, any claims of Jesus to divinity, the virgin birth, most of his miracles and his bodily resurrection: all should be rejected.

This is very much in keeping with the redefinement of Jesus, the man, beginning with his virtually unknown life for about thirty years in the insignificant town of Nazareth. He was apparently so like his uneducated relatives that the townspeople who knew him were astonished when Jesus suddenly began his ministry.

His bemused neighbors are quoted as saying at the time: "This is the carpenter's son, surely. Is he not the son of the woman called Mary, and the brother of James and Joseph and Simon and Jude? His sisters, too, are they not all here with us?" (Matt. 13:55–56). And there is Mark reporting: "They would not accept him" (Mark 6:4). So great was the feeling in Nazareth that this son of a carpenter had no place doing what he was now doing, preaching, that they expelled Jesus from their synagogue (Luke

4:28). And when he persisted in continuing with his ministry, his family "set out to take charge of him, convinced he was out of his mind" (Mark 3:20–21).

Only much later, when Jesus had consolidated his position as a preacher throughout Galilee, did his family see the advantages of his fame. "His mother and brothers now arrived and, standing outside, sent in a message asking for him. A crowd was sitting round at the time the message was passed to him. 'Your mother and brothers and sisters are outside asking for you.' Jesus replied, 'Who are my brothers and sisters?' And looking at those seated in a circle around him, he said, 'Here are my mother and my brothers. Anyone who does the will of God, that person is my brother and sister and mother'" (Mark 3:32–35).

From this fragment of human biography, the revisionists argue that Jesus never really said who he was. When John the Baptist asked Jesus, through his disciples, "Are you the one who is to come, or have we to look for another?" Jesus sent a message, "Go back and tell John what you hear and see; the blind see again, and the lame walk, lepers are cleansed, the deaf hear" (Matt. 11:3–4).

But that was all Jesus said. Even in response to Peter's question, "You are the Christ?" Jesus gave them "strict orders not to tell anyone" (Mark 8:30). All this, say the revisionists, only confirms the doubts that Robert Funk has articulated.

Understandably the traditionalists fulminate against what they see as heresy in which matters of fundamental importance are being distorted. Against their traditionalism crashes a tidal wave of relentless claims. Surprisingly some of them are made from within the very bastion of traditional faith, the Roman Catholic Church.

Typical are those made by John Meir, a biblical scholar at the Catholic University of America in Washington, D.C. Along with many of his academic colleagues, Meir argues that the New Testament Gospels have a limited value as historical records, but what information they do contain enables a number of conclusions to be made: that Jesus was born in Nazareth, not in Bethlehem; that Jesus had four brothers and at least two sisters; that the virgin birth "cannot be proven or disproven." Meir concedes that you cannot mix theology and historical research without causing tremendous confusion.

Equally vehement in his rejection of the conventional Jesus are the views of Dominic Crossan, a former professor emeritus at St. Paul University in Chicago. Born and raised in Ireland, Crossan sees himself as "Catholic through and through," despite revising some of the core teachings of Rome. He perceives Jesus as preaching "God's radical justice" and living by this concept so totally that if the true clarity of his life and message could be grasped today, the world would be a better place.

By using modern sociological and anthropological studies of Palestine at the time of Jesus, Crossan argues that the evidence he has interpreted within the Gospels, together with other noncanonical texts from the early Church, means we should reject some of the most important teachings of Christianity. The Last Supper and the appearance before the disciples of the risen Jesus, argues Crossan, are no more than attempts by them to express their "continued experience" of his presence after the crucifixion.

It has been left to another Roman Catholic, Luke Johnson, a professor of New Testament and Christian origins at Emory University in Atlanta, to lead the charge for the traditionalists. Religious knowledge is not the same as historical knowledge, he says; the faith of most Christians is a matter of bearing witness to the Holy Spirit in their present-day lives. Johnson argues that the four Gospels, together with the letters of Paul, do offer a credible history of Jesus' life and ministry, including some firsthand accounts. Those may indeed be patchy, but they do show that Jesus was a Jew who preached love and selflessness and was tried under Pontius Pilate, crucified and later appeared before witnesses who went on to dedicate themselves to spreading the Word. In Britain this comforting assessment for the faithful has been buttressed by two distinguished scholars, James D. G. Dunn and N. T. Wright.

All three argue that while it is interesting to examine the social, political, anthropological and cultural life and times of Jesus, that is hardly the point of Scripture. The point, of course, is that many Christians do find blasphemous the idea of making a distinction between the Jesus they pray to, and someone called "the Jesus of history." In the United States the ever-expanding fundamentalist and evangelical congregations—who are also increasing their numbers in Britain and even in traditionally Catholic Ireland—maintain that the Gospels, the Acts of the Apostles, and Paul's Epistles are the best history of all: that a believing Christian should no more dare challenge whether Jesus had raised Lazarus from the dead than question his own status as the risen Messiah. For them, the words of Martin Luther, who pioneered Protestantism, that it was sufficient for every Christian to establish his own relationship with Christ simply by reading Scripture, act as a leitmotiv. The very idea of using the precise calibration and cool scepticism of scientific rationalism is anathema for all those who believe that Jesus cannot be subjected to the tools of historical or literary analysis.

In following this theological battle since my original publication, I am struck that while much in religious thinking has changed, certain fundamentals have not.

The birth of Jesus Christ remains the starting point of all real history for more than 1.5 billion Christians. Primarily they worship him as a divine being. Many find it comforting to let it be so. For these devout it is probably of lesser importance that there is a persuasive argument that the four Gospels were not actually written by the apostles, but were more likely authored by their anonymous followers, or even their followers' followers.

The devout prefer to point to yet another discovery which continues to divide the rarefied world of biblical scholarship. Three papyrus snippets have been preserved in the library of Magdalen College, Oxford. The scraps contain passages from chapter 26 of the Gospel according to Matthew. Written in Greek script they were originally bought at the turn of the century by an obscure British chaplain at a market stall in Luxor, Egypt. Conventional wisdom among experts was that the papyrus dated from some time in the middle of the second century A.D.

Then, in 1995, the German papyrologist, Carsten Dieter Thiede, announced that the three scraps actually dated from about A.D. 70. The implications were stunning. It would mean that Matthew's Gospel, as well as Mark's, on which it is generally accepted it is in part based, is not an account separated by some two centuries from the time Jesus walked this earth. Matthew's is actually close to an eyewitness account.

Taking that as his starting point, Thiede argues that all four Gospels were written before A.D. 80; that a scroll fragment discovered at the Essene community of Qumran in 1972 was almost certainly a fragment of Mark's Gospel and can be dated as A.D. 68; that another fragment in a Paris library is part of the Gospel of Luke, and was written between A.D. 63 and 67.

More intriguing still is that Thiede found in three places of the Matthew fragments, the name of Jesus written as KS. This is the abbreviation of the Greek word, Kyrios, or Lord. Thiede argues that the shorthand—KS—is proof that early Christians regarded Jesus a *nomen sacrum*, a sacred name, much in the way devout Jews of the time emphasized the holiness of God's name by shortening it to the tetragrammaton, YHWH. From this Thiede concludes the very idea of Jesus' divinity is not a development of later Christian faith, but was an entrenched belief of the early Church.

Inevitably Thiede has come under severe attack by other experts who challenge both his credentials as a papyrologist and the methods he used to arrive at his conclusions. To which Thiede has replied:

> If the Gospels are more authentic than we thought, then perhaps the gap between the Jesus of history and the Christ of Faith is not so great as academics have claimed, and Christians have feared. For non-believers these findings are not going to force anybody to become a Christian. But the testimony of eyewitnesses of Jesus' generation does make the Gospels more credible, at least as a historical account.

Like so much else in the increasingly superheated arena of current biblical research, Thiede's claims have further fueled the controversy.

Looked at from another standpoint, the Gospels offer only minimal insights into the earthly life of Jesus. The narratives are so featureless that Jesus appears to be moving in a vacuum; there is no glimpse of what his daily life was like, almost nothing about his relations with those he met. And we know almost nothing about them. All too often his parables and sayings appear to hang in the air; even when the symbolic point is clear, their positioning within the Gospels varies significantly from one account of the same incident to another. The fourth Gospel, John's, covers no more than the three public years of Jesus' life; the other three add up to a mere few months. Again, if we calculate the time it would actually have needed for Jesus to deliver all the words attributed to him, we are speaking only of hours; if we add up all the actions attributed to Jesus, they cover no more than a few weeks.

More difficulties emerge. Christ is presented in the Gospels as the quintessence of goodness—yet he arouses a terrible violence that ends in his horrendous death. He is called eternal and divine, yet detailed genealogies not only connect him with the royal house of David, but he has a family who, from time to time, regard him as dangerously delusional. His views on the faith of his mother, Judaism, is conventional, even unexceptional. Jesus seems to be meek, yet claims to have more wisdom than Solomon, and even claims the right to sit on the right hand of God. He condemns the use of invective, yet he constantly attacks his opponents by the same means. Baptism is constantly praised, but we are told that Jesus never baptized anyone himself. Crowds acclaim him one day, reject him the next. When his disciples hail him as the Messiah, he urges them not to do so. If nothing else, the Gospels present puzzles and contradictions which do demand an unshakeable faith.

To all this, the conservative answer is: it happened; don't challenge. The differences between the Gospels are waved aside as "omissions and paraphrases" that were a natural part of the oral culture of the time. Accept that, we are urged, and the portrait of Jesus that the Gospels offer is fundamentally correct.

The truth is, as Geza Vermes, Reader in Jewish Studies at Oxford, has pointed out in his compelling study, *Jesus the Jew*, almost everyone when they read the Gospels does so with preconceived ideas. Christians read them in the light of their faith; Jews do so inured with ancient suspicion; agnostics turn to them ready to be shocked; the professional New Testament experts approach them wearing the blinkers of their trade.

When I first sat down to write this book, I did so in the hope that I had emptied my mind of prejudices and misconceptions, and that I could come to the Gospels as if for the first time. That seemed the only way to deal with my premise that everyone has a Jesus of Nazareth. It still holds true.

There is a Catholic Jesus, a Protestant Jesus and a Jewish Jesus, as well as a Jesus of the Celts, Latins, Greeks, Nordics, Russians and Chinese. There is a Muslim Jesus, a prophet born indeed of a virgin and second only to Mohammed, and the Jesus of Africa, Asia and Latin America—symbol of imperial power that conquered in the name of religion. Colonialism is dead but the memory remains of what that Jesus figure brought: an iron hand carrying the cross; a Jesus figure for whom millions faced violent death, either because they believed, or did not believe. For that crucified figure seas were crossed, continents conquered and empires founded.

Much evil is still done in the name of Jesus by those who claim to preach his word and live by his commandments. Who has not recoiled at the evil of ethnic cleansing in Bosnia? Or the continuing horror committed in the name of Catholic or Protestant bigotry in Northern Ireland which continues to spill over into England with terrible incidents such as the bomb which ripped out the guts of Manchester in June 1996? And who has not felt a sense of despair at the violence that still permeates the very homeland of Jesus?

Every new church since the Reformation has created its own Jesus. So have the atheists and agnostics, the charismatics, the ecumenicists and the Jesus People of all persuasions. Yet increasingly, believers—and for that matter, nonbelievers—grapple with what they can accept about Jesus of Nazareth. They face an increasingly confusing and often contradictory task. It is a sobering statistic that more has been written about Jesus in the past twenty years than in the previous two thousand.

The result of all this outpouring is that the earthly fate of Jesus is no longer used as a crude excuse to vilify Jews. There has been a dramatic reduction in the intense hostility between two religions bound by a common tie which can never be severed. It is accepted that ties to Judaism have always been there in all claims made for the coming of Christ; remove the history and tenets of Judaism out of the New Testament and Christianity will seem to have no purpose. The New Testament, like the Old, will always be with us, and the story in the former will always produce pain, sorrow and anguish for Christians. But the anger against the Jews has been reduced.

In part, this has been due to the bridge-building between Rome and Jerusalem. There are plans, well advanced, for the present pope to visit the Holy Land in the year 2000. On the diplomatic front there has been an exchange of envoys between the Vatican and Israel.

The great stumbling block that was the "gospel truth" for Christians and manifestly not gospel truth for Jews—that the Jews had full responsibility for the crucifixion of Jesus—has been eased, firstly by that wonderfully brave prayer by Pope John, and later by some vigorous scholarship which persuasively argues that many of the harshest passages in the New Testament should be seen as part of an essential propagandizing by the early Christians. This school of reinterpretation claims that Jesus' hostility towards the Jews, as stated in the Gospels, was in reality the feelings of the Gospel writers themselves who had used Jesus to convey the hostility towards the Jews of a later age.

Nevertheless, many Jews remain convinced that the anti-Semitism which has blighted their lives for centuries—the expulsions, the pogroms, culminating in the Holocaust—will linger on until the central theme of the Gospels is also removed: that Jesus was arrested by order of the high priest of the Temple; that he was tried before a Sanhedrin of other priests; that he was handed over to the Roman procurator by the high priest; that he was condemned to crucifixion for claiming to be the King of the Jews. Throughout the entire process, Jews are in the forefront of all the Gospel accounts.

Today it is widely accepted that responsibility for the death of Jesus can be equally laid at the door of the Roman imperial system, and specifically its procurator in Judea, Pontius Pilate. It was the Roman emperor who appointed him; it was Pilate who chose the high priest, Joseph Caiaphas, effectively making him a vassal of Rome. It was the harsh sanctions of the Roman occupation which led to unrest throughout Judea, which bred revolutionaries and produced charismatics.

In a judgment that is hard to challenge, the distinguished Jewish scholar, Ellis Rivkin, professor of Jewish history at Hebrew Union College in Cincinnati, argues that Pilate and Caiaphas were both motivated by two common interests: the preservation of imperial power in the face of any challenge—ensuring the continuance of the high priest's office—and the uninterrupted collection of tribute for Rome's coffers, guaranteeing Pilate's tenure. All else in the story of Jesus and his death would flow from that alliance.

It was Caiaphas and a handful of his priests who set in train the events that would enable them to hand Jesus over to Pilate for execution. They acted not in the name of the Jewish people, but purely from self-interest. From perceived threat to final judgment, Caiaphas and Pilate acted out of personal expediency. Two weak men condemned a strong man to an inhuman death. To otherwise lay that great crime at the collective door of the Jewish people is a calumny that it took Pope John to finally recognize.

And Jesus himself understood this all too clearly. As he hung suspended in agony on his cross—the ultimate symbol of Rome's method of dealing with its enemies—he lifted his head skywards and asked God: "Father, forgive them, for they know not what they do" (Luke 23:34).

The search for new answers to old questions has inevitably accelerated with the approach of the third millennium of the Christian Church. The year 2000 has become an emotive beacon for both theologians and exegetes. By the late 1990s—today—the historical data has been reinterpreted to suggest that Jesus may actually have died on the cross without any intention of ever founding a new religion.

Yet totally convinced that he loves them and they him, hundreds of millions of ordinary people still manage their daily lives in his name. They ask no more than, just as he gave them hope through his own death, that they, in turn, can await their own earthly ending with a certainty no other figure has ever come remotely close to instilling.

Many of these Christians continue to look at the New Testament as their only guide. Yet there are other, equally important scriptural writings. These were once accepted when the Church was young, but subsequently rejected in the formation of doctrine that often grew from intolerance, persecution and bigotry.

While the New Testament can still be read without an understanding of the prevailing political, social and economic portents, a simple and inescapable truth does remain: there must, inevitably, be a limit on how thoroughly the language of Scripture can be fully accepted without a clear grasp of the world in which the Word was written.

It is particularly important in understanding Jesus, the man and his mission, to see him in the context of his times; to try and understand how he and those around him lived—his immediate family; Mary and Martha and their brother, Lazarus, in Bethany; the priests in the Temple; Pontius Pilate and his wife, Claudia Procula; the Jewish aristocracy; the Romans in their fortresses. That understanding requires knowing their lifestyles, their dress and eating habits, their legal systems; it requires re-creating, in all fidelity, the world in which the Word was first preached—and to understand its effect on those who heard it firsthand.

Equally, it is perfectly true that faith does not stand, or fall, on the details of history. God, inspiring individuals, allowed them to write within the framework of their own time, mind and culture. What they created was not—as some churches insist—simply a series of unchallengeable and eternal truths. To promulgate that is to reduce Scripture to little more than theological principles, virtually devoid of the true revelations of God. Instead, Scripture conveys its own unique truth—in the case of the New Testament it can properly be called gospel truth—by mingling parables, anecdotes, deeds, formal statements, laws, miracles, poetry and hymns. The richness of it all is part history, part hagiography, part biography and something else: the message of God's revelation, while indeed founded on fact, does not depend on each precise detail of fact.

That explains why, for example, the Garden Tomb in Jerusalem is not the tomb of Jesus; the pavement in the basement of the convent of the Sisters of Zion in the Old City is not the site mentioned in John 19:13, where Pilate judged Jesus; nor was the Ecce Homo arch spanning the Via Dolorosa built when Christ was presented to the high priest of the Jews and his cohorts with the procurator's cry: "*Ecce homo*—Behold the man." Or was it, "Behold—the Man"?

Yet, pilgrims continue to journey to these sites, filled with a deep longing to be close to where Jesus spent his last days. Religious pilgrimage has bestowed a sanctity which does indeed show that faith does not depend on purely historical fact. May it always be so.

In my writing about Jesus, it is essential for the reader to know what lies behind another attempt to try and explain.

For as long as I can remember I have always wanted to believe. My interest in his life and death began when I was taken as a child to the Holy Land. The map of what was then Palestine became the first I drew and colored: the straight line of the coast, the central mountain range and beyond the River Jordan, all given their hues, from copper to purple, colors which are unforgettable to those who have lived there. As a young man I began seriously to study the life of Christ; my Scripture graduation prize is the only one I kept from schooldays.

Through a career first as a journalist—much of it spent in the Middle East—and then as a full-time author, I became deeply interested in the Protestant exegetes who emerged in the 1950s. Men such as Günther Bornkamm, Hans Conzelmann, Ernst Käsemann and Ernst Fuchs offered differing and challenging new theological concepts about how and why the four evangelists came to include certain material and leave out other data. Those German critics, Protestant to a man, were at the center of high wrangling which frequently brought religion onto the front page of the newspaper I worked for. I played a part in promoting the debate—and I am certain I did not escape its influence. I was quite ready to accept that the Gospel form in which Jesus' life and death had been set down was assailable; I was the willing victim of other, more persuasive minds: Huxley's claim that "miracles did not happen" and Matthew Arnold insisting there could be such a state as a "non-miraculous Christianity."

Yet when it came to the person of Jesus I retained a deep and properly respectful regard that my mother implanted on those first trips through the Holy Land. Much later, when I had experienced war, pestilence and famine, the workload of any foreign correspondent, I still felt a sense of shock and anger at the misuse of his name. It was naive—and I only mention it now as part of an attempt to try and explain how and why I came to write this book.

Nor is this the first attempt to put on paper my account of his life and inevitable crucifixion. Some thirty years ago, when I was going through a difficult crisis, I wrote a play based upon his trial. It was never performed, but writing it did encourage me to continue my research, leading eventually to this book.

Now, as a result of writing it, my own interpretation of Jesus—a portrait of a man of powerful eloquence and magnetism who became such a threat that his fate was sealed by a thoroughly self-serving political process—is to receive a far wider audience than I could have imagined. It is to be filmed, from a screenplay I wrote. Supported by the Bible Society, this is their first major venture into the commercial world of feature film. That it has overcome all the many hurdles which inevitably face any such project where many millions of dollars are committed to two hours of screen time, is largely due to the energetic drive of Clive Manning, its executive producer.

If nothing else, I hope it answers that question Jesus put to his disciples: "Who do men say that I am?" Seeking that answer brought me into contact with scholars who encouraged and deepened my interest in the trial and execution of Jesus.

If the birth of Jesus is the starting point of all real history for 1.5 billion Christians, then it can be said, without fear of serious challenge, that his trial is the most notable in the history of the world. No other trial—notably that of Socrates, condemned for introducing strange gods and corrupting the Athenian youth; or Joan of Arc, sentenced to be burnt for her belief that God entrusted her with a special mission for her people—while memorable for the moral heroism of the condemned, comes anywhere near to acquiring the religious significance attached to the trial and execution of Jesus.

In one of our many meetings, S. G. F. Brandon, then Professor of Comparative Religion at the University of Manchester, laid down for me the guideline I should follow if I was to make any sense of the events leading up to the death of Jesus: "assess the various, and obviously, complex factors which lie behind the composition of the four Gospels of that tragic event."

Over several subsequent years, having acquired along the way the collective wisdom of many eminent scholars, both Protestant and Catholic, I realized that no matter how long I remained on the trail, I could never hope to reach its end unless I discussed the matter with Jewish scholars.

I returned to Jerusalem. I read on the flight the words of a man, Frank Morison who, almost sixty years earlier, had set off on a quest not dissimilar to mine. His *Who Moved the Stone* was devoid of a single source note. Nor did he encumber himself with a line-by-line defense of, or attack on, the Gospel passion narrative. In the end he produced a book which was both his personal testament and yet had a considerable universal appeal to common sense. He had concentrated on the resurrection. But Morison's approach struck me as a worthy model for tackling in many ways the more difficult task of making sense of Jesus' trial.

In Jerusalem I received a number of challenging reinterpretations of that trial from Jewish scholars. Haim H. Cohn, a ranking authority on Jewish legal history and a judge of the supreme court of Israel, guided me through ramifications of his trial that I had hitherto not suspected. Judge Cohn's complex argument can be distilled into a belief that almost certainly Christianity would have begun and developed very differently if that trial had been conducted in a way other than it was—and, equally important, if it had been reported more fully in the canonical Gospels. Ze'ev W. Falk, then Professor of Family Law at the Hebrew University in Jerusalem, was among those who offered a lengthy catalogue of what Falk called "the historical carelessness of those Gospels." I quickly became convinced, as a Christian, that the Jewish interpretation of his trial must be given full credence.

I began to make other judgments. They were based on my own quite extensive reading. For those who wish to follow my trail, they can do so in the bibliography. What that list cannot, of course, explain is the judgmental criteria I used. But then, what use would it be for anyone if I indicated that, for example, I favoured Kung's interpretation of a point at the expense of a claim by Bultmann—or vice versa? My judgment is not anyone else's; how could it be? Much of the scholarship of the past few decades, brilliant though it has often been, has, in the end, so it seems to me, concentrated far too much upon demythologizing—and at times debunking. Some of the most unkind judgments have been left to the footnotes.

In preparing this book I decided, knowing the risk of attack was great, that I would not burden, or bore, readers with foot or source notes. What would they really serve? My sources are the Gospels—and not just the canonical ones, but those discarded in the wake of the councils of Nicea and Chalcedon. My research also includes a respectable body of Jewish and non-Christian literature, such as the tractates of the Mishnah, the Tosophta, Talmud, the Midrashim and the Tarqamin. A list can be found at the end of this book. But they still do not go all the way to unraveling the tangled skeins of prejudice, passion and political intrigues which govern the life and death of Jesus. That, ultimately, must be a matter of interpretation. In this case, and I say so with all humility, it is mine.

From beginning to conclusion—if I only take as a starting point that meeting with Brandon—this book has taken me twenty years of constant thought, intermittent research and many drafts. In between I wrote other books before returning to this one story which I felt compelled to write.

With each draft the interpretation I placed upon the facts inevitably differed. But in some indefinable way my perspective was changed by facts that could not be altered. Jesus had lived his brief life during a period in which Judaism was gripped by traumatic developments on the political and social fronts. For me to fail to take account of that would be to try and understand Dante without grasping conditions in medieval Florence.

Whether or not Jesus was actually born in Bethlehem is, in the end, of small consequence. Whether as Mark says (6:3) that he had brothers—James, Judas, Simon and Joses—about which we know almost nothing—is of no real import. Whether it was in 26 or 27 B.C.—or according to Jewish reckoning, in the year 3788 since the creation of the world—that Jesus was baptized, is not ultimately significant.

Yet such issues are portrayed as providing the ultimate key to Jesus. Scholars of many disciplines begin and end their careers trying to prove, or disprove, among other matters how many times Jesus visited Jerusalem and what route he traveled; who were the disciples closest to him and in what order were the Gospels set down: did Mark's version precede Matthew's, Luke's come before John's? Increasingly clinical procedures are brought to bear to try and discover his height, weight, the color of his eyes and hair—as if any of this will make Jesus more understandable.

When Jesus asked his disciples that most important question, "Who do you say I am?" he surely could not have wished the debate to have developed the way it has. Wilfred Sheed's remark, "another damned theologian comes grunting out of the Black Forest," has never been more apt. There is a growing, determined and, at times, disturbing move to demythologize, to replace faith with scepticism and even disbelief. Somewhere along the way the Jesus of ordinary people has been lost. Those who have tried to expropriate Jesus, his words and involvement with humanity have often left him further removed from the real understanding of Christianity. All that finally matters is that a deeply sensitive religious Jew was convinced he had been born first to reform Israel and then launch the kingdom of God.

It is that Jesus that these pages are concerned with; the man as well as the God-man. In every thought and deed Jesus showed that his life and death remain the greatest story to ever be told—and that the only way to tell it is to present him, in the true sense of the words, as a real man, as well as the only perfect one. He would surely have asked for no more. I have tried for no less.

THE PRINCIPAL PLAYERS

Our playwright may show in some Fifth Act what this wild drama means.

Alfred, Lord Tennyson, *The Play*

The Immediate Family

Jesus

(of Nazareth). *Yeshu*. His given Jewish name etymologically means "Jehovah is the Savior." Exact birth date unknown, but definitely not 25 December. Scholarly presumption points to late summer, 12 B.C., around the time Gospel "star in the east," later called Halley's Comet, seen in sky over Bethlehem. Makes Christ close to forty when his ministry began and approaching middle age when crucified. Spoke four languages but left no written personal record. Mesmeric public orator in spite of broad Nazarene dialect mocked by sophisticated Jerusalemites. Confined his ministry largely to countryside. Immediate followers numbered no more than seventy, including twelve he designated apostles. All deserted him in Garden of Gethsemane.

Mary

His mother. Only child of Anna and Joachim. Born to them during early part of reign of Herod the Great after long barren marriage. Her father one-time servant to Jerusalem Temple priests; mother member of well-established Bethlehem artisan family. Given name of Egyptian origin, Miriam, but raised in strict Hebrew tradition, ensuring word perfection in Holy Scripture. Law pronounced a girl could only marry when physically ready, usually at age of twelve and a half. May have waited a few more months before betrothal, but bore her son when still under the age of fourteen. Typical regional physiognomy would give her remarkably dark eyes and hair, olive skin. Died some time between death of Emperor Caligula (A.D. 41) and before Matthew wrote his Gospel (A.D. 50). Fifteen hundred years after having been designated Mother of God (A.D. 431), and pronounced totally without sin, officially proclaimed as having ascended into heaven body and soul (A.D. 1950). Only her son has the same status.

Joseph

His putative father. Son of Jacob, carpenter. Mother unknown. Settled in Nazareth some time between end of turbulent rule of Jewish Queen Salome. Alexandra and Pompey occupying Jerusalem. Took over family business around the time Caesar assassinated on Ides of March. Onset of reign of Herod the Great and crowning of Emperor Augustus almost certainly had little effect on his lifestyle. Knew Mary's parents through common artisan background and regular synagogue worship. Details of courtship circumstantial, but married late in life, defying rabbinical warning about such age-gap unions—in this case perhaps as much as fifty years. Died during period of ruthless oppression of Jews around time Pontius Pilate appointed procurator. Although not converted to Christianity subsequently sanctified by Catholic sainthood and currently patron of thirty-five religious orders.

Joses, Juda and Simon

All younger blood brothers of Jesus whose biographies have so far escaped history, along with his two sisters, whose names remain uncertain. Their existence shows that after the annunciation—that one event which was to make their mother blessed among women and unique of all her sex—the Virgin Mary enjoyed a full married life with her husband.

Their Relations and Friends

Elizabeth

First cousin and close confidante of Mary, the mother of Jesus. Well beyond childbearing years. Married to equally aged Zachary, village priest. Zachary reportedly struck dumb by angel when given news Elizabeth would bear a son. After the birth Zachary immediately recovered speech and called infant *Yochanan*, "Wished by God"—later known as John the Baptist.

John

(the Baptist). Born a few months before Jesus. Physical distance kept them apart in childhood. John confined his ministry to the banks of Jordan. Discarded conventional dress of short-sleeved *kolbur*, vest and *subrikin*, trousers, for shift of camel hair girdled at loins. Lived on locusts, wild honey and river water. Garment and diet fitted style of ascetic prophets from days of the exodus. Strong elements of Essene radical influence in John's doomsday preaching. Core of his teaching was repentance only possible through baptism after full confession of sins. His use of water in liturgy not new: centuries prior to John, Indian Brahmanism taught immersion in the holy river Ganges exorcized evil. John largely responsible for spearheading the rebirth of prophecy that "kingdom of God" finally at hand. At same time singled out Herod Antipas, tetrarch of Galilee, for sustained attack. Finally imprisoned by his tormentor after John railed against Herod Antipas' seduction of sister-in-law, Herodias. Her daughter, Salome, asked for the Baptist's head on a platter as reward for dancing at her stepfather's banquet.

Mary Magdalene

Born at Magdala, tiny fishing village on Sea of Galilee, famed for preparation of muries, salt-cured fish exported as far as Rome. Worked for a time as a hairdresser; versed in use of dyes, especially fashionable auburn and black tints. Controversy over why, but drifted into life of prostitution while still young. Abandoned immoral life after rescue by Jesus when she anointed his feet during dinner with Simon the Pharisee. Died before Nero became emperor (A.D. 54). Details of her relationship with Jesus raised subsequent speculation of whether she had grounds to hope they would marry.

Mary

(of Bethany). Born and raised in village fifteen *strades*, or just under two miles, from Jerusalem. Parents died shortly after birth; raised by elder sister, Martha, and brother Lazarus—immortalized as the man brought back from dead by Jesus. His exact relationship with Mary also a matter of intense conjecture.

The Apostles

Simon

(called Peter). Born *Shi'mon*. First and eldest of disciples to answer call "Come, follow me." Early on Jesus changed his name to *Kephus*, Aramaic for "stone"; through translation into Greek and Latin became "rock" and thus Peter—from which Catholicism and papacy trace their origin. Like his master, Peter wore a full beard as a symbol of resistance to clean-shaven

Roman occupiers. Gave Jesus a home at outset of his ministry around Capernaum on Sea of Galilee. Died a martyr in Nero's Colosseum. Left unresolved tantalizing question whether Peter was married and if his wife suffered a mysterious fate.

Andrew

Name of Greek origin. Younger brother of Simon-Peter and second apostle recruited. Crucified in Patros, Greece. Survived three days on cross. His last words: "Accept me, O Christ Jesus, whom I saw, whom I love and in whom I am."

James

Eldest son of Zebedee, patriarch of devout Jewish family. James middle-aged and a widower when he joined Jesus. Executed by Herod Agrippa in A.D. 44.

John

Younger brother of James. Subsequently credited with authorship of Gospel that is not only most mystical and dogmatic of all apostolic accounts, but one apologists insist holds priority over Matthew, Luke and Mark. Almost two thousand years later controversy still rages among scripturalists who devote entire careers, and reputations, to debating how untutored Palestinian fisherman acquired deep knowledge of Greek philosophy and theological reflections that give John a primal vision of Christ. This learned image in marked contrast to other Gospels which suggest John was quarrelsome, indolent and a self-seeker eager to usurp Peter's position as closest apostle to Jesus. John executed alongside his brother.

Philip

Greek-named, meaning "lover of horses." Barely out of teens when answered call of Jesus. Remained a constant companion up to the Last Supper. Subsequently went to Asia Minor, preaching in Turkish city of Hierapolis. Married after death of Jesus and fathered three daughters. Passed closing years in Ephesus, where early Fathers of the Church were subsequently to elevate Mary to status of Mother of Jesus. Finally crucified on order of local Roman proconsul whose wife became Christian.

Bartholomew

Name means "son of Tolmai." Family tree possibly traceable back to revolt of the Maccabees (200 B.C.). By all accounts devoted and caring. Went to Turkey with Philip, ministered at southern end of Caspian Sea. Finally fell into hands of heathen brigands who skinned him alive.

Thomas

Also known by the Greek, *Didymus*, meaning "twin." No record of his having identical brother or sister. A fisherman born and raised on banks of Sea of Galilee. Moody, suspicious, despondent and a questioner, earning him accolade: "Thomas doubted that we might have no doubts." After long eventful life as a missionary died in Mylapore, now suburb of Madras in India.

Matthew

Born *Matthai*, itself shortened version of *Mattaniah*. Roman-appointed tax collector, scorned by fellow Jews until he became eighth disciple. Fluent in Greek and Latin but wrote his Gospel in Hebrew after a long life of ministry in Ethiopia, Persia and Macedonia. Died peacefully and buried in cathedral in Salerno, Italy.

James

Born *Ya'kob*, but known among the disciples as "the Less," because of small body. Genealogically the most fascinating of all the apostles. Blood brother of Jesus and second eldest of Mary's children, only sibling to believe without question in him. Became one of the most authoritative figures in the Christian community in Jerusalem, the city's first bishop and author of the hotly disputed Protevangelion of Birth of Jesus. Finally martyred by procurator Caspius Farus (A.D. 44–7), hurled from clifftop and remains buried on Mount of Olives. Continuing controversy over James equaled only by one other disciple—Judas Iscariot.

Jude Thaddaeus

Often called *Trionius*—the man with three names: his own, Matthew's *Lebbaeus* and Luke's *Judas-ben-Ya'kob*, meaning "son of a man named James." Grandson of Zebedee, followed his widowed father James and uncle John into ranks of disciples. Was missionary in Syria and northern Persia where he died and was buried at Karg Kalesia. Disinterred almost five hundred years later and bone fragments brought to Vatican where they are mingled with those of apostle Peter and remain under papal edict in tomb sealed until Day of Judgment.

Simon

(the Zealot). Also called *the Canaanite* or *Canaanean*. Former member of Zealots, Galilean-based, outlawed patriots who continually resisted Roman occupiers. After Jesus' death preached throughout North Africa before crossing Alps into France and sailing Channel to reach England in A.D. 60, onset of Boadicean war. Evangelized Britons and castigated Romans. Arrested and crucified at Caistor, Lincolnshire, on 10 May, A.D. 61.

Judas Iscariot

The last to be called. Only apostle not from Galilee. Born in region of the Ghor, geological trench close to whose brink stood the accursed cities of Sodom and Gomorrah. Appointed treasurer because of his expressed business acumen. Undoubtedly originally loved Jesus but somewhere along the way, perhaps as late as during that last journey into Jerusalem, became dangerously mentally confused, convinced time had come to force Jesus into confrontation with both Roman and Jewish priestly aristocracy, thus hastening the coming of the kingdom of God, his infamous act of betrayal swiftly followed by suicide. Was treachery or misguided belief the motivation?

The Establishment

Joseph Caiaphas

High priest of the Temple and president of the Great Sanhedrin, the supreme court of the Jews in Jerusalem. Physically puny but with remarkable skills in political chicanery. Placated Romans and Jewish civil administration through fawning and manipulation. Almost twenty thousand priests, acolytes and soldiers under his command. As soon as Jesus emerged as a public figure, he assigned spies and *agents provocateurs* in attempts to entrap him into scriptural breaches. But initially did not regard him as a serious threat. Only when Lazarus was raised from the dead was the full danger to established religious life recognized, and Jesus elevated to status of prime threat to public order, paving the way for the most notorious show-trial ever held. Died about ten years afterwards.

Pontius Pilate

Roman procurator for Judea. Debated with Jesus during legal proceedings. Cultured, introverted, self-taught expert on Judaism. Initially found Sanhedrin charges failed to meet requirements of Roman law, yet fatally flawed personality resulted in crowning blunder that blighted hitherto promising career. Was he already a secret Christian when he condemned Jesus? Six years later banished to Gaul. Committed suicide.

Herod Antipas

Tetrarch, ruling prince of Galilee and Perea. Fifth son of Herod the Great. Inherited paternal traits for violence, wanton impulses and behavior verging at times on insane. Since murdering John the Baptist obsessed with idea of being constantly plotted against. Disliked and feared Caiaphas. After Jesus publicly insulted him became convinced he must die. After death of Jesus banished; died in exile.

The Other Women

Claudia Procula

Imperious granddaughter of Emperor Augustus. Married Pilate the year before they came to Judea. An increasingly empty, childless union which would have avoided historical record but for one momentous event. She dreamt about Jesus on the night before his death and sent her husband a message that could have changed history. The desperate intervention of a woman who loved Christ secretly—or a calculating response to use her husband to promote her social ambitions? Promulgated saint by Greek Orthodox Church.

Joanna

Wife of Chuza, chief steward of Herod Antipas. Middle-aged convert to Jesus' teachings. Constantly risked her life to provide him with information about the tetrarch's growing fury. Fate unknown.

Mary

Aged widow of Zebedee and mother of apostles James and John. Devoted camp follower, ready to endure severe hardship on his account. Fate unknown.

28 ANNO CHRISTI: THE CONTINUING PREPARATION

O Jerusalem, Jerusalem, thou that killest the prophets, and stonest them which are sent unto thee, how often would I have gathered thy children together, even as a hen gathereth her chickens under her wings, and ye would not!

Jesus, contemplating Jerusalem
from the Mount of Olives,
Matthew 23:37

1

JESUS

> Whosoever will come after me, let him deny himself, and take up his cross, and follow me.
>
> Mark 8:34

The hour of ritual sacrifice and celebration was once more close. As evening approached the entire community began to gather around the twin plots. The fields were roughly equal in size, each separated and encased by low walls of rock. At the center of one was a hewn boulder upon which the rabbi would stand, as priests had done for centuries, to offer prayers when the time came.

Though it had less than a thousand inhabitants, Shechem was classified by the Romans as a medium-sized city and one of strategic importance: it was on the main road from troublesome Galilee to Jerusalem, and revolutionaries in northern Judea intent on marching on the capital would have to pass this way. In less than a day troops from the imperial coastal citadel at Caesarea could be deployed between the two hills in whose lee Shechem lay, cutting the trail at the first sign of further civil insurrection. In the ninety years since Pompey had first led his legions southwards between the hills into Jerusalem, Roman forces had regularly been rushed here. When the soldiers returned to barracks, the village elders resumed their talk about the nation being rescued from foreign tyranny. In recent years people in Shechem had spoken again of a Jewish king who would one day come and free them. Increasingly, they used the old biblical name for such a deliverer—the Messiah.

This longing for liberation was further reflected in the game Shechem boys played: Zealots and Romans, patriots and tyrants. That part of the game which depended on the capture of Mount Gerizim always ended in defeat for those luckless enough to be cast as Romans. Legend said Noah had erected the first altar after the flood on top of Gerizim. Those playing Zealots invariably managed to drive their attackers away from the mountain shrine towards the nearby slopes of Mount Ebal. Joshua had placed a curse upon its summit a thousand years earlier; since then evil spirits were still reputed to haunt its peak. Shechem's other claim to fame was the well, as Holy Scripture related, which Jacob had dug, going down seventy-five feet to reach one of the sweet-water springs.

There was tremendous competition among the children to be on the Zealot side and particularly to play the roles of the two most recent heroes of Israel: Judas of Gamala, called simply the Galilean, and Sadduck the Pharisee. Twenty-two years before, in A.D. 6, they had led their followers against the Romans when another of the hated Imperial head-counts had been ordered. The Jews detested a census designed to suck more taxes from them. While Rome's gubernatorial appetite for enrichment was common throughout the empire, the population of Judea was not only more financially impoverished than other occupied lands, but was also the victim of the capricious methods employed by Rome. Pontius Pilate, the latest Roman procurator, had made it clear he intended to extract the last possible shekel of tax—and that defaulters would be imprisoned, their lands seized, their families driven out of their homes and, if need be, sold into bondage to pay off debts. He had also ensured that the once powerful Zealot movement, while maintaining public sympathy, had been greatly reduced numerically by ruthless Roman search-and-destroy operations. Now there were only a few hundred Zealots left, partisans operating for the most part in Galilee and Samaria. They attacked the enemy at night, cutting Roman sentry throats with their short daggers, the *sicarii*, and then slipping silently through a legion encampment, butchering as they went. Their exploits continuously excited the passions and hopes of the Jewish people.

During one of their mock battles near Mount Ebal the Shechem boys saw a group coming down the track from Thebez to the north. Their first instinct, a well-developed one, was to turn and run. Romans were not above snatching a handful of Jewish youths and using them for spear practice. But the boys quickly realized these strangers were not soldiers. Except for their leader, who was dressed in a cassock-like garment with wide sleeves reaching to the ground, the men wore the traditional *haluk*, a long woollen garment, girdled with a thong at the waist; over it was a cloak woven either from goat or camel hair. Behind them, at a distance, trudged a group of women, each robed in a voluminous *istomukhuium* and girdled either with a plain black *pinzomata* or a colored *zonarim*, waist sashes.

For months now the people of Shechem had heard stories that far beyond where they would ever dare venture was a man who performed astonishing feats around the shores of the Sea of Galilee. Was this leader the man? He was becoming as celebrated as that other extraordinary preacher, a physical giant who spent his time ministering on the banks of the Jordan, and who was known throughout the land as John the Baptist. Watching the approaching group each boy could have recounted how the thrilling story of John once more graphically illustrated the truth of the scriptural texts they were taught as they squatted round the rabbi behind the Shechem synagogue. As well as memorizing all the ceremonies connected with the sabbath and the various festivals, especially Passover, each child also learned that Yahweh was capable of anything. The entire story of John, from his birth to his emergence as a prophet, confirmed this omnipotence.

It was known to them that John's father was a country priest in a village so small that its only claim to recognition was being on the dirt track which eventually led to that historic spot where David slew Goliath. John's mother was called Elizabeth, respected within the tiny community for three reasons: her great age, the lineage she claimed with the royal house of David, her long and happy marriage to Zachary. Their union had entered its fiftieth year and the couple had long come to accept they would end their days alone, without the joy of their own child to disturb the dignity of their home beside the synagogue where Zachary continued to marry, circumcise, and bury the dead.

Each year they made the pilgrimage to the Temple in Jerusalem for Passover. There they would meet Elizabeth's cousin Joachim and his wife, Anna, who traveled south on foot from Nazareth. When she was born, they brought with them their only child, Mary. Elizabeth and Zachary had wistfully watched her grow from an infant in swaddling to a pretty olive-skinned and dark-eyed girl. While Zachary and Joachim, like men everywhere in the Passover crowds, spoke feelingly about the Roman oppression, Elizabeth, Anna and Mary explored the latest delights of the city. Jerusalem was a three-day walk from Nazareth—and the wonders of the metropolis were far removed from those of the isolated mountain village. On each visit there seemed to be new stalls selling even finer silks from all over the Orient: the Street of the Perfume Makers in the Lower City grew longer and more aromatic. At the end of the celebrations, the two families would go their separate ways, exchanging kisses and promising to meet in twelve months.

As the years passed, Elizabeth and Anna both agreed Mary was approaching the time when she would take a husband. The news stirred an old longing in Elizabeth for a child of her own.

One year, Anna had sent word to Elizabeth that they would not be coming to Passover; Joachim was still recovering from a long winter illness. She also had one other piece of news. Mary had been promised in marriage to one of Nazareth's carpenters, Joseph, son of Jacob. Though Anna admitted there was a considerable difference in their ages, something the rabbi of Nazareth was unhappy over, Joseph was a fine and honorable man, abstemious and devout. All in all, she and Joachim had decided he would be a good husband for their daughter.

The news of the betrothal must have been a talking point between Elizabeth and Zachary as they made their slow way to Jerusalem for another festival, but as for a child of their own whom they could give in marriage, God had decided otherwise—and Yahweh's will was not to be questioned.

Elizabeth had, as usual, stopped in the Court of the Women, beyond which any female was forbidden to go within the Temple. Her husband, reputedly stiff-legged from rheumatism, had slowly climbed the steps which allowed him, as a priest, to enter the inner courts. In one of them he had put on ceremonial robes, ready to join all the other rabbis in leading the religious ceremonies. Seventy and more years Zachary may have been, but he had never lost his reverence for the rubric of the sacrifice, the utterance of the ancient prayers, the swinging of his censer that held the burning, pungent spice whose smoke cast its own spell over the worshippers. Dressed and ready to perform his functions as an anointed servant of the living Lord, Zachary had waited his turn to approach the great altar where the high priest, the legendary Annas, ruled supreme.

What happened then had produced a spate of stories. In one, Zachary had suddenly turned and stumbled back into a robing room. In another, he had gone to the vault where the solid gold candlesticks for the high altar were stored. A third report had said he disappeared into the kitchens under the Temple where votive cakes made of wheat and barley were baked along with the twelve loaves of holy shewbread. Wherever he had gone, Zachary had emerged, divested of his raiment and censer, a dazed look on his face, and had fled past the altar, one hand pointing to his open mouth from which came no sound. He had found Elizabeth and clung to her speechlessly. She had taken the stricken husband home. There, Zachary had motioned for a wax tablet and *stilus*, writing implements. Squatting on the floor, he had carefully formed the characters which would ensure them both a place in history.

"An angel spoke to me at the Temple."

Then, watched by his wife, the old rabbi's *stilus* had bitten at speed into the wax, forming further astounding words. These, too, would become legendary, to be quoted and paraphrased as veritable proof of the truth of the Scripture that angels did speak with humans. His winged messenger had made a prediction.

> Fear not Zacharias: for thy prayer is heard; and thy wife Elizabeth shall bear thee a son and thou shalt call his name John. And thou shalt have joy and gladness; and many shall rejoice at his birth. For he shall be great in the sight of the Lord and shall drink neither wine nor strong drink; and he shall be filled with the Holy Ghost.

Elizabeth's reaction would be variously recounted. She had laughed in hysterical disbelief. She had wept. Finally she had asked whether the angel had given his name. Zachary had scratched the word: "Gabriel." Husband and wife were overcome by the enormity of the revelation. Gabriel was one of the four archangels of the heavenly host; he had been the divine messenger who was sent to reassure the greatest of all the prophets, Daniel. Zachary resumed writing, explaining that Gabriel had struck him dumb as verification that he was indeed God's principal herald and that he would not be able to speak again until his son was born.

Zachary's congregation had been stunned; what had happened was beyond their comprehension. Then, in the sixth month of Elizabeth's pregnancy, a young and attractive girl arrived alone in the village. She was covered in dust and her feet were swollen—and the sharp-eyed village women noticed that she was also with child. She walked towards the house of Elizabeth and Zachary, and the older woman had waddled forth to greet her cousin from Nazareth.

"Hail Mary!" Elizabeth had cried, her face alive with pleasure. "Blessed art thou among women, and blessed is the fruit of thy womb!" Then she had delivered a further unforgettable outburst. "Whence is this to me that the mother of my Lord should come to me? For, lo, as soon as the voice of thy salvation sounded in mine ears the babe leaped in my womb for joy."

Then, sensing the openmouthed stares of her neighbors; Elizabeth had taken Mary by the elbow and led her into the small house: a construction of stone, covered with white plaster.

Inside the dwelling Mary had revealed her momentous decision. She too had been visited by the archangel Gabriel, who had told her she would conceive, and already she felt as if she was a new person, someone filled with glory and humility; she felt strong and wonderfully protected.

Staring at Elizabeth she had spoken. "My soul doth magnify the Lord! And my spirit hath rejoiced in God my Savior. For he hath regarded the low estate of his handmaiden: for behold, from henceforth all generations shall call me blessed. For he that is mighty hath done me great things; and holy is his name. And his mercy is on them that fear him from generation to generation."

When she had finished, tears rolled down her travel-weary face. How, she asked Elizabeth brokenly, could she still expect Joseph to believe that she had not been with another man? How could she hope he would marry her now? Then Elizabeth had quietly told her how she had conceived. Sobbing in relief, Mary had clung to the old woman. Later, she had left the house, walking proudly out of the village, never once looking back.

Elizabeth's pregnancy had been normal, and on the predicted day she was delivered of a baby—a lusty, screaming son. Zachary helped to bathe his son, then rubbed his body in salt to harden the skin, and wrapped the child in swaddling clothes. On the eighth day he circumcised the boy, and upon writing upon his tablet that his son's name was John his speech returned.

All this had begun to be recounted when John started his ministry, dipping converts into the River Jordan and assuring them that the Messiah was finally on earth. The news had been passed on with muted voices. Spies were everywhere. It was dangerous to repeat anything which could be construed as a political or religious threat to the Romans, the Temple authorities or the tetrarch. But the word had spread: the Expected One was here.

To the youths of Shechem, their game forgotten, eyes on the approaching strangers, their assumption was that these were more converts making their way to where John performed his baptisms. They had heard how he would stand in the water, raising his massive bronzed arms heavenward, and uttering through his tangled beard words which had become a chant for Jews throughout the land. "The kingdom of heaven is at hand. I indeed baptize you with the water unto repentance, but he that cometh after me is mightier than I, whose shoes I am not worthy to bear; he shall baptize you with the Holy Ghost, and with fire."

John had uttered them a year ago when his cousin had walked from Nazareth to the spot on the banks of the Jordan where the Baptist ministered. Many had been present at their encounter. The story of what happened had been endlessly repeated around the campfire of the caravan routes and in the squares and souks of Jerusalem and a hundred other cities and towns. To the youngsters of Shechem, already steeped in the local folklore of Noah, Jacob and Joshua, the meeting had taken on an unforgettable aura.

They had finally stood face to face: John, knee-deep in the water, his hair a damp tangle from his exertions, his voice hoarse from hours of shouting about the need for repentance; Jesus, slimmer, features tranquil and free of any exhaustion in spite of the long trek from Nazareth, had walked into the river until the water reached his thighs.

The crowd had suddenly fallen silent, as if they, too, recognized the historic importance of the meeting. Those closest to the two men strained to hear every word. There was a quiet certainty about the request from Jesus to be baptized by John, whose response was a simple, unequivocal statement: it was he who should be immersed by his cousin. Jesus' answer was filled with implication. "Suffer it to be so now, for thus it becometh us to fulfill all righteousness." Then John had baptized Jesus.

The brief ceremony over, the silent, watchful gathering were convinced they saw a snow-white dove suddenly descend and hover for a moment. Folding its wings, the bird perched on the shoulder of the new convert. Then it flew away, finally only a speck that vanished from view. The stunned crowd would later swear that at that moment an unseen voice had cried out from the cloudless sky: "This is my beloved Son in whom I am well pleased."

John had led Jesus from the river and brought him to the cave where he, the hermit prophet, lived. The spectators crowded close to the entrance, straining to catch the quiet exchange between the two men, hoping for an explanation of the celestial events they had witnessed. Among them were the brothers Andrew and Simon, soon to be called Peter; James and John, the sons of Zebedee; as well as the youthful Philip. They were all from Capernaum and knew each other well.

Inside, almost lost in the gloom, John and Jesus squatted opposite each other, the Baptist hunched forward, intent on what his cousin was saying. Jesus was describing the circumstances of his birth. After leaving Elizabeth, Mary had walked back to Nazareth, a trek of a few miles through some of the most dangerous terrain in Judea, a route along which Roman patrols had been known regularly to take women for their pleasure. But, filled with the reassurance that she would be protected, she had safely reached home. Her parents, who assumed her lengthy absence had been to help Elizabeth through her confinement, had only too clearly observed the condition of their daughter. Their stricken looks had turned to wonder when she told them what had happened.

Jesus had continued to take his cousin through the sequence of events. Joseph, too, had been dismayed at her condition and had even thought of breaking off the betrothal until the night he experienced a dream so vivid that it seemed to be actually happening as he lay tormented in his bed. Jesus described how, in that dream, "the angel of the Lord" had gently spoken to Joseph and told him not to be ashamed to take Mary as his wife, for the child she was carrying was not from any other man, but had been placed there by the Holy Spirit, God himself, and that she would bear his son so that he could come into the world and redeem its people from sin. John had uttered a prophecy which had sustained generations since the prophet Isaiah first spoke them: "Therefore the Lord himself shall give you a sign. Behold a virgin shall conceive and bear a son."

The cousins had come out of the cave and the crowd had drawn back in respectful silence. Jesus had looked at the faces of the men from Capernaum, searching each in turn, before telling them to wait on the bank of the Jordan near where John baptized until he returned for them. Jesus had then walked south, away from the river delta into the greatest of all Judean deserts—the one simply called "the Wilderness."

Jesus led the disciples, Mary Magdalene and the other women into Shechem to where the activity around the two plots had gathered pace. In front of the rabbi's boulder-platform was a trench about four feet wide and nine feet long, lined with scorched-black unhewn stones. This was the sacrificial pit, where since noon a fire had burned. Resting on wooden poles across the top were several cauldrons of steaming water. In the adjoining plot was a circular pit about ten feet deep. It, too, was lined with stones, glowing from the intense heat.

The first stages were completed for a sacred ritual which went all the way back to God's covenant with Abraham. What was about to happen was part of the endless process of spiritual development of the Chosen People: it was as important as their pledges of righteous behavior, brotherly love, moral worth and justice. It had a deep mystical meaning of holy purification. Abraham had called it "the mark of the flesh"—the circumcision of every newborn Jewish male child, a requirement so binding that the operation could be performed upon the sabbath.

Originally Abraham had circumcised his firstborn and the rite had remained for centuries the responsibility of the father. Then, when Joshua had descended the Hill of the Foreskins—named after its phallus-like shape—and led his people into the Promised Land, circumcision had been elevated to a profession. Each town had a *mohel*, a practitioner trained to perform the delicate operation. Working only with a flint knife, an experienced *mohel* was a revered figure, allowed to partake in the special offerings that the family of the newborn made to the priest. All of Shechem was jostling around the plots when the boys arrived with Jesus and his party. They may have been in time to see the *mohel* follow the precise sequence demanded in the tractate: "The making of the cut, the tearing of the skin, the sucking of the wound and the placing of a plaster of oil, wine and cumin upon the wound."

The strangers were promptly invited to join in the forthcoming feast. There was nothing unusual in this: Jews were traditionally generous with their hospitality, and indeed Abraham had invited God himself to sup with him at Mamarea.

The host, the father of the circumcised child, received each of them with the kiss of peace and ordered water to be brought for their feet to be washed. Separate pails were provided so that each right hand, the one used for eating, could be carefully cleansed. Then, to show the importance of the feast—a circumcision celebration ranked with a wedding banquet as a cause for rejoicing—scented oil was sprinkled on the heads of the men and the headdresses of the women. Those who performed the ritual reacted as they did towards all strangers—looking into their faces, taking their measure; and among the strangers this day was Jesus.

The stories of what Jesus had done had grown to a point where no one could be absolutely certain which event followed the other. There had been so many miraculous happenings. But it was generally agreed that the first one had been at Cana. What occurred there had been witnessed by many. Caravan traders carried the news to Jerusalem and the ears of the high priest, Joseph Caiaphas, and the tetrarch, Herod Antipas. Shortly afterwards there had passed through Shechem rabbis from the Temple and agents of the tetrarch hurrying to Cana to probe further the extraordinary event which had finally plucked Jesus out of obscurity. It would once more be the sheer detail that would defy rejection; if it had not happened as recorded, how else could it have occurred?

Jesus had spent the time in the Wilderness walking through that desolate area where David had cut off a strip of Saul's coat; where Samson had reputedly slain ten thousand men with the jawbone of an ass; where Abraham had had his unhappy encounter with Abimelech; where Jacob had stolen Esau's blessing: a distance perhaps of two score zigzagging miles, trudging through an enervating landscape of deep ravines, beds of treacherous shale, and acres of blistering sand, seemingly empty of life except for prowling leopards and wild pigs. At night when the sun set, it was icily cold. Jesus had remained here for forty days, facing and overcoming temptations he would never speak about—but which others would ascribe to him. Here, they said, he had encountered Satan and rejected his blandishments. Satisfied at what he had achieved, Jesus made his way past the eerie mists of the Dead Sea and the Herodian fortress atop Masada, on up along the left bank of the Jordan and finally back into Galilee and Nazareth.

His family was now sadly depleted. His father, Joseph, had died a few years after Zachary succumbed. His aunt Elizabeth was also dead. His brothers and sisters were grown up; before he died Joseph had arranged marriage contracts for several of them. They were settled in Nazareth or the other towns in the fertile plain of Estraelon bordering the Sea of Galilee.

Over the years the gap between Jesus and his family had widened, with two exceptions. He still had a close and loving relationship with his mother and the eldest of his brothers, James, who openly adored him. But from now on the familial ties would further loosen under the sheer pressure of what he had to do and the time he had left in which to accomplish it all.

If Jesus' mother was shocked at her son's appearance after his lengthy stay in the Wilderness she gave no sign to those men he had brought home, the first five of his recruited apostles: Peter, Andrew, James, John and Philip. Returning from the desert Jesus had met them on the route to Galilee and issued for the first time the command: "Come, follow me." His brother was the sixth to respond; to avoid confusion, he was known as James the Less.

Mary had made them all welcome. Now, into middle age, and her figure that much fuller after years of childbearing, her life had become no different from that of any other Nazarene widow: an endless round of housework, shopping and sabbath candles to be lit; her spare time spent gossiping with neighbors about the focus of her life—her growing number of grandchildren. If she felt it, she had hidden any sadness that her eldest son had not produced any babies for her to nurse and spoil. She realized that few still understood him—especially why he had felt it necessary to spend almost six weeks in that desolate region far to the south. She was one of the few who knew that as well as conquering temptation he had spent time contemplating the events which had made his life so different from that moment she had first felt him moving in her womb. When, ran the story, he had been old enough to understand she had told him how, on the eve of his birth, she had been forced to ride on a donkey, one of those stubborn Galilean asses, down to Bethlehem to comply with the latest Roman edict. The governor of Syria, who then had jurisdiction over neighboring Judea, had announced that its population was to be counted, tribe by tribe, for tax purposes. Those who failed to register would be severely punished. Joseph had known he would have no alternative but to expose his young wife to the lengthy journey as she came to termination. His own lineage went back to King David, Bethlehem's most exalted son; therefore Joseph had to register himself and Mary in that ancient seat of the tribe of David. In a cave, on the outskirts of Bethlehem, she had finally been delivered. Afterwards, Joseph had settled them both on the back of the donkey and led his wife and baby son far beyond the Dead Sea and into the Sinai Desert, where their ancestors had wandered for forty years after Moses had told a Pharaoh to let God's people go. Joseph had brought his family back into Egypt to avoid another tyrant, King Herod. In the city of Alexandria, where Cleopatra had fallen in love with Julius Caesar, his parents had waited until Herod the Great was dead. They had then returned to Jerusalem only to find themselves amidst the tyrannical rule of his son, Herod Antipas. So the Gospels would retell.

Much else had happened to them both since Mary watched him grow into maturity. But she never questioned her son's actions or motives—nor had she done so when he returned home with those five men who, he calmly told her, would carry on his work. Instead, she had invited them all to the wedding of a distant cousin at Cana.

They had left Nazareth in the early afternoon to give ample time to arrive for the marriage feast on a fine autumn evening. The harvest had been gathered, the vines stripped, and the grapes were fermenting; it was a time when everyone was content and it was pleasant to sit up late and enjoy oneself.

Jesus, his mother and the apostles arrived as the bridegroom's procession went to fetch the bride from her home. Scrubbed and dressed in his finest clothes, the groom wore a crown as Solomon had done at his nuptials. The bride, veiled and her hair freshly hennaed, was carried on a litter through the streets lined with people singing songs which went back to King David's days. When the procession reached the bridegroom's house, the rabbi offered traditional scriptural blessings, each invocation intoned in turn by the crowd. After the religious service the celebrations began. There was dancing in the street; as dusk fell the bridal couple sat under a canopy, the *huppah*, surrounded by the usual ten bridesmaids. The guests squatted around low tables stacked with platters of boiled meats and vegetables either raw or cooked in oil. Nathanael the caterer and his staff moved with practiced ease, refilling pitchers of red and white wine and jugs of water for the children. Jesus and his mother were seated at the table of the bride's father. Like John the Baptist he had no desire for alcohol. But around him the atmosphere was becoming increasingly rambunctious under the heady influence of the wine.

Suddenly the caterer was at the host's elbow, whispering urgently. The wine was about to run out. To bring more from Nathanael's cellars would take time. No doubt crimson with embarrassment the host murmured to Mary what had happened. At several tables she saw guests draining their goblets and beginning to pound the table for more drink.

John would recount that Mary turned to Jesus and "saith unto him, 'They have no wine.'"

Jesus had answered: "Woman, what have I to do with thee? Mine hour is not yet come."

The singing and laughter had begun to be matched by growing demands for the caterer and his staff to refill the pitchers. A look of determination on her face, Mary rose to her feet and motioned for Jesus to join her near where the waiters were draining the last of the vats. What passed between mother and son in their brief conversation would be a moment of significance for the future of all history. Here, in the tiny square of a town, virtually unknown beyond Galilee, an event was about to happen which would forever remain beyond human comprehension. Mary turned to Nathanael's men. Once more John would remember her words. Pointing to her son, she ordered: "Whatever he saith unto you, do it."

Jesus asked the waiters to fill the wine vats to the brim with water. They did as bid. He then invited the caterer to dip a ladle into one of them. Nathanael, perhaps shaking his head at such time-wasting futility, did so. He withdrew the spoon. The water had changed to a rich red color. He lifted the ladle to his lips and sipped. It was the finest wine he had ever tasted.

Even before the caterer had delivered his verdict, the story had spread, as Jesus knew it would. He also knew, and accepted, there could be no turning back.

Following Cana, Jesus preached in the open air, in synagogues and the courtyards of private homes. His message was simple and compelling. The kingdom of heaven was drawing ever closer; people must repent and believe the good news. Every sermon was designed to encourage his listeners to achieve a greater awareness of the immediate presence of God—not as a distant divinity but as a life-force among them. He attracted a growing and varied following, including the Twelve finally chosen as his closest confidants. Among his devotees were a number of women—whom Jesus treated with a respect and seriousness which was exceptional for the times. He often motioned for them to come from the edge of the crowd and sit at his feet. They looked up at him in astonishment and delight when he attacked the dual morality which often allowed a man to be forgiven his transgressions and yet branded a woman for life who had succumbed to the smallest of temptations. When he led them in prayer he invariably called God "Father," an old Jewish concept, but one to which he gave a new intimacy. Everywhere Jesus went he reaffirmed that the dark inner forces which ravaged the souls of every man and woman could be exorcised by faith. "If by the power of God I drive out the demons, then be sure the kingdom of God has come upon you." To enter it, all they had to do was to accept that the old order was being swept away.

Jesus spoke a great deal about love, illustrating its meaning with stirring stories and parables: the Prodigal Son; the Good Samaritan who rescued a victim of highway robbery. In a score of different ways he stressed that love meant being tolerant, patient and always seeking to help others without thought of self-reward. He was laying out an ethical commitment, a direction, a standard of behavior that was radically different from previous concepts.

His listeners were exhilarated. But among the crowds were mischief makers trying to entrap him. He had first challenged them over the sabbath. Jesus made it clear he did not oppose the concept that it was a day of rest, not only for those in authority but for those whom they exploited; that it was a pause for everyone to pray and remember that God was the Creator of all things. What he objected to was that the sabbath had been demeaned by being surrounded with rabbinical restrictions. He steadfastly attacked these as pointless dogma. Where was the sense, he asked, in a law that said it was permissible for a person to travel twelve miles but not a yard further on the sabbath? Where was the logic that allowed someone to write one but not two letters on that day? What religious basis could there be in a regulation that allowed a housewife to fasten a rope to a bucket but not draw water from a well during the hours of the sabbath? How was it justifiable for a musician to tie the ends of a broken lute string but not replace it; for food to be eaten but not prepared; for vinegar to be used to relieve headache but not spat out? How could these everyday actions offend God on his day of rest? He had demanded where was any of this rooted in Holy Scripture? Jesus had summed up his attitude in one memorable sentence: "The sabbath is made for man, not man for the sabbath." Sensing his opponents ready to attack, he silenced them on that occasion with a resounding challenge: let them show where he was wrong. There had been no response. But Jesus knew they would return.

Soon everyone around the fifteen-mile length of the Sea of Galilee had their favorite story of his determination to alleviate suffering and sorrow. The miracles which he began to perform were an integral part of his ministry.

There had been that unnerving moment in the township of Gergesa, on the west bank of the Sea of Galilee, when a raving lunatic had rushed to Jesus, teeth bared, howling; he would kill him. Jesus had extended his hands and gently asked the man to kneel. After a tense wait while the man remained half-crouching, as if he was about to spring, snarling like a wolf, Jesus had quietly asked him his name, and the demented reply had driven some of his disciples to move forward protectively. Jesus had motioned them back and again addressed the man. "'What is thy name?' And he said, Legion: because many devils were entered into him. And they besought him that he would not command them to go out into the deep."

The wretch had flung himself on the ground rolling and sobbing uncontrollably. Jesus had knelt beside him, one hand on the man's head, who was suddenly still, asleep. After a while Jesus rose and stepped back, commanding the man to rise. When he did so, and opened his eyes, the madness in them was no longer present.

Then who could forget—certainly not Peter—what had happened when he asked Jesus to help his dying mother-in-law? The doctor in Capernaum, held to be the cleverest physician around the Sea of Galilee, had prescribed every known remedy for her sickness: swallowing the brain of an owl, pounded and strained, to alleviate her crippling bouts of stomach cramps; chewing toads' legs boiled in vinegar to end her blinding headaches; massaging the urine of unweaned calves into her legs to reduce the swelling. Nothing had worked. One by one her bodily functions were failing.

Jesus had gone to her bedside and held her hand. For a moment, just like the madman at Gergesa, the old woman had stared with hostility at him. Then her face had cleared and she had smiled. Her sickness had gone. Within an hour she was out of bed and cooking supper for her family—something she had been unable to do for years.

In all he continued to say and do Jesus made it clear that he perfectly understood the correct interpenetration and intermingling of the human and the divine. Never far from his mind was the realization that his methods must one day provoke a final clash with the ruling religious authorities in Jerusalem. That was inevitable: what he had come to do was to demonstrate the power and the pity of God experienced solely through love. No high priest or tetrarch, let alone a Roman procurator, could do that. Yet it had been difficult at times for Jesus to convince even his immediate followers that they must see what he was doing not merely as a passing phenomenon but as part of a new eternal truth which was both supernatural and human.

Those Jesus had brought to Shechem knew how intensely human he was. There was the balding Peter, called Simon until Jesus had changed his name, and his brother Andrew. Both still had the rolling gait of fishermen. They would come down through history depicted as standing shoulder to shoulder with Jesus, intensely proud they were the first he had called. James and John might well have been the siblings of folklore: James short and portly, the belt around his waist barely meeting, older than his forty years, sometimes a sadness in the eyes that was ascribed to his wife having died shortly after the birth of their son, Thaddaeus; John tall and spare-framed, his slimness accentuated by the breeches and close-fitting vest he invariably wore.

The Twelve were comprised of other differing personalities. Philip, whose beard was reportedly the blondest of them all, supposedly born a year after the last Zealot uprising, and still fired with the impetuosity of youth. Legend would insist he had been drawn to the older Matthew, the former tax collector, depicted as a patient and thoughtful man, who spent the time on the road teaching Philip the rudiments of Greek and Latin. Bartholomew was muscular, with a warrior's stride and a face made to appear more pale by his thick jet-black beard; James the Less, a small figure whose robe was frayed at the hem and trailing in the dust; Thaddaeus, given his father's stout figure. Matthew, for a reason no one understood, called him Lebbaeus. Then there was Thomas, whom Matthew had nicknamed Didymus, the twin. A popular view would survive that Thomas' belligerence was never far from the surface. True or not, the nickname stuck, just as Thomas remained, perhaps by choice, a man alone.

Simon the Canaanite was reputedly taller and broader than even Peter or Andrew. Closer to seven feet than to six, winter and summer Simon wore a woven cloth wrapped tightly around the loins and reaching to the knees, with one end flung over his shoulder. Even in his bare feet he must have looked every inch as imperious as an emperor. Simon had been a Zealot and still saw himself as the group's natural protector with his knowledge of Roman tactics and those of the soldiers of Herod Antipas. No doubt he knew the safest routes through the countryside infested with hostile patrols.

Judas Iscariot would survive in mythology as a slight, dark-skinned man, dressed in a short-sleeved *kilbur*, the linen garment which was the usual garb in that village he had been born in on the edge of the Ghor. He would be given darting eyes that never failed to return to the large money-purse the treasurer clutched to his person. It contained the shekels which paid for the group's needs—a new pair of sandals, a girdle, the barest necessities of their lives. Tradition would have Judas a tireless bargain hunter, his enthusiasm for driving a deal matched only by sustained praise for the ministry of Jesus. Why not?

After a year some friendships were closer than others; harmony was frequently broken by outbursts of anger, pettiness and jealousy. Peter and Matthew made no secret of their dislike of Judas; John often bickered with Thomas. The others squabbled over who should sit next to Jesus at meals, walk beside him on the road, sleep near him under the starlight. The Gospels would hint at no less. When it became too irksome Jesus chided them for their childish behavior. He must also have understood that, being simple country men, they had no previous experience of the wiles of the Temple agents from Jerusalem and their cunning questions, or the spies of Herod Antipas, who pretended they were eager to overthrow the Romans and urged Jesus to give one, just one, encouraging sign. He had ignored these marplots—just as he had sidestepped those Jews who had taken the Roman coin and stood on the edge of the crowd hurling questions designed to provoke treasonable responses they could report to Pilate.

Facing crowds—increasingly larger groups of mostly impoverished men, women and children come to hear him preach, bringing with them their sick, lame and infirm for him to cure—Jesus had shown the Twelve more than ever that he would need their sustained and selfless support if he was to succeed. People came from everywhere: running the gamut of the Roman patrols on the coastal plains and avoiding the troops of Herod Antipas inland to make their way to the Sea of Galilee; from the northern Phoenician ports of Tyre and Sidon; from the west, far beyond the Jordan; from as far south as the Valley of Salt in the Wilderness of Idumea, reaching Galilee after a walk of a week or more. What was happening was both awesome and sobering.

Jesus decided he must escape momentarily from the incessant demands for healing and ministering, and had brought the disciples away from the port towns and villages around the Galilee lake. Shechem was only a stopping point on the way to the secluded place where he wanted to take them and finally explain what he expected them to do.

Shortly before sunset the crowd parted to allow shepherds through, each leading a tethered unblemished white-fleeced sheep to the enclosure. The rabbi rapidly checked the animals; this was part of the precise rules governing sacrifices: a brown mark on an animal's head rendered it unfit to be an offering. After passing inspection the sheep were led close to the pit with its steaming cauldrons of water. The priest resumed his position and began to chant further prayers. The crowd joined in the responses. Before the rock were the parents of the circumcised child, the *mohel* to one side.

The rabbi beckoned into the crowd. Youths vaulted over the wall to stand behind the shepherds, two to each man. When they were all positioned the priest nodded. The trio assigned to each animal moved swiftly, throwing the sheep to the ground; one youth pinned it down, the second held fast its legs and the shepherd pressed back the head to expose the throat. The rabbi produced a knife from under his robes. He stood beside the first animal and with one swift deadly slash, a back and forth movement of the blade, severed the head from the body. The shepherd turned the carcass on its side allowing the blood to drain into the earth. The priest moved to the next prostrate sheep and repeated his action.

While the slaughter went on, the singing resumed, prayers were offered and blessings evoked upon the infant who had just been admitted into the community.

When the last animal lay inert the shepherds carried the carcasses to the edge of the pit, lifted down the cauldrons and poured boiling water over them. Then they began to pluck away the wool, tossing it into the pit, sending a stenchy smoke spiralling into the cool air. As the process continued the infant's father brought pieces of unleavened bread to the priest and *mohel*. When they pronounced it to their satisfaction servers went among the crowd distributing the offering. Among the first to be served was Jesus and his group, a sign of respect after the cure of Peter's mother-in-law.

Jesus had gone on to complete his first tour of the lake towns, healing as he went; preaching, as was his right, in every synagogue around Galilee. He was only too aware of the agents from Jerusalem still dogging his footsteps. Yet they had been unable to find a single fault in what he said, claimed or did. His preaching was rooted in impeccable doctrine; not a word of heresy passed his lips.

The more deadly the verbal traps, the greater his skill in avoiding them. Increasingly, though, he began to speak in apocalyptic imagery of the coming new age. Before it dawned, he said, there would be disasters, war, the emergence of false prophets, pestilence and the persecution of those who believed in him; there would be tribulations at every turn. But for those who remained true to the faith which he had given them, their reward would be salvation. The choice was starkly clear: there was no middle road. Jesus was describing an eschatological vision that even the shrewdest of Temple agents could not easily challenge; there was nothing in their holy books from which they could mount one.

When the spies became too irksome Jesus avoided them by slipping away under cover of darkness, walking with the apostles through the moonlit Galilean landscape, reappearing the next morning at some new venue. He had done this several times on the tour of the lake. On one occasion he had backtracked, following the banks of the Jordan. As dawn had broken over the river Jesus had asked the disciples what people were saying about him. They had scuffed their feet in the dust, each anxious not to be the first to speak. Finally, Thomas had blurted out that many were convinced he was the reincarnation of Elijah. Thaddaeus reported that in Magdala some firmly believed he could be Moses. Andrew said that in Capernaum the talk was that he was really Jacob. One by one the apostles had made their reports. Finally, Jesus had turned to Peter: "Who sayeth thou am I?" His first follower had not hesitated: "The Messiah." Jesus had quietly praised Peter for his perception. It was the first time he had admitted his claim to divinity. He had firmly cautioned them to keep the knowledge secret: the time had not yet come for the world to be told such a shattering truth. Jesus added a somber warning: those willing still to follow him must be prepared to shoulder the cross. They all knew that crucifixion was the ultimate Roman punishment, the cruelest of all forms of death, and his words almost certainly were received with foreboding. Without waiting for their decision, Jesus turned and headed towards Capernaum. He may indeed have only walked a few yards before they caught up with him. The details, as such, would be unimportant. What would not be in dispute is that, as so often in the past, after facing them with reality, Jesus had commanded their loyalty.

He had once more led them into Capernaum where he had a room in the home of Peter's mother-in-law. One claim was that the apostle's wife had died in childbirth, her first baby stillborn. Another report said she had drowned in the Sea of Galilee. A third postulated that she had run off with one of the caravan traders who regularly passed through the town. Her exact fate would be lost to history.

Outside the town they found a now familiar gathering waiting patiently. At every stopping point around the shores of Galilee people had entreated Jesus to stay. The crowd, spotting his approach, began to surge forward. The apostles, themselves very possibly tired after another long day, bundled him into a nearby inn and bolted the door. Too late they must have realized their mistake: several of their tormentors from Jerusalem were lodging there. They began to ask more questions. With the crowds outside clamoring for Jesus to preach there was no way to leave. The agents grew more confident as they challenged him about the basis for his teachings. Where did Scripture say this or that? The deadly probing was interrupted by an overhead disturbance. The occupants of the crowded room were startled to see the ceiling steadily torn away, and in the ever-widening hole appeared expectant faces. A woman pleaded to be excused for such behavior, explaining it was the only way to bring her paralyzed father to Jesus. The throng outside had made it impossible to reach the door. With the help of friends the daughter had brought her father's pallet up a rear staircase that led to the flat roof. Jesus ordered the hole to be widened and the pallet lowered down by ropes. John would record how Jesus knelt beside the old man, laying his hands on his brow. Bending closer and speaking in a clear distinct voice Jesus said the man's sins were forgiven.

Sudden exultant cries came from the Temple agents. After months of fruitlessly stalking their quarry, they finally had something. Only God could forgive sins. Jesus, they shouted, had committed a blatant blasphemy. Matthew would note how Jesus turned and faced the agents and asked: "Wherefore think ye evil in your hearts?" Before they could answer, he fired further questions. What was easier to say: that sins were forgiven? or: arise and walk? Without waiting for a reply Jesus turned back to the cripple, his voice gentle: "Ye may know that the Son of man hath power on earth to forgive sins. Arise! take up thy bed and go into thine house!"

The man's body began to stir, almost indiscernible movements at first which rapidly grew stronger. Slowly, then with growing confidence, he raised himself on one elbow. From that position he delivered his first words: "Glory be to God."

The man eased himself off the pallet and stood on the floor, also looking dazedly upwards at the rapturous cries coming from his daughter and her friends. When his gaze turned to Jesus, tears ran down his face. Then, doing as he had been commanded, the cured man lifted the bed and waiting until one of the apostles unbolted the door, left the house.

Jesus and the disciples followed, leaving behind the stunned agents. When they finally began to speak, they asked one question. What had he meant by "the Son of man"? The oldest and cleverest of them, a scholar respected even by the high priest, remembered. Daniel the prophet had used the words to encourage the belief that one day the Messiah would come: "I saw in the night visions, and, behold, one like the Son of man came with the clouds of heaven." The import of what Jesus had said was only too clear. It was heresy. It had to be. But, even so, the words by themselves were not enough; he could always claim he was merely quoting Daniel. But by the time the spies had forced their way through the joyous crowd, Jesus and the disciples had once more vanished. They had taken the road south, finally to reach Shechem.

The last sheep was plucked, fastened to a short pole and carried on the shoulders of two boys to the adjoining enclosure where the village butchers were cutting off the right foreleg of each animal, drawing the sinews from the hind legs and disemboweling the carcass. Care was taken to ensure not a piece of flesh fell to the ground. The shepherds zealously collected the entrails and placed them on the wooden poles where the cauldrons had stood. The innards sizzled and shriveled before dropping into the pit. The severed legs and the edible offal were placed in pots of fresh cold water; these would be taken home later by the rabbi and *mohel* as their reward.

The butchering completed, a pole about fifteen feet long was inserted lengthways through each carcass. Its skin was then cut in a series of gashes on either side of the ribcage and salt rubbed into the openings. A final check that each animal was securely fastened, then, at the command of the rabbi, the stakes were lowered into the pit—kept clear of the growing ash bed by inserting the pole tips in gaps between the hot stone walls. A large wooden grid was positioned on top. Grass was spread over this and finally panniers of mud layered over the greenery until the opening was airtight.

Among the select number of women who had accompanied Jesus was one who followed him everywhere. In spite of all she had done, recklessly and deliberately, lore would ensure there was an innocence and purity about her, a chasteness which men who had once used and abused her no doubt would have found clearly bewildering. She had once been a spoilt, bejeweled and painted wanton; a whore to whom they had always returned, making her the richest harlot in the town of Magdala. More than its fortress and its fleet of fisherboats, she had spread the port's fame throughout the province. Clients brought her silks from Arabia, jewelry from Egypt and spices from India. Her reddish hair had been braided with pearls; her arms once weighted with bracelets and her fingers glittered with rings. She had been wealthy enough to afford slaves and brazen enough, rumor had it, to have doubled her normal fee to share the bed of any woman. For a price she had even slept with the odious Simon the Pharisee, one of the wealthiest men in Galilee. Mary Magdalene had agreed to do so again on that night her life changed irrevocably.

When Jesus received Simon's invitation to dinner, the apostles had been of one voice: this was another trap. Simon was a lawyer versed in all the subtleties of biblical precepts; an advocate who knew which arguments to cite, depending on whether he was appearing for the plaintiff or for the defendant. Once, calling upon a precedent dating back to Solomon, he successfully argued that a Capernaum landowner who had killed a thief who entered his home at night should be acquitted. Conviction for murder was only possible if the offense had taken place in daylight when the robber might have been taken alive; in the darkness there would have been no way of knowing if he was armed or alone.

Apart from his thriving criminal practice, Simon was an expert on other serious crimes—the lengthy catalogue of offenses against religious law which had always demanded the severest punishment. These included idolatry, necromancy and the performance of sorcery. Each, upon conviction, automatically carried the death penalty. So did blasphemy, which included not only the smallest infringement of the sabbath, but also misusing the Holy Name. The apostles had warned Jesus again: to eat at this man's table was to run the very real peril of being ensnared by legal tractates. Jesus had assured them that he feared nothing—and there was no need for them to be afraid.

Simon's house overlooked Capernaum and the road to Magdala. It was a place of inner courtyards and rooms furnished without accounting for cost. He had arranged for Mary Magdalene to arrive before Jesus. The servants knew her as an habitué, and the prostitute was escorted to the long paneled gallery overlooking the dining area. Leading down from the balcony was an enclosed staircase; when he was bored with his guests Simon used it to slip away to his bedroom—and Mary.

From her vantage point she saw Jesus led in by a servant. Simon motioned him to be seated, making no attempt to offer the traditional kiss of welcome. She immediately sensed tension. The lawyer further broke with normal social mores by having no other guests present—a studied insult to Jesus. The meal offered was frugal: boiled rice and vegetables served with wine from a pitcher she had once noticed the servants use. The lawyer's conversation was immediately taunting. Did Jesus see himself as some sort of unqualified doctor who had to treat the outcasts of society?

Jesus answered equably: "They that are whole have no need of the physician, but they that are sick."

The guest was an equal match for his host. Simon persisted. What did Jesus mean by those words? The reply might well have sent a shiver of excitement through the listening woman. "I came not to call the righteous, but sinners to repentance."

The lawyer pounced. Jesus sounded like a disciple of John the Baptist with no original thoughts of his own. Was that what he was? A blind follower of a man most people thought was mad?

Jesus would not be drawn.

"Why," demanded Simon, "do the followers of John fast often . . . but thine eat and drink?"

Jesus' reply had likely brought a smile to Mary Magdalene's lips. "Can you make the children of the bridechamber fast while the bridegroom is with them?"

The image of the lawyer slumped back on his divan, annoyed and nonplussed, survives with his next questions. Was Jesus trying to diminish the Baptist's importance? Were his words a clever polemic?

Jesus answered with a reply that he had used before, and would do so again, when faced with such a challenge. "Verily I say unto you, Among them that are born of women there hath not risen a greater than John the Baptist: notwithstanding he that is least in the kingdom of heaven is greater than he."

Simon pressed. Jesus was still just using words, clever phrases that might well impress an ignorant proletariat, but ones that the lawyer could see through. Was not the truth that Jesus perceived himself as greater than John? Was he not guilty of self-aggrandizement? Or did he really believe he was only one step away from God?

Where such questions might have led remained unresolved. Simon's interrogation was interrupted by the arrival of Mary Magdalene. In her hands she held an alabaster box. Her eyes, fixed on the penniless mendicant Jesus, began to fill with tears. Simon remained too stunned to move; his mouth worked but no words came.

Weeping copiously, Mary knelt at the feet of Jesus and, using a finger bowl from the table, washed in turn his calloused soles, drying them with her long red hair. Then, after tenderly kissing the insteps, she massaged cream into the skin before she resumed kissing it.

The lawyer finally managed to speak. Visibly out of control, forgetting the reason why she was in his house, Simon screamed at Jesus. Did he not know who this woman was? That she was a whore more infamous than any found even in Babylon? Anywhere in the Roman empire!

Jesus stared steadily at his angry host. Then he asked Simon to ponder a parable: a moneylender had two debtors. One owed a thousand shekels, the other one hundred shekels. Neither could repay their debt, but the moneylender forgave them both. The question, Jesus concluded, was which of the two freed debtors was the more grateful? Simon had replied that it must have been the one who had owed the most; anybody could have deduced that.

For the first time Jesus moved to the attack. "I entered into thine house, thou gavest me no water for my feet." He pointed at Mary Magdalene. "But she hath washed my feet with tears, and wiped them with the hairs of her head. Thou gavest me no kiss: but this woman since the time I came in hath not ceased to kiss my feet. My head with oil thou didst not anoint: but this woman hath anointed my feet with ointment. Wherefore I say unto thee, her sins, which are many, are forgiven; for she loved much." Then, ignoring Simon, Jesus helped Mary Magdalene to her feet and closed the alabaster box. He addressed her directly for the first time. "Thy faith hath saved thee."

The next certainty is they both left Simon's house, and she became his bondslave, selling off her home and possessions and distributing the proceeds among the poor, offering herself as a living example of the positive value of his love, which had been strong enough to overcome the evil of her former life. Never once had she flaunted her newfound purity and modesty, but time and again had shown an infinite capacity for comforting those who grieved, encouraging those who felt disheartened, guiding those who appeared lost. She always gave without demanding, and recognized the weaknesses in others without judging. In that way she was as close to Jesus as any apostle.

The pit was uncovered and the lambs removed. They were cooked to perfection, and laid on prepared beds of dried grass. Once more the butchers fell to work, carving and slicing. Pitchers of wine were distributed. Then the meat was hastily devoured, a rite that spanned the gulf of ages, linking the past of the Jewish people with the present.

Next morning, after bidding Mary Magdalene and the other women to await their return, Jesus led the apostles out of Shechem to lay the final foundations for a new chapter in that story.

Jesus took them on their longest journey so far. For a while they traveled east into the desert land of Decapolis, where even Herod Antipas' troops rarely patrolled. Then they headed north, keeping well clear of the Roman-built road to Damascus and its camel caravans and imperial checkpoints. In the distance was the permanently snowcapped Mount Hebron, blessed among all mountains: from its topmost peak Gabriel had banished Satan and later the she-devil, Lilith; on its slopes God had spelled out the covenant to Abraham. The ancient book of Zerubbabel promised that, when the time came for the redemption of the Israelites, heralded by the advent of the Messiah, the Temple would be miraculously transported from Jerusalem and divided between Hebron and the four other holiest of mountains—Lebanon, Moriah, Tobor and Carmel. Fording the Jordan, Jesus led them back into northern Galilee to their final destination, the altogether more modest Mount Hattin, a mere fifteen hundred feet above the Sea of Galilee and so far with no religious significance. Jesus had chosen Hattin for one speech to the apostles which would crystallize all his teachings, ensuring forever a complete and indisputable explanation of his message.

At some isolated point, Jesus found a place on the mountain relatively sheltered from the wind—one of the many ledges which act as stepping stones to the top. The disciples squatted in a ring around him.

He began to speak.

From the outset, Jesus made it clear that this was not a sermon but a succession of unchallengeable and inviolate maxims, each given its explanatory illustration. His listeners could hardly have needed reminding that not since the days of Moses had anyone promised to be so explicit. But the commands of the ancient patriarch had mostly been a catalogue of prohibitions: about not coveting, stealing and killing. Jesus' prescription for the future—not only for the apostles but for the whole world—was a very different kind of divine revelation: a carefully ordained philosophical system and a practical charter for all future human behavior. He promised them at the outset that when he had finished, they would know all that was required to fit God into daily life, to understand that beyond today lay a far more rewarding tomorrow—by accepting his vision of the future.

Just as there would be an endless search to identify his physical features and voice—was it high or low pitched, broad and heavily accented or mellifluous and compelling?—so in time to come passionate argument would try to prove, or disprove, what Jesus said on Mount Hattin was far from original; that his mantle of a lawgiver had been sewn together from passages in the Psalms and Proverbs of the Old Testament. All these future exegetes in the end would only provide a very unexpected denouement—that Jesus was not an iconoclastic revolutionary, nor did he look with contempt upon the people of his day. Neither had he come to destroy. The Law and the prophets remained valid for him as the ultimate expression of God's will. What set him apart on Mount Hattin was challenging not the law, but its interpretation. He had come to offer a penetrating new insight into God's will. His secret, the power of his magnetism, was his unique ability to take familiar expressions of faith and redefine them with a compelling certainty. Most important of all, he made it clear that everything he would promise was on the verge of realization: the kingdom of heaven would begin here, on this mountain. Yet when he began to speak—the wind tugging at his robe—he did not cozen the apostles with illusory hope of a new national prosperity for their nation, a fresh political resurgence; he would not discuss whether the Romans could be driven from the land, along with the Herodian dynasty. Instead he concentrated upon personal justice and human happiness. There was nothing demagogic in his approach—though his strictures against the rich and powerful would subsequently be seen as such. Instead, to the dozen men clustered around him, Jesus expressed himself in the only way he knew—from the background of his own impoverished upbringing, in which there were no luxuries for his brothers and sisters, let alone for his mother and putative father. Mary, very possibly, had sown the seeds of the argument for a brave new idyllic world, where the brotherhood of man could live in perfect harmony if certain basic rules were followed. Jesus began to unfold an uncompromising manifesto.

"Blessed are the poor in spirit: for theirs is the kingdom of heaven. Blessed are they that mourn: for they shall be comforted. Blessed are the meek: for they shall inherit the earth. Blessed are they which do hunger and thirst after righteousness: for they shall be filled. Blessed are the merciful: for they shall obtain mercy. Blessed are the pure in heart: for they shall see God. Blessed are the peacemakers: for they shall be called the children of God. Blessed are they which are persecuted for righteousness' sake: for theirs is the kingdom of heaven. Blessed are ye, when men shall revile you and persecute you, and shall say all manner of evil against you falsely, for my sake."

In summarizing all he represented so succinctly Jesus was clearly aware the apostles still vied with one another to impress him of their worthiness. Such behavior, he said, must stop. The rules he was laying down allowed for no further conflict among them. Equally, he could offer them no immunity from the threats and railing of the world that still existed beyond the mountain ledge. They would need all their belief to combat the pressures.

Matthew recorded how, having outlined the broad concept, Jesus developed it, expanding it into a stunning new interpretation of the law, choosing as his first example the Mosaic commandment: thou shalt not kill. "But I say unto you: that whoever is angry with his brother without cause shall be in danger of the judgment."

Even *thinking* harm about another required an act of reconciliation with that person—and asking forgiveness from God. Jesus warned that the same stricture applied to lust: an adulterous thought was as bad as the act of unfaithfulness itself; a potential libertine should pluck out an eye before being led into temptation. The continuous demand to resist all temptations was embedded in the reward of infinite succor.

There followed rules which opposed everything the men around him had been taught from birth. From now on they were not to answer force with force; above all they must ignore one of the most revered teachings of the Bible about demanding an eye for an eye or a tooth for a tooth. This was a hallowed principle of revenge, one which a community could evoke or a family claim or a single injured person demand. For centuries it had been enshrined as the ultimate vengeance of God, a counterbalancing of divine punishment. The disciples were given a radically different instruction.

"Whoever shall smite thee on the right cheek, turn to him the other also."

Once more Jesus stressed this was the state of mind essential for even being *considered* worthy to enter the kingdom of heaven. But there was more; an end to praying as hypocrites did, striking exaggerated poses, making sure everyone around was aware of their piety. It was better to pray alone. God would hear: that was all that mattered. No more complaining about obligatory fasting: it should be regarded with eager anticipation, a further chance to sacrifice a part of daily living to him.

Through all these commandments ran a consistent theme: *agape*—love. That was the core of the life he was proclaiming: the outer mold for a new kind of inner living, a pattern of personal conduct. Rather than judge, people must love; rather than condemn, people must love; rather than criticize, people must love. Yet—and he made the distinction clear—this love must not be the possessive, clinging kind. It must strive to come as close as humanly possible to God's love. Jesus was asking no one to feel blind affection for an enemy; rather, that a foe be prayed for, his crime forgiven, and his punishment left to God. That was what he meant by love.

Jesus reminded them they must concentrate on ending their criticism of others and try to improve their own defects. He told them the story of the two brothers: one only saw the mote in the other's eye, totally failing to see the beam in his own. He reminded them never to squander the treasure of spirituality—illustrating this with the futility of casting pearls before swine. He cautioned them again always to be on the lookout for false prophets. They would soon come to know them—just as easily as they would recognize a wolf covered in a sheepskin. He told them they must always assume full responsibility for every word and thought. All this formed part of the only basis for the kind of living he envisaged, where everyone served God and no one else. In the future there could be no place for the tiniest division of loyalty: no one could serve two masters.

But even then there was no absolute promise: a person could appear to live by all these precepts, and yet in the end be refused admission into heaven because God would know it had all been a sham; the disciples must learn to discern. "By their fruits ye shall know them." For miscreants genuine repentance was never too late. That was their only hope of salvation.

Always seeking an example they could readily grasp, Jesus recounted the foresight of the man who built his house on a rock. It survived storm and flood while his neighbors who erected theirs on sand saw them swept away. For Matthew the message was again clear: to those who believed in him, their faith—like that house—would survive. Others would be consigned to spiritual oblivion.

Jesus cautioned that this new lifestyle would not be easy; it was not meant to be. But in return for making every effort to follow it, Jesus made them promises which he guaranteed would be honored: "Ask and it shall be given you. Seek and you will find. Knock and it shall be opened unto you." Then he asked them to rise, bow their heads and repeat after him the prayer he wanted them to use from then on—and encourage everyone else to use. It was the "Our Father."

So ended the Sermon on the Mount—and Christianity was born on a hill overlooking a land occupied by pagans, possessors of the greatest empire the world had yet known. Within a year its emperor, Tiberius, a living divinity, would make a pilgrimage to another summit, close to the very center of imperial power, to beseech his gods. Not for a moment would he suspect there was nothing they could do to preserve him and all he ruled over from fate.

29 ANNO CHRISTI: THE WORLD OF ROME

This Agglomeration which was called and still calls itself the Holy Roman Empire, was neither holy, nor Roman, nor an empire in any way.

Voltaire

2

THE EMPEROR

Depart from me, ye cursed, into everlasting fire, prepared for the devil and his angels.

Matthew 25:41

The first light of a new day revealed the procession climbing Palatine Hill. Its approaches were guarded by the arch erected in memory of the emperor Augustus, stepfather of the short, bull-necked figure sprawled in the litter. The recorders of such detail would be no less sparing elsewhere.

Since that day in A.D. 14 when the consuls had sworn their loyalty to him after Augustus' death and Tiberius had taken the sacred emperor's oath of office, he had regularly been carried to the hilltop. There were those in the Senate who said that upon his accession Tiberius continued to act out a role he had perfected early in life: that of dissembling hypocrite. Others claimed the emperor was obsessed with the thought that the gods made a mistake in allowing him to be elected.

He had never found it easy to reconcile the various factions within the Senate and, from the outset of his reign, was overawed by the sheer size and responsibility of the empire. He had tried to cope in the only way he knew: vacillating between placating and threatening, provoking servile smiles from his aides. Everyone in Rome knew that behind the emperor's outward arrogance lurked a deeply insecure man; that while he had ample blood on his hands, that which flowed through his veins was tainted with venereal disease after a lifetime of sexual indulgence. Finally, tired of being dominated by his mother, the empress Julia Augusta, and inconsolable since the death of his favourite son, Drusus, Tiberius had, three years earlier, in A.D. 26, virtually relinquished imperial responsibility and retired to Capri. The funeral of his mother had brought him briefly back to the capital.

The emperor had been effusively welcomed by the man he had entrusted with the daily affairs of state, Aelius Sejanus, the prefect of the Praetorian Guard. Sejanus had organized the procession with the same relentless efficiency with which he managed everything. But he was more than a ruthless administrator. In a city of natural plotters the prefect was the arch-manipulator: controlling by continuous persecution, treacherous friendships and the ruin of the innocent. It was widely whispered that, to bring him even closer to Tiberius, Sejanus had first seduced Drusus' wife, Livilla, before persuading her to poison her husband, whom Tiberius had hoped would succeed him. The prefect had then coolly asked Tiberius if he could marry the widow. The emperor was still considering whether the gods favored the idea. Sejanus had hesitated over enlisting the imperial astrologers to manipulate Tiberius. This time they might refuse—unlike a previous occasion when they had collaborated in sending Pontius Pilate to Judea, removing another threat against Sejanus' burning ambition to sit on the imperial throne.

At that time Pilate had been back in Rome awaiting a new posting after service in Germania, where he had met his wife, Claudia Procula, the granddaughter of the Emperor Augustus. She had introduced her husband to imperial society as part of her campaign to obtain for him an important post in the capital. Pilate had been flattered to be treated as an equal by Sejanus. The prefect had eventually inquired whether, with Tiberius already into his dotage, Pilate had any interest in the highest office in the land; with his wife's connections he would have a good chance of being considered by the Senate. Pilate had finally admitted that the prospect of one day wearing an emperor's toga was certainly attractive. Shortly afterwards, he had been summoned before Tiberius and told he was being appointed procurator of Judea, one of the remotest and most insignificant of imperial postings. To refuse would have ended Pilate's career. Sejanus had been placatory—Pilate should see it as an interlude—and suggested he consulted the court astrologers to see what portents the move indicated. The soothsayers were reassuring. Not only should Pilate go to Judea—but he must take his wife with him. The astrologers had merely faithfully repeated what Sejanus had ordered them to say. With Claudia Procula out of the way, her husband had lost a Roman power base to run for emperor; her formidable connections would be dissipated by distance.

To make absolutely certain Pilate's chances of being a contender for imperial succession were forever destroyed, Sejanus had set out to ruin the procurator's credibility. He had instructed Pilate to submit regular and detailed accounts of events in Judea: nothing should be too insignificant to go unrecorded. From Caesarea had come a stream of scrolls dealing with every aspect of social, religious and political events impinging upon the Roman occupancy. Tittle-tattle mingled with affairs of state. Pilate's pedantic mind missed nothing. They were the boring outpourings of an isolated bureaucrat who increasingly felt the world revolved around his pettifogging accounts of warring Jewish sects and the scheming of the tetrarch, Herod Antipas, who in any event sent his own confidential reports to Tiberius. These were in turn intercepted by Sejanus; many were critical of the procurator. Increasingly, Pilate's own assessments had a complaining tone: the Jews were always trying to stir up trouble; their high priest was a charlatan; their rites were revolting. Nevertheless, the prefect was careful: proof of consistent and sustained stupidity on Pilate's part could see him being recalled to Rome where, with the help of his wife, he could set about redeeming himself. Sejanus ensured just enough material came before the emperor to make Tiberius shake his head.

The procurator may have mentioned John the Baptist or Jesus in his reports. To the prefect the pair would in any event have sounded about as threatening as the ants scurrying across his path on Palatine Hill. Soon the gods would once more awake and begin manipulating the all-important seven planets which bore their names: the Sun, Saturn, Jupiter, Mars, Venus, Mercury and the Moon. It was a Roman article of faith that each heavenly body had some lordly or terrifying influence on all earthly lives. Sejanus knew that the emperor shared his view that no Roman should take Jews seriously; in no way could their religious claims ever threaten Rome's invincible gods.

To bring Tiberius to the summit of the Palatine Hill required several hundred men. Ahead of the main procession marched a cohort of eighty infantry, led by the signifier carrying their legion's standard, its symbol drawn from paganism. There followed a squadron of cavalry, wrapped, like foot soldiers, in the long red cloaks of the Imperial Army. Immediately behind rode a legate, commander of the procession, and three tribunes, younger men, highborn citizens of Rome who had chosen military life. Distanced from them, mounted on his Arabian stallion, rode Sejanus. He was unusually tall for a Roman, swarthy and thin-lipped, dressed in his *toga praetexia* bestowed by the Senate as a mark of distinction. Over the heavy woollen wrap he wore the embroidered cloak of his high office. His feet were encased in a pair of hand-tooled riding boots.

Next came two cohorts of the Praetorian Guard, one hundred and twenty of the finest fighting men in the empire. Each had sworn a personal oath of allegiance to Tiberius when he gave them their shields, embossed with ancient protective symbols and curved to deflect spears and slingshot. They wore short capes fastened around their shoulders with silver chains. Scabbards sheathed short-bladed swords, designed for close-in fighting; these men were always the last line of defense between the emperor and any threat on his life. To further emphasize their status they marched with two standards, the personal emblem of Tiberius and their own, far older, banner, dating from the time when the praetor, a Roman magistrate, commanded them. Tiberius formed them into the Guard in A.D. 23 when he detected the first plot against his life. They marched on either side of his litter. Twenty-four slaves supported the huge ornate sedan upon their shoulders.

At the rear in a smaller sedan rode Livilla, hidden from view behind heavy lace curtains. Once more Sejanus had called upon her to further his ambitions. She had always seen Claudia Procula as a rival to her position as Rome's leading hostess and needed no encouragement to damage her rival. Livilla had mentioned to Tiberius she had heard a story that Claudia Procula was becoming captivated with some wild prophet in Judea. She knew, instinctively, there was no need to press the matter. The poison had been planted. The emperor's mind would do the rest: nurturing the tidbit, trying to fit it into all the other pieces which nowadays never quite seemed to come together in his brain.

The procession was completed by the emperor's astrologers, a dozen men in cloaks covered with a variety of mystical symbols. They had decided Palatine Hill was the most favored by the gods for Tiberius.

The group moved at a pace which ensured the emperor reached the summit before Jupiter, the greatest of all the gods, ordered the sun to appear. It was a cherished belief of the astrologers that, if Tiberius basked in the first glow of sunrise, the omnipotent ones would continue to look upon him benignly, thus ensuring the emperor remained the ultimate authority in nearly all of the known inhabited world.

Only China was a comparable power. From within its remote borders came the silks for the highborn women of Rome, brought by a series of camel caravans over alps, through jungles and deserts, a journey that took almost a year. From Asia came spices and grain, jewels and precious stones, conveyed across the Indian Ocean in Arabian dhows and up the Red Sea to the great Roman warehouses in Syria, at Antioch, Damascus, Palmyra and Petra. From there they were shipped to Rome. Every nation, occupied or free, supplied the needs of the emperor and his subjects—and was glad to do so. Yet there were those in the Senate and the Forum who had begun to urge Tiberius to abandon his frontier policy of nonaggression and once more to extend the boundaries of empire in all directions. Why should Romans have to pay exorbitant prices for elephant ivory, hides and slaves from the depths of Africa when they could be there for the taking once the land was conquered? Why not send Rome's famed war galleys to capture and hold in the name of the emperor the Persian Gulf? Why not go even further—into India, and perhaps, ultimately, China itself? Rome, insisted those senators, had the military resources; the risk would be high, but the rewards greater.

Tiberius had rejected the arguments. Rome's twenty-eight legions were fully occupied with containing existing frontiers. Even then, there was continuous skirmishing along the Rhine and the Danube. In North Africa Roman-held territory was regularly attacked by savage nomadic tribesmen. Gaul was still restless in spite of the crushing of a rebellion in A.D. 21; the country's fanatical Druids could rise again at any moment.

On the climb up the Palatine slope the emperor lay inside the litter, his massive round head reclining on pillows stuffed with soft plumage plucked from under the wings of partridges, and his flabby body motionless upon blankets dyed purple and embroidered with gold. Over fifty years of age when elected, Tiberius had steadily developed an old man's fears of plotters stalking the corridors of power. Only the gods could protect him.

The procession reached the hilltop. The soldiers and cavalry formed a protective circle around the litter. The legate ordered it lowered on to its stubby legs. That done, the slaves remained motionless: to move without further command would mean being sentenced to savaging by lions in the arena. Sejanus dismounted before the emperor. Tiberius' protruding red-rimmed eyes were those of a man in the depths of his winter who appeared an even more vulnerable figure under the brightening sky. The once jet-black hair, kept short and combed forward from the crown to the forehead, Roman style, was wispy and gray. The formality of his *toga picta*, with its distinguishing purple hem and golden embroidery, contrasted with the *udo*, a pair of homely felt slippers.

Yet, from that summit, Tiberius knew that when he looked north he ruled in an unbroken line of over twelve hundred miles, across the River Po, over the Italian Alps and on into northern Europe. From there came iron and timber for his warships, along with pigs and sheep for his banquets. A shuffling turn to the west and he could picture the six-day sea journey to the northwest coast of Spain and the longer voyage to Cadiz, at the very tip of Iberia, where a large, unnamed rock guarded the exit to the unknown wastes of the Atlantic. From this region came the olives he preferred to the Italian ones, as well as stonemasons to chisel idols and whores to stock the brothels of the capital. Peering south, Tiberius, on a clear day, could glimpse the trading ships, sails fully rigged, plying between Rome and Carthage, a four-day sea journey, taking legionnaires back to their North African posts and bringing home salt and dates. A half-turn would bring him in line with the long sea route from Rome to Alexandria, a twenty-day voyage that could be twice as long if the wind veered. From the Egyptian port came perfume, papyrus, linen, exotic fruits, granite, marble, grain and asphalt. Another full turn would bring him northeast, to face out across the great overland trading route that began in the center of Rome and ended sixteen hundred miles away in Byzantium; it was the busiest and most diverse of all the trading routes within the empire's borders. Finally, facing fully east, Tiberius could look towards the furthest extremity of his empire—the frontier that incorporated Syria and Judea.

He had never understood why his predecessors had clung with such stubbornness to Judea, the second smallest of all the Roman provinces, probably the poorest and certainly the most troublesome. A succession of procurators had done nothing to quell the rebellious nature of its people. Nothing seemed to work—tact, an iron hand, appeasement, mass execution; there was always trouble. Part of the problem was that Judea was not fully integrated into the empire. Its foreign and military affairs remained in the hands of the locally appointed representative of Rome, Herod Antipas. The emperor was represented by Pilate. In theory the procurator had the last word; in practice the tetrarch and, even more so, the high priest, wielded considerable responsibility over their people in all matters which did not impinge upon direct Roman concern; two indigenous legal and religious systems existed side by side. When he appointed Pilate, Tiberius had delivered a standard reminder: the Jews enjoyed autonomy in legal affairs except for political offenses; Roman policy also totally distanced itself from all local crimes of a religious nature. Julius Caesar had granted these freedoms; from time to time the Jews had fought for more concessions. There had been bloodshed. Tiberius had often considered withdrawing all privileges, but had been counseled against this by Sejanus—to do so would provoke further unrest. Roman blood would be spilt quelling it and there would be more angry debates in the Senate. The cantankerous emperor reluctantly decided to let matters stand. He could only have hoped that Pontius Pilate would absorb some of the native cunning Herod Antipas displayed.

From when he had first come to Rome, a dark-skinned slip of a boy, the Herodian prince had impressed Tiberius. He bore the mark of a scion of Herod the Great: the same coal-black eyes, thick lips and short-cropped crinkly hair. He had demonstrated what he had learned at his father's knee on that day when they had sat together in Tiberius' box overlooking the Roman arena. Invited by his host to choose whether a group of Jewish gladiators who had shown particular bravery should live another day, young Herod Antipas had given the thumbs-down sign. The fighters had been disarmed and then devoured by lions. Tiberius had decided here was a Jew who knew his place and accepted Roman mores—and history would have another footnote.

Isolated on Capri, tired from a long life of wasted opportunities, an object of mockery in the streets of Rome, Tiberius had increasingly turned to mysticism to sustain his last years. The predictions of his astrologers were of paramount importance. Through them he sensed matters that his faded political acumen no longer divined. They had alerted him that something unusual was about to happen. Whatever it was, his astrologers must have assured him it would have nothing to do with Pilate's reports about those Jewish preachers. No one had the power to overcome the gods of Rome.

Suddenly, the astrologers dramatically extended their hands towards the horizon. Gaining size by the second came the fiery planet that Jupiter had once more commanded to rise. The sun's rays reached out and touched the emperor, the power of its light forcing him to close his eyes, its warmth removing the chill from his body. The veneration over, the procession descended towards the city, itself now a burnished glow of terracotta roofs, marble colonnades and stone arches.

While Romans continued to speculate how long the gods wished to provide their emperor with his reassuring sunrise, few wondered what lay behind Tiberius' increasing preoccupation with other portents. He had ordered his seers to study the miraculous powers of Pythagoras, dead for six hundred years, to discover if he really had foretold the future by geometric symbols. Imperial soothsayers had traveled to Alexandria, home of the greatest library in the East, to pore over the words of the most celebrated of all the Persian *magi*, author of two million verses in which magic merged with philosophical speculation. Had he also been able genuinely to forecast happenings? Closer to home, in the records of the Roman Senate, astronomers continued to search for signs of a forthcoming comet similar to the one which had plunged across the sky after Caesar's murder. Still other investigators sought evidence for another unscheduled eclipse—as timely as the one which had once quelled a mutiny by one of his own legions on occupation duty in Germania. The suddenly darkened sun had convinced the soldiers the gods were angry at their behavior.

Everything Tiberius did nowadays was based upon fallacious associations which linked to the gods all human doings, as well as the physical properties of the earth. He found a satisfying neatness, completeness and total indisputability about the method. His astrologers had recently interpreted the way the entrails had emerged from a slaughtered hen to mean the time was right to deport some four thousand Jews from the comforts of Rome to the inhospitable rock of Sardinia. His other advisers had observed that since then the emperor had become still further obsessed about the movements of the sun, moon and stars and the way they affected the life and death of all humanity. For him they were the controllers of the human race; they determined its future—and his.

Even in gossipy Rome—where sharing a sworn secret was a sacred duty—few realized that Tiberius was driven by a real and growing panic that the gods would one day soon casually take away what they had bestowed: his supreme power over every man, woman and child in an awesome empire, conquered and established in little over a hundred years. A fear of impending death had become another fixation. He tried to rationalize to himself and others his feelings but this often created a terror that left him a gibbering ruin of a man. But nowadays it was not only death which frightened him: somewhere within his great fief was a threat which had no shape or form. Yet it was there. This certain knowledge had come to him in a dream. He had first experienced it thirty years before when Augustus had exiled him to a lengthy period of lonely duty on Rhodes. There Tiberius had consulted the legendary Thrasyllus of Alexandria, an astrologer who was an outstanding Platonist and the author of a standard text on numerology. Thrasyllus had not only predicted that Tiberius would become emperor but had also interpreted the vision as meaning that during his reign "a great challenge would arise in the East."

Recently the dream had returned. Yet, in spite of all their skills in creating elaborate patterns indicating what the disposition of the heavenly bodies meant at any given time, his astrologers had not been able to identify the form this challenge would take. He had urged them to search harder for signs that would reassure him he had not offended the gods. He could never forget they had demonstrated their power to take terrible revenge upon Julius Caesar, who until then had been their most favored son on earth.

In 45 B.C., three years before Tiberius was born, Caesar had met and seduced Cleopatra in Egypt. She was a nubile twenty-two-year-old; he well into middle age, virile and battle-scarred, until then more at ease around chariot steeds than in a boudoir. Romans had smiled understandingly when Caesar confirmed his mistress as Queen of Egypt; a hero was entitled to his peccadilloes.

Many, however, felt he had gone too far in tampering with the calendar. They waited uneasily to see how the gods would respond. Rome had calculated the year by a lunar method which lagged behind solar reckoning. In 45 B.C., Caesar saw the Roman year was shorter by sixty-seven days than the solar one. Displaying his renowned impetuosity, he decreed that every ensuing imperial year would contain 365 days. This still made the Roman calendar different from the one used by the Jews. Their rabbis had told Caesar's astrologers that in the Jewish holy *Book of Jubilees*, God had ordained that "man must observe a year of 364 days and those that do not bring upon themselves misfortunes." Caesar learned that another essential of their religion was believing that one day their God would visit earth and walk among them as a man. To a Roman this was pure nonsense. Why should a god ever want to assume the shape of a mortal? Caesar had not been given long to ponder such a question. Three months after changing the calendar he was murdered on the Ides of March in 44 B.C. by Brutus, Cassius and others upon whom he had bestowed favor and pardon.

Anarchy had subsequently befallen Rome and the empire. Hundreds of senators were executed for conspiring in the death of Caesar. Cleopatra committed suicide. For three years the world trembled as factions in Rome fought for control. From the carnage emerged Augustus. Many now said his achievements were greater than even Caesar's. Augustus had streamlined the cumbersome Roman administration and ruled through careful delegation. But on the advice of his astrologers he did not reinstitute the old lunar calendar. When he became emperor Tiberius was counseled that the gods had forgiven the great Caesar and were content that the solar calendar should remain on the statute books.

Perhaps it was the return of Tiberius' dream, once more with its hint that the threat lay in the East, which had aroused the emperor's interest in the way the Jews calculated their year. They regularly added an extra month, Vaeder, inserted between the spring months called Adar and Nisan. An important date was the spring equinox called Tisni, celebrated by Jews throughout the empire. The emperor had learned that during the last Tishnin Jews started again to refer openly to the most mysterious of all figures in their religion, the one they called in Aramaic "the Messiah"—the Expected One.

For the past five centuries—dating around the time the code of the Twelve Tables had been given to Rome by the gods so that its citizens would know how to order their lives—there had been almost no mention of when this Messiah would come. Instead, throughout the empire—from the mountains of Armenia overlooking the Caspian Sea to the wastes of Pannonia and on to the verdant coast of Gaul—Jews had chanted their mournful lament: "There are no prophets left now, none can tell us how long we must endure."

But in the carefully screened news Sejanus forwarded to Capri, the emperor's consuls, procurators and tribunes reported that within the empire tantalizing whisperings had continued to seep from within their closed communities. The Messiah was coming.

On previous occasions when they had been angered, the Roman gods had exacted tribute in the form of massacres upon this people who worshipped a single God without an image. In the past forty years there had been no fewer than fifteen pogroms against Jews. Never far from the surface was a virulent anti-Semitism which Tiberius resolutely believed the Jews brought upon themselves with their clever schemes to avoid paying taxes, and their refusal not only to enter a Roman home, but even to touch, by as much as a handshake, anyone but their own people. They rejected pork on the grounds that their holy books called it unclean—a further affront to Romans, who regarded suckling pig as essential for any feast. They included in their religion the degrading ritual—performed in the name of their God—where the foreskin of each male child was removed. Tiberius had nevertheless been astonished to learn that, in spite of massacres and exile, there remained within his empire an estimated seven million Jews; one out of every ten he ruled over professed a faith and adhered to customs he regarded as repugnant and profane. Unlike all other races—Greeks, Gauls, Cyrenaicans, Africans, Britons, Germans and Iberians—the Jews steadfastly clung together in a remarkable way. Even in Rome they remained in close-knit ghettos living by their own strict regulations. They gathered together every week on their holy days to pray and sing psalms. They called this place the *kinneseth*. Tiberius preferred the Greek, *sunagoge*. Whenever they could, if only once in their lifetime, Jews returned to Judea to partake in great feasts and pray at the Temple. Then, imbued with fervor, many would spread their religious propaganda, patiently explaining the virtue of a weekly day of rest, their festivals, their custom of lighting lamps and rules about food. This proselytizing, when it stretched the forbearance of the gods too far, led to renewed bloodshed. Yet, in spite of this, attempts to Romanize them had failed. The greater the pressure, the more determined the resistance.

The humblest Jew displayed a mysterious pride suggesting that he or she not only belonged to a people far superior to the Romans, but was also a member of the greatest race to walk the earth. Even in the literal jaws of death facing the lions in the arena, Tiberius had watched, both baffled and impressed, how Jewish gladiators accepted their fate unflinchingly. Sometimes they had even fallen to their knees and cried a last prayer to their God, assuring him they were glad to be a part of his greatness. The emperor had once ordered a thousand Jews in succession into the hippodrome sands to see if one of them would show fear. None had. He could not understand such reaction. Neither could he grasp why so many Jews, having claimed they had been given a piece of land by God, should leave it. This incessant movement was their Diaspora.

Like much else associated with Jewish history, Tiberius discovered their restless dispersion had its origins long before Rome laid down a history. Having come out of Egypt, the Exodus, they soon returned there. Caesar had brought back to Rome evidence that the equivalent of a legion of Jews had borne arms for a Pharaoh in the sixth century and had captured and held a vast tract of desert around the oasis of Aswan. They were given honorary Egyptian citizenship—but steadfastly clung to their own religion. Later, tens of thousands of Jewish warriors enlisted in Alexander's army to capture Mesopotamia. They had been similarly rewarded, taking from Greek culture what they saw as worthwhile, like its language, but never its religion. The Romans had themselves found their fiercest opponents often were Jewish fighters. As a token of respect some had been spared upon capture and offered the chance of settling in some new and inhospitable part of the empire. The opportunity had been accepted, the areas had prospered.

Gradually the Diaspora took on a new meaning: the wandering peddler Jew became absorbed as a successful businessman into every town and village under Roman domination. Within the past fifty years Rome had joined Alexandria as one of the two main centers of the Diaspora. The Egyptian metropolis contained as many Jews as lived in Judea; three-fifths of the city's population worshipped the God of Abraham. In Egypt there were over a million who did so.

Caesar had encouraged them to settle in Rome, allowing them to build their underground cemeteries and openly worship before the seven-branched candlestick of their faith. Many, through favor or purchase, had acquired Roman citizenship—though Tiberius still resisted the idea of Jews holding any imperial appointments. Denied any official authority, Judaism continued to wield an influence that clearly strengthened the mood of those of its people who remained in their tiny homeland. Scattered to all corners of the empire, the Jews, unlike any other of Rome's subjects, had a well-established communications network which kept them in touch with each other and events in Jerusalem. Again, at the core of that bond was their religion. Jews could never forget that, no matter how well they did living among the heathen, the Diaspora was still their *galut*, the exile: a curse God put upon them for the sins of their forefathers. No Roman, least of all an emperor, could understand how foolhardy they could be.

Upon the death of Herod the Great, Jews had launched an uprising against the Roman forces. In spite of an early success in all but overwhelming the small garrison, the revolt was doomed. Within a week's march were two legions in Syria; from Cyprus and Egypt scores of Roman war galleys were swiftly sent with further forces. Yet the insurrection had gone ahead. The quick-thinking Jerusalem garrison tribune had ordered the Temple to be put to the torch. Thousands of Jews perished, including a large number of priests. The population then surrendered. For the next three months the predominant sound in Jerusalem was the hammering of crosses to hang some two thousand men and women judged to have been involved in the rebellion. To reduce the risk of further revolt the country was divided between three of Herod's sons: Archelaus, Philip and Herod Antipas. The brothers had fought and plotted against each other. There had been uprisings. Jew had killed Jew. High priests had been replaced. There had been further fighting. The final victor in the family battle for power had been Herod Antipas. In the face of his political maneuvering some procurators had lasted only months. The emperor had not intervened in the matter: if a Roman was not skilled enough to withstand the machinations of a Jew he had no place in Judea. If nothing else, Pontius Pilate had learned that much.

30 ANNO CHRISTI: THE UNHOLY TRIUMVIRATE

How would you be if He, which is the top of judgment,
should but judge you as you are?

Shakespeare, *Measure for Measure*

3

THE PROCURATOR

Thou art not far from the kingdom of God.
Mark 12:34

What would endure of his biography, as well as in the memory of those who knew him, however slightly, would be that punctuality remained one of the many inflexible rules of Pontius Pilate. He had awoken when the level of liquid, released a drop at a time, had reached the fifth marked division on the side of his bedroom *clepsydra*, the most elaborate of all the water clocks in Judea. This was one of the few hours he enjoyed in Jerusalem, when the infinity of shades were at their most captivating, the tints moving from black to mauve to the first hint of yellow.

During the night he had slept fitfully as he often did when Claudia Procula was not there; he blamed his insomnia on the bed, even though it was identical to the one in his palace in Caesarea, his wife having arranged for a pair of these elaborate beds to come with them from Rome. Whenever Pilate traveled on duty to Jerusalem he brought one with him. Like the *clepsydra*, it was far superior to anything available in this godforsaken land. The frame was carved from the best wood, the mattress and pillows were stuffed with wool, the coverlet came from Corinth and was the handiwork of the finest seamstresses in the empire. Yet perhaps alone, away from her, he did indeed brood that in Rome his future had been finally settled: that he was destined to end his days as a forgotten cipher of imperialism.

Claudia Procula would upbraid him for such defeatism; reiterating that while they were both victims of Sejanus' machinations he must never forget her imperial pedigree. She would fight for him; all he had to do was listen to her. Her connections in Rome assuredly had sent word that in the past year Sejanus had begun to overreach himself, becoming embroiled on too many hostile fronts; that a groundswell was developing against the prefect's intrigues; that the emperor no longer blindly trusted him. A wise woman, she might well counsel that this was not the time for her husband to go to Rome and confront Sejanus. Let others do that. Far better to bide his time.

Their marriage, for all its outward signs of harmony, was, in its third year, an empty barren union, sustained only by her determination to see him elected to the highest possible office.

Despite her coldness and indifference, his wife was the only person to whom he could speak freely. On this trip she had promised to join him in Jerusalem, showing no reluctance to do so, as she had in the past. Nor had she expressed detestation of Jews since she had begun to read his reports on Jesus and John the Baptist. He had never asked her to explain her interest in them. She could certainly be imperious and secretive when she chose. Those were the times he felt most keenly the gulf between them.

Overnight more drovers with their sheep, cattle and caged birds—all to be sacrificed—had camped out on the hills around the city. Mingling with them were thousands of new pilgrims. Their presence gave credence to the ancient Hebrew expression "next year in Jerusalem," the one promise which had brought Jews here down the centuries. Huddled around the campfires they waited for the city gates to open. Then they, too, would converge upon this capital standing in the center of the Judean land, amongst hills which not only presented a formidable physical barrier, but also in the eyes of every Jew held a special significance. For them, those mounds, when finally seen, were a reminder that their journey was almost over; that behind the slopes and escarpments lay the holy courts of Jerusalem, whose glories they had chanted about while on their journey. The closer they came to Jerusalem, the louder grew their Hebrew psalms of ascent, as they picked their way upwards to the high plateau, almost three thousand feet above sea level, where the city stood. No matter which way they approached—over the top of the Mount of Olives, along the Valley of the Cheesemakers, across the rocky slopes of the Gereb, through the bleak Kidron ravine or traversing the Mount of Scandal where Solomon had allowed altars to be raised to the gods of his heathen wives—they still had to climb. Pilate understood why their scriptures constantly called it the "city of the high place."

He could have recited word-perfect the passages about Jerusalem not being "rebuilt in its entirety until all the children of Israel will be gathered from exile"; that the city was "The tent God will spread forth in all directions"; that "in the end of time Jerusalem will become the metropolis for all lands." No doubt it was about as realistic to Pilate as the claim that "one day" this invisible Jewish God would surround the city with seven walls: including one of silver, another of gold, a third of precious stones, finally an outer wall of fire to ensure that the existence of Jerusalem "will radiate to the four corners of the world." Even Saturn would not have dared to make such a promise. Yet those people out there on the hillsides and within the city wall believed it all implicitly. Pilate had never understood how they could seriously think for a moment that this city would ever replace Rome as the center of global influence; it was another example of their arrogance.

No doubt, too, they would be astonished at how much he knew about their holy writings and the rituals controlling their daily lives; of customs peculiar to Jerusalem such as displaying a flag at the door of a house where a feast was being held; of doubly fining a caterer who produced a bad banquet for the disgrace he had caused the host and the upset to guests; of city ordinances which included a ban on renting out private homes to pilgrims and forbade an oven because the smoke would blacken the Temple: all baking was done in the Tower of Ovens, a huge edifice in the Lower City. He was above all aware of the special significance Jews attached to one particular gate in the Temple walls, built by King Solomon to await the day when the Messiah would enter.

To Pilate this was as foolish as the popular Jewish belief that deep inside the Temple was a stone which miraculously hovered in the air and would only fall to earth when the Messiah came. Pompey had thoroughly searched the Temple and never mentioned such a phenomenon. The procurator understood the need for such legends: the Jews, for all their innate violence, were a weak people. He knew they saw him as inflexible and stubbornly relentless, ready, if the occasion demanded, to act with pitiless savagery. While he never hesitated to do so, they totally failed to understand that his response—like that of any Roman—was a natural reaction to their attitudes. All things Rome held sacred Jews regarded as profane: every Roman was the living incarnation of idolatry and debauchery, sensuality and materialism, power and tyranny. While in the rest of the empire Jews were content to remain aloof from their neighbor, here, in Judea, they displayed an open revulsion that no self-respecting Roman could tolerate—let alone the appointed representative of the emperor. It was all there in his accounting to Tiberius.

Well into his forties, Pontius Pilate, after a career representing the empire in various provinces, was used to total respect—not to being ostracized, or treated with barely disguised contempt and hatred. What made it particularly galling was that these reactions were not the natural responses of the conquered to the victors: the Jewish attitude seemed to be rooted in an ancient superiority complex that was an essential part of their religion.

Pilate possessed a highly developed mind and was a voracious reader. In his four years in Judea he had mastered Hebrew and among Jewish works he had read was the *Sybilline Oracles*, written around the time Rome had really begun to expand its empire. The procurator discovered within its pages a prayer which could only have infuriated him. "A holy king will come and reign over all the world—and then his wrath will fall on the people of Latium and Rome will be destroyed to the ground. O God, send a stream of fire from heaven, and let the Romans perish, each in his own home. O poor and desolate me! When will the day come, the judgment day of the eternal land of the great king?"

That awesome entreaty historically reaffirmed Pilate's strong sense of mission. Not only was he the ultimate representative of the emperor, he was also an emissary of the gods. For all of Sejanus' trickery he also believed he had been sent to this forsaken land to continue to make its people bow, to break their will further, to reinforce the authority of Rome upon them with a rigor and severity in a way no previous procurator had done. But he had not made the mistake of his predecessors and acted impulsively. Every step he had taken had been calculated: reporting to Rome the renewed talk of a coming Messiah, the emergence of preachers in Jerusalem and Galilee; strengthening his surveillance on Herod Antipas and around the Temple. From whatever quarter trouble might erupt, Pontius Pilate believed he was ready to overcome it.

This time he had been in Jerusalem a week; as usual it already seemed like a year. To him it was a dirty, smelly city, not to be spoken of in the same breath as Rome. Yet Jews continuously used the syllables of its name in their prayer life. Every year at Passover pilgrims from the farthest reaches of the empire traveled to what they called the Lord's home—the massive Temple edifice adjoining his quarters. Some had actually wept at the onset of their journey here to celebrate the greatest of all their feasts. It drew vast throngs from all parts of the Diaspora: Jews from Babylon with black robes trailing in the dust; Jews from the steppes of Anatolia in their goat-hair cloaks; Jews from Phoenicia dressed in tunics and striped trousers; Jews from Rome in togas; Jews from Gaul in leather skins; Jews from Spain with sheep pelts around their shoulders; Jews from Persia in their silks, brocades and adorned with gold and silver. Battening on them were the peddlers of sacrificial animals and the money changers, scandalously overcharging—just as in Rome the purveyors of votive offerings to gods doubled their prices at certain times.

Pilate hated coming here not only for Passover, but also for the Feast of Weeks, the Day of Atonement and the Feast of Tabernacles. At these times the air was particularly filled with the sickening smell of burning animal and bird flesh from the sacrificial altars and the cloying aroma of incense. Each festival was a highly dangerous time, when popular sentiment could overflow and the air fill with talk of insurrection and revolt. These were the occasions when the Jews felt most keenly the yoke of foreign rule and their patriotic motivation was closest to the surface. Pilate was certain there would be the usual rabble-rousers, whispering that any Roman presence in the city—especially at this hallowed time—was the ultimate and never-to-be-forgiven insult.

Yet informers had reported that the indignation of Jesus continued to be directed at what happened in and around the Temple. He had increasingly challenged what went on within its hallowed courts and rooms, where the rabbi-scholars taught amidst the shrieks of the sellers of sacrificial birds and animals and the din of the money changers offering pilgrims coins which had been ritually cleansed in exchange for their pagan currency.

The difficulty in trying to assess the response to Jesus, like all else reported to Pilate about him, was the system the procurator had inherited. Paid on the importance of their information, he found the network of spies notoriously prone to exaggeration. They often brought tales to his headquarters at Caesarea which bore the hallmark of lengthy sojourns in village taverns, where Hebraic mythology was rife. In one, shortly after he was born, the parents of Jesus had come to the Temple to partake in the ritual observances which accompanied the birth of every Hebrew baby. A Jewish woman was considered ritually unclean for forty days following the delivery of a son and eighty in the case of a daughter. To purify herself she made a sacrificial offering of two doves to a Temple priest. He cut one bird's throat allowing the blood to flow down the side of the altar, removed the crop and feathers, broke the wings and threw all the remains into a fire. The blood of the second dove was sprinkled over the altar. The ritual was completed when the rabbi pronounced the woman cleansed, and the husband handed him five shekels—the prescribed payment for the sacrifice. This commonplace occurrence had, according to one informer, in the case of the baby Jesus, an unusual twist. Leaving the Temple, cradled in his mother's arms, they had been confronted by an old man—"just and devout"—named Simeon. He had peered at the infant and at once hailed him as the Expected One. A few minutes later an old woman named Anna, who lived on the charity of the faithful, spending her days in the Court of Women, had repeated the prediction. Both Simeon and Anna were long dead. There had been no way for Pilate to have that particular report verified. For his soldiers to question the mother of Jesus would almost certainly have proven fruitless. She would no doubt have denied any such happening.

There had been another incident.

At the age of thirteen Jesus had come to the Temple for the custom of *bar mitzvah*. For a Jewish boy this meant being embraced as a son of the law—forever responsible for observing all religious and civic duties; from now on an adult who acknowledged sacred commitments. Once more an informer had offered an account which made Jesus exceptional, describing how the boy had come with his parents who had once more paid for a sacrifice to mark the occasion. When the ceremony was completed, Jesus had disappeared. After spending three fruitless days searching for him they had finally returned to the Temple to offer prayers for his safety and found him debating with the priests over their interpretation of faith. The story ran that he had challenged and corrected them on numerous points—and they had been astounded and fearful of this prodigy. When Jesus' angry mother had chastised him for such behavior the boy had reportedly given a puzzling reply: "How is it that ye sought me? Wist ye not that I must be about my Father's business?" Pilate had concluded at best it was no more than a determination by Jesus to give an early sign he intended to devote himself to a religious life. To try to give it any deeper meaning was nonsensical.

The reports about Jesus which had reached Pilate after the wedding feast at Cana could neither have alarmed nor seemed exceptional to him. The poetry of Homer and Virgil was filled with similar fantasies. Besides, many of the accounts of his miraculous powers had taken on a suspicious similarity; his curing of a possessed madman was very close to a subsequent account of his healing an epileptic boy.

The procurator had come to recognize that his spies were rich in metaphors and imagery but short on case histories which would warrant the slightest accusation that Jesus had set out to show he was in any way equal to the empire's gods: they could inflict plagues, deflect the arrows of an entire army, make men fall in love or go mad, change one person into an animal and another into a rock. Compared with them, Jesus was no more than the object of harmless adoration mostly still confined to Galilee.

While he had continued forwarding details of the less farcical stories about his work to Rome, Pontius Pilate regarded Jesus, three years after he had first come to the procurator's attention, as still a curiosity rather than a threat. However, it did not explain to Pilate the attitude of both the current high priest, Joseph Caiaphas, and Herod Antipas towards Jesus. They had still made no move to silence his sustained attacks against the Jewish establishment.

The relationship between Pilate, Herod Antipas and Caiaphas had never been smooth. The procurator had expanded the infamous system of tax gathering through private contractors. These men reviled as "publicans" and "sinners" by Jesus—often had their own armed men to enforce their demands; they could also call upon the imperial army for support. While many were Roman citizens, imported for the task, a growing number were Jewish. These collaborators were treated by other Jews as outcasts, denied any place in Jewish society and disqualified from giving evidence in any Jewish court. Their families were equally ostracized. Herod Antipas and Caiaphas had appealed to Pilate to stop using Jews to collect taxes. He had refused. The tetrarch had asked the emperor to intervene. The response from Capri was that in this instance matters must remain as they were. On learning of Herod Antipas' intervention Pilate ended all pretense of treating him on anything resembling equal terms. To the procurator the prince was no more than a Jew aping his betters, and he regarded Caiaphas with similar contempt.

Pilate now only met the high priest when the official came to collect his vestments. The expensive stole and other regalia were kept in a stone-lined chamber in the base of the Antonia Fortress which the procurator used as his headquarters in Jerusalem. The door of the chamber was triple sealed, one affixed by the high priest, the other by the chief of the Temple guard—an official named Jonathan—and the third by Pilate himself. The seals had been broken a few days ago in preparation for Passover. Keeping the apparel of the high priest under Roman custody and handing it over only for high festivals, reclaiming it immediately after a feast ended, was a deliberate measure to curb Caiaphas' authority and protect Rome against any surprise move he might attempt in his capacity as the most senior Jewish dignitary in the land. Under certain circumstances, Caiaphas would need his full religious regalia to enforce his authority—such as presiding over a session of the Great Sanhedrin, the supreme court of the Jews.

The procurator knew the restrictions over vestments not only rankled Caiaphas' own highly developed sense of personal pride but painfully reminded him he could not exercise his power without the permission of Rome's representative. To salt the high priest's wound—and to increase his own wealth—Pilate had continued the custom of his predecessors by demanding from Caiaphas a substantial annual payment to remain in office. This further soured daily contact between the two administrations.

From his bedroom high above the Sheep Gate, Pilate had an unsurpassed view of one of those stretches of water Jews regarded as holy; this one was called the Pool of Bethesda. Winding between the Mount of Olives and Mount Gereb were the roads to Jericho, Bethlehem, Shechem and Caesarea.

A hundred feet below where he stood came the measured tread of sentries patrolling the stairways and the entrances to the secret passages which led from the fortress under the Temple and into the heart of the city. In one of these the quick-thinking tribune's men had broken out a hole and started the fire which quelled the revolt of A.D. 6.

Pilate could be certain that any rebellion would now be even more swiftly crushed. All Jerusalem's gates had been further fortified under his order. At each entrance the massive wall had been deepened to three times its depth and heavy iron gates replaced wooden ones. Above each was a platform from which defenders could rain down spears and slingshot upon attackers. The Golden Gate had five hundred lances permanently racked in its guardhouse. The Fountain Gate had the natural defense of the Kidron Valley before it; few Jews would want to wage war by crossing their hallowed cemetery of Jehoshaphat, where the prophet Joel had predicted all souls would gather on the Day of Judgment. In the west of the city were the Gate of Ephraim and the Corner Gate, already strong defensive positions, but now permanently manned by two cohorts of Roman soldiers. Another cohort protected the Dung Gate, leading to the foul-smelling Valley of Hinnom where child sacrifices had been made to the Phoenician god, Moloch, and the Temple courts had been filled with prostitutes. Hinnom was also a place to be avoided. Finally, there was the Fish Gate, where the roads from the coastal villages converged. These tracks were constantly patrolled by cavalry who ran spot checks on Jews; anybody carrying an unauthorized weapon was invariably executed. In the event of trouble in Jerusalem's narrow streets and alleys, the horsemen could ride to Caesarea to summon more troops. Force-marching they could reach the city in under sixty hours.

Caesarea was a Roman port. Within its walls Jews were barely tolerated and Romans could walk streets which were filled with statues to their gods and emperors. Here in Jerusalem such totems were forbidden under what the procurator complained was yet another sop to the Jewish faith. In Caesarea coins were struck bearing the portrait of Tiberius. But they could only be used within the city limits—and never displayed in Jerusalem because their image offended Jewish susceptibilities.

The longer he lived amongst them, the more intolerable Pilate found the Jews; they were full of incomprehensible prejudices and exponents of intrigue. At every opportunity they sought to make Judea almost ungovernable. Pilate had six thousand troops to deal with any insurrection. Five hundred of them formed the Jerusalem garrison. The remainder were in Caesarea. Like the procurator, they hated duty in Jerusalem, which at times like Passover contained more potential troublemakers than would be found in all Rome.

At this hour of the morning within the city wall—ringing it for three unbroken miles—all was virtually silent. The only sign that people lived here was the stench of excrement, decaying refuse, cooking grease and, from the west, the reek of diseased animal carcasses thrown on the city's rubbish dump. The smoke from its perpetual fire reminded Pilate of the place to which the gods of Rome regularly consigned those who had displeased them. The stench reinforced his distaste for this country, its people and its leaders. Pilate had learned they could be as ruthless towards their own kind as Sejanus. The fate of John the Baptist proved that.

It had been in the month the Jews called Iyar when news reached Pilate of what had happened at Machaerus. In his squat and menacing fortress, Herod Antipas had kept John the Baptist imprisoned for over a year. Yet, brought from his dungeon, the prophet had continued to reproach the tetrarch over his relationship with Herodias, the wife of Herod Antipas' brother. Several times the tetrarch had made the uncomfortable journey from Jerusalem to his hilltop keep far beyond the Dead Sea to try to persuade the prophet to cease his attacks. Groomed and scented, dressed in all his finery, he had sat with John, clad in his shirt of camel skin, hair matted and tangled, beard flowing and unkempt. Alternately cajoling and pleading, then threatening and screaming in fury, Herod Antipas had tried to persuade John to accept his relationship with Herodias. The more the tetrarch talked the greater John's intransigence. God, he insisted, told him he could not remain silent. Herod Antipas should be an example to his people, instead his behavior had aroused divine anger. Deeply troubled, the tetrarch had discussed the situation with Herodias. She consulted the high priest.

To celebrate his forty-ninth birthday Herod Antipas moved his entire court to Machaerus. Invited, too, were Jerusalem's most important businessmen and traders. Pilate had ordered no Roman could attend. But he had his informers in place. The birthday festivities lasted a week, culminating in a sumptuous banquet which kindled memories of the day the tetrarch's father had been crowned: then a thousand lambs had been roasted and a hundred of the loveliest dancing girls had performed. His son also had a similar number of lambs slaughtered as well as importing delicacies from all around the Mediterranean. At the height of the revelry, a shocked murmur had swept through the women seated at the far end of the huge banqueting hall. Herod Antipas had urged his stepdaughter, Salome, barely fourteen years of age, to dance before the drunken men at the tetrarch's table. The women were stunned into silence when Salome rose to her feet.

Pirouetting slowly at first, then gaining speed, she swirled barefooted before her stepfather. Skillfully she removed one silken veil after another, tossing each one to the clamoring men. Finally, she stood almost naked before them. Herod Antipas promised Salome any reward she cared to name for her erotic performance, even, he added, half of his kingdom.

She, perhaps a child seeking guidance, or possibly acting out a role rehearsed with her mother, hesitated. Her stepfather repeated that she could have anything. Salome walked across to the table where Herodias sat with the other women. After her mother had whispered in her ear, she walked back to stand before Herod Antipas. He paled at her request, and appeared to hesitate, to be on the verge of refusal, when she repeated the words more firmly. He had promised, she reminded him in her little-girl voice, now he must not disappoint her. Two guards were dispatched to the dungeons. There, below the marbled floors where Salome waited, silent like everyone present in the hall, one guard had held John the Baptist's head over a block, while the other severed the neck from the body with a sword. The two men returned with the head on a brass tray. Salome reportedly screamed. Herodias had smiled and raised her glass towards Caiaphas who was seated with a select number of his priests at a table adjoining that of the tetrarch.

Even in death—so his spies had told Pilate—John the Baptist's face possessed an expression that chilled their hearts. Herod Antipas had offered to bring the head to Caesarea so that the procurator might try to have his astrologers interpret its meaning. Pilate had coldly refused. The tetrarch had then thrown the skull to his mastiffs.

Arriving in Jerusalem, Pilate's agents had brought news of a growing rumor that Jesus intended to confront Caiaphas during Passover concerning the death of his cousin. If that was the case it would remain a matter for the Temple authorities. Caiaphas had his own efficient force policing the Temple; he could also call upon the tetrarch's troops. That sort of superiority should be enough to deal quickly with Jesus and his followers should they create trouble. But to apprehend Jesus in the name of Rome when there was no evidence to show he had committed a crime under imperial law could provoke the wild backlash the procurator was here to prevent.

Pontius Pilate recognized only too clearly that if the Temple authorities moved against Jesus or indeed any other preacher in the superheated emotionalism of Passover without the greatest skill and stealth, coupled with the strongest of legal reasons—instead of the personal vindictiveness which had led to John the Baptist's death—the whole country could again be plunged into bloody revolution. The chances at the best of times of avoiding this were not improved by the position of Caiaphas. On the one hand he represented the supreme ancient authority of the Temple administration, the chief spokesman for the nation and ultimately the most important Jew in the eyes of the Romans. Yet, largely because he remained in office solely at the pleasure of the procurator, the high priest was no longer regarded by the people as the symbol of Jewish pride and hope, or irrefutable living proof that Judaism was superior to all religions. Many saw him as a puppet and a collaborator, a quisling who clung to the most sacred of Jewish national and religious posts through simony. Pilate realized that if Caiaphas misjudged the mood of the people over Jesus, no matter how strong the provocation or how certain the high priest was of his facts, there could still be trouble. That would involve the use of Roman force. The procurator well knew how easily aroused the masses became over anything that threatened or offended their religious susceptibilities.

After his first visit to Jerusalem, Pilate had decided to replace the unadorned standards raised over the Antonia Fortress. He felt they did not reflect the authority of Rome. He already knew it was a basic and sacred precept of Judaism, clearly stated in the Book of Exodus, that "thou shalt not make unto thee any graven image or any likeness of any thing that is in heaven above or that is in the earth beneath." But, determined to show his power over, and contempt for, such hallowed belief, something no previous procurator had done, Pilate went ahead with implementing the Roman custom of displaying, on all public buildings and monuments, standards and insignias which bore the face of the ruling emperor. These were raised overnight, Pilate gambling that, once in place, the Jews would allow the image of Tiberius to flutter beside the Temple. Dawn saw the full force of Jewish rage. A deputation, led by no less than a thousand priests from the Temple, marched to Caesarea, demanding the removal of the offensive emblems. Pilate refused.

For five days thousands of Jews had surrounded his palace, chanting prayers and squatting on the ground in an act of peaceful civil disobedience. The procurator had turned a legion loose on them; the Jews were driven at swordpoint into the local hippodrome where gladiators fought once a week. Pilate ordered the soldiers systematically to beat the Jews. Hundreds of lacerated bodies littered the arena. Still the demonstrators refused to concede. Finally, Herod Antipas had arrived and suggested to Pilate that such important emblems warranted a more deserving site than Jerusalem could offer and would be better displayed at the magnificent Temple of Augustus in Caesarea. Pilate had at the time reluctantly admired the tetrarch's face-saving solution. The offending banners were removed from Jerusalem, and Herod Antipas attended the dedication ceremony which saw them raised over Augustus' Temple. He had then sent a report of the incident to Tiberius. When Pilate had thankfully thought the matter forgotten, from Capri had come a stinging rebuke. Pilate's instinct had been to move against the tetrarch as he had successfully done before with local opposition, but Claudia Procula cautioned against action. Her Roman sources had already told her about Herod Antipas' favored position in the emperor's eyes. Not for the first time Pilate had been grateful for his wife's advice.

It was an autumn morning when Pilate had stepped ashore from an imperial galley and stood for the first time on the soil of Judea. His dark deep-set eyes had surveyed the guard of honor and, beyond, the silent, watchful throng of Jews. No doubt he knew they were measuring him. The conquered always did; trying to gauge whether he would be strong or weak, fair or unjust, a meddler in their affairs or indifferent to their ways. The first moments of a new posting were always like that. Each time he had tried immediately to stamp his personality on the onlookers, showing them the way he intended to behave.

Less certain can be the motive for the action ascribed to him on that blustery day in Caesarea. After inspecting the drawn-up cohorts, the procurator had walked to the huge sundial on the jetty. Under a cloudy sky it was useless. He ordered it to be removed and replaced with a water clock.

Later he had ordered checks to be made on the *clepsydrae* in Roman law courts throughout Judea. They had been installed to curb the speeches of lawyers who were paid by the hour. The clocks governed the length of time permitted to prosecutors, who had two hours to state a case, defense counsel were allowed an extra hour. For grave offenses—the murder of one Roman by another or Jews being tried for insurrection—the prosecution was permitted six hours to present their facts while the defense were entitled to a full nine hours to call rebuttal evidence. Trials could be conducted—if a Jew was involved—in Aramaic and Greek, but judgments were always recorded in Latin. Jews condemned to death had brief details of their crimes nailed in all three languages to their crosses. Such attention to detail was in the best tradition of the Roman administrative class—and had ensured Pontius Pilate was even more hated in the eyes of the Jews. A lifetime in imperial service, hoisting the standards of Rome over distant colonies, hardened him to such responses.

Pontius Pilate had a distinctive physical characteristic, the result of an imperfectly healed shoulder injury suffered when he had been rescued from a sinking war galley driven on to the rocks of Sicily during one of the sudden storms that made the Mediterranean so treacherous in winter. His skin had been darkened by desert sands and blistered in icy mountain passes. Born and bred in the colder uplands of the Apennine mountain spine southeast of Rome, he possessed the racially classical round head of antecedents who, centuries before, had migrated from Asia Minor over the Alps. His family name was a distinguished one among the Samnites, the clannish mountain people who, since the First Punic War—twenty years of fearsome battles—had provided Rome with administrators to rebuild and exploit shattered lands and peoples. Before governing Judea, Pilate had seen service in Spain, Greece and Gaul. In all these territories—in spite of his reading and other knowledge—he had displayed, along with his punctuality, a massive indifference to local culture and customs. For him the social mores of the longhaired Gaul were no different from the peculiarities of Spaniards or Greeks. They were all subjects of Rome.

He would have preferred the governorship of a province where the seasons were more pleasing than those of Judea: two abruptly divided periods of a long broiling summer and a winter when the nights were so cold that the law of the Jews required a creditor to give back any clothes, taken as a pledge, before darkness. During Adar, the third month of the Hebrew calendar, there was heavy frost at dawn, sweltering heat at noon, and at dusk ice once more rimmed the ornamental ponds in the grounds of his palace. No one had warned him of the winds. His Homeric scrolls had spoken of wafting breezes, little more than zephyrs. While it was true they made the heat of high summer almost tolerable, there was also the winter *qadim*, howling from the east, icy and dry, cleansing the air and chilling the bone marrow with its blast. Most unbearable of all was the *khamsin*, roaring in from the desert filling the sky with a gritty grayness that could bury a horse and its rider in an hour. A squadron of Rome's finest cavalry had vanished forever on border duty beyond the Ghor, swallowed by drifting sand. Then there were the rains. A year's downpour fell in a few days, storms so severe that entire villages were washed away. Afterwards the sun would settle in the sky and the temperature would rise dramatically, leaving the ground fissured over large tracts.

Only in certain parts, especially in Galilee, was the land fertile and forested, a place of fragrant acres of brushwood, where myrtle, broom, lentisk and acanthus grew. Where these had been cleared were fields of mustard and the smaller cultivated patches of mint, camomile, cumin, flanked on either side by meadows grazed by sheep. Here, too, grew the staple olive, the fig tree, the grapevine and the exquisite almond whose early flowers signaled another spring. Cereals, nuts, pomegranates, dates, lentils and beans, onions and peppers: all thrived in Galilee.

Several times in the past year, claiming she was bored with the garrison-town atmosphere of Caesarea, Claudia Procula had visited Galilee, traveling with a handful of servants and a small escort of soldiers. She had assured her husband that no one—not even the most fanatical Zealot—would attack her retinue, let alone kill her: Jews did not slaughter women. Pilate could have assumed the agents of the high priest and tetrarch had observed her and no doubt Herod Antipas would have reported the matter to Rome. Yet no reminder had come from the emperor or Sejanus that such behavior was not in keeping with her position. Pilate had not asked her why she had gone—let alone whom she may have seen or met. That could only have led to an embarrassing confrontation with her. Within their relationship the procurator had learned that there were some matters best left unexplored.

Among the black-eyed Semitic women, her Romanness, like that of her husband, was unmistakable. Claudia Procula came from a military family which for over two centuries had supplied tribunes and legates to command legions. Her life had been punctuated by fine funerals for uncles and cousins killed in action. When her father died some believed the loss had killed off her own soul, leaving intact only her ambition and lust for position and power. She was lean, strong jawed and forthright, and had ruled the domestic side with a grip as steely as Pilate's. On one occasion a slave she caught stealing had been sent to the great stadium in Caesarea, to die in its arena in combat with a lion—such a spectacle always drew huge crowds of non-Jews. The slave's amulet had been left hanging in her servants' quarters as a reminder of the fate awaiting all miscreants.

In Jerusalem further flocks of animals were being driven through the Sheep Gate. Traders' stalls were beginning to line streets, so narrow that two donkeys laden with panniers could not pass at the same time. From the maze of alleys and lanes people were emerging, almost all on foot; only the very rich could afford litters. Already, legionnaires—each man in his crested helmet and cuirass, red cloak worn on the shoulder—had begun a new day of patrolling.

Pilate would not leave the Antonia Fortress until it was time to return to Caesarea after Passover. From his vantage point he could stare down upon the Temple courts. He firmly believed an acquiescent Temple with firm control over its people was a prerequisite for effective Roman governance.

Yet, at the last Feast of Tabernacles, there occurred an incident showing Caiaphas had backed away from ruthless action as far as Jesus was concerned. Incomplete and no doubt distorted, as such stories always were, Pilate's spies had emphatically reported that Jesus had suddenly emerged in the Temple and claimed his right to teach, and had caused a great stir with his astonishing attack on the priests over their hypocrisy in allowing circumcision on the sabbath yet condemning him for healing on the same day. From the rapidly growing crowd in the courtyard had come protests that here, indeed, was the man whom the Temple agents had sought—yet he was being allowed to speak freely with no one making a move to apprehend him. Jesus had silenced the cries with a furious and extraordinary phrase that his "time had not yet come," and calmly walked past the guards and out of the Temple.

Pilate had little difficulty in assessing such behavior: Jesus had simply been carried away by religious fervor. These past years the procurator had heard of numerous examples of such behavior by itinerant preachers. What interested the procurator now was the truth of yet another report—that Herod Antipas was finally going to act against Jesus.

4

THE TETRARCH

> Go ye and tell that fox, Behold, I cast out devils and I do cures today and tomorrow, and the third day I shall be perfected.
>
> Luke 13:32

The vast caravan of Herod Antipas and his entourage stretched back through the Wilderness of Judea and skirted the shores of the Dead Sea. While its rear echelon was in the shadow of Masada, the most impregnable of all his father's fortresses, the vanguard was in sight of the Kidron brook that spewed winter rains from the Mount of Olives outside Jerusalem into the still waters of the vast lake, so heavy in minerals that no one could sink beneath its surface. Curious to prove this point, the tetrarch had once ordered a group of slaves to be slashed with swords, bound hand and foot, and thrown into the Dead Sea. They had remained floating, screaming in agony from the salts penetrating their wounds before they finally bled to death.

Herod Antipas transcended mere folklore, and his instability makes plausible the claim that for months he had plotted the death of Jesus for the stinging insult of branding him a fox. Ezekiel had called the false prophets of Israel foxes for ruining the nation, and no doubt Herod Antipas relished the prospect of subjecting Jesus to the torture the tetrarch's numerous executioners devised. But after delivering his rebuke Jesus had once more mysteriously vanished from Galilee.

Herod Antipas' strong sense of survival must have been a constant reminder that Jesus should have been dealt with like any other activist and killed when his followers had numbered scores, not thousands. Then, his devotees would have done nothing. They were country people, far from

Jerusalem, well beyond the center of influence. Now Jesus was expanding his power base.

He had attracted growing support from the Pharisee party—the committed religious opponents of the Sadducees, who were seen as collaborationists for accepting official posts under the Romans. Caiaphas was a Sadducee, the only bond he shared with the tetrarch; and just as Herod's relationship with Pilate was at a nadir, his contact with the high priest was strained since the death of John the Baptist. Caiaphas had begun to speak about the tetrarch having abandoned himself to a purely licentious life. Herod Antipas had sent word to the Temple not to meddle in his morals. The warning was a reminder that the Herodian dynasty had always controlled the high priesthood for its own ends. But the tetrarch knew Caiaphas was more devious and adroit than many previous holders of his office. That could explain why he had not acted against Jesus. Caiaphas was merely biding his time, wanting to be absolutely certain that any action he took would not involve the Romans.

The Sadducees were bent on keeping Judaism simple, intending it should remain centered on the bulwarks of Scripture, the priesthood and the Temple. All other matters—particularly economics and politics—should be kept out of the religious arena. Sadduceeism had created a holy, dead relic of Judaism, though the party's conservatism had given it a natural appeal to the rich and powerful. Its doctrine had a strong attraction for both the Romans and Herod Antipas: it made for easier rule.

The Pharisees argued that the Torah applied to the whole of Jewish life—and that included the right to express a strong political commitment. They had become the natural critics of the Roman occupation. When the Herodian dynasty was founded with the connivance of Rome, and later the compliant high priesthood of Caiaphas came into force, the Sadducees became further natural enemies of the Pharisees who, for all their vociferous opposition, still only numbered around six thousand, mostly in Galilee.

The Pharisee party lacked real leadership. Many of its members increasingly felt Jesus could provide it, that he would unite the many paradoxes which surrounded them: the desire to be both traditionalist and reformist; the wish to be at the same time the core of national religious authority and the center of political dissent; the belief they had a sacred role to perform as critics of society and the protectors of the faith of Abraham. Jesus was the authentic voice of their kind of Judaism; his teaching was a brave and honorable defense against tyranny and misused power, coupled with a well-thought-out appeal for the return of the old standards of decency and compassion; his words held the strongest possible attractions for the oppressed masses to whom the Pharisees increasingly appealed. Jesus was literally their Godsend. To murder him could be the precursor to a Pharisee uprising.

But with Jesus alive and at their head, any insurrection would also end in unsurpassed bloodshed as hundreds of thousands of other Jews would seize the chance to try to overthrow the Herodian dictatorship and drive out the Romans.

There were a couple, Chuza and Joanna, husband and wife, somewhere in the midst of the caravan who had a special interest in what action Herod Antipas would take against Jesus. Chuza was the tetrarch's chief steward; Joanna was housekeeper to the royal household. In the past year they had become devout followers of Jesus. In their privileged position of personally cooking for and serving Herod Antipas they would have overheard more than most in his vast entourage. The more the tetrarch had dismissed the reports of cures and healings by Jesus the greater had grown Chuza and Joanna's belief in their validity.

Seated astride his magnificent horse, a birthday gift from Herodias, the tetrarch knew that the vast inheritance from his father—military powers no other Jew held, a string of fortresses, theaters where he could enjoy some of the finest tragedy and comedy in the empire, amphitheaters and stadiums for contests to the death—in the end was in the gift of Pontius Pilate. For all his Roman education and embracing of its customs, to Pilate the tetrarch was still a barbarian, someone whose background had never been formed by the great cultural influences of Athens, absorbed and adapted by Rome.

To kill Jesus before or during the coming Passover would virtually guarantee a riot leading to Roman intervention. The tetrarch certainly knew how serious that would be. The procurator would not hesitate to use an uprising as an excuse to end the Herodian dynasty. Already Pilate could confiscate any Herodian property as punishment for any of a wide-ranging number of infractions of Roman law: criticism of anything Tiberius had ever said or done; wearing garments which resembled imperial robes; carrying a ring or coin bearing the emperor's image into a brothel; accepting any honor that had ever been voted to Tiberius.

As well as being a natural survivor Herod Antipas inherited other paternal attributes. He was hard and unforgiving, raised to know the value of cunning, deviousness and brutality. Shedding the blood of others without remorse was something he learned in infancy probably when he first witnessed Herod the Great slice off the head of a slave who failed to show proper servility. The tetrarch lived as he rode, without fear, knowing his lance or his arrow rarely missed, inspired to emulate his father.

King Herod, when still only a young Jewish nobleman, became embroiled on the side of the Romans in one of their periodic skirmishes with the Parthians. His small army had been quickly routed and pursued to the safety of his Masada refuge, situated on a plateau overlooking the Dead Sea. He had erected the massive fortifications, palaces and storehouses some years before. He had left his family in this redoubt and continued with a handful of men across the Sinai Desert to Alexandria. From there he sailed to Rome. Grateful for his support, the Senate appointed Herod King of Judea and provided him with two legions to protect his title. The first of Rome's vassals in the province, he showed considerable political dexterity in pleasing his imperial masters, yet retaining his position as absolute monarch by ruling with viciousness, using murder and banishment to impose his will. There had never been a more cruel Jewish despot, at heart a pagan and filled with an unshakeable belief Judea would be ruled by Herodians for Rome until the day came when its leaders would destroy each other, leaving the country ripe for total Herodian domination. His son had been raised on this creed.

However, Herod Antipas was not born to be a natural ruler. Lacking an important requirement—patience—he had not taken time to work out his relationship with the Romans: when to be deferential; when to recognize that something could not be achieved without their help and favor. Instead he had a strong conviction in his destiny, one which included a preternatural acceptance that he was meant to be preserved from the dangers that beset others. Behind his impetuousness, unreasoning anger and wild rage—that could degenerate into terrifying madness—was a highly developed sense of superiority. Jesus was a threat to that entrenched belief; the authentic voice of opposition to the tetrarch's violence, corruption and dishonesty. Jesus' was the one clarion call that rocked the very core of the festering rottenness prevalent in the Jewish establishment. Yet the tetrarch's instinct to kill him with the same lack of compunction he displayed as a huntsman had been checked by the growing fear such a move could set in motion a reaction that would wreck his ambition to go down in history as a figure greater than his father.

Riding past Herodium the issue of Jesus again bore upon him like a physical burden. The tetrarch's caravan approached Jerusalem from the most incomparable vantage point of all, coming up through Bethlehem to the top of the Mount of Olives. The mound offered a view which never failed to impress him. Across the Kidron Valley Jerusalem looked as unassailable as always, a fortress city defended by a wall that rose from sheer bedrock to nearly two hundred feet. This barrier was topped by towers rearing a further hundred feet into the blue sky. Behind them was the Temple, its golden spires rising a full three hundred feet above its cyclopean foundations. On its northern flank stood the massive square block of the Antonia Fortress from each of whose four towers fluttered Pilate's standard, unadorned in deference to Jewish demands. To the west, the tetrarch's destination, stood his palace, an imposing conglomeration of fortified walls and, behind them, colonnades and towers. As Herod Antipas began the descent from his vantage point, his entourage still tailed back to Bethlehem. Even now he could not be certain what had happened there over forty years ago when he had been a small boy, living at the top of Masada with his maternal grandparents.

When he first heard the story Herod Antipas had been enthralled by a saga that held all the ingredients of a superb fantasy, and guaranteed to excite the mind of any child, one in which the mystery of the heavens combined with earthly power and wealth.

It had centered on a star that appeared and vanished at will, on wish-fulfillment and a glorious dream of expectation which ended in a slaughter. It had been recounted by his grandparents, seated high above the silent Judean Wilderness, in the moonlight over Masada, while far below them the Dead Sea sparkled, and it had indeed been possible for him to accept that a celestial sign had foretold a special birth.

Simple and believing nomads, they had said that Herod the Great personally witnessed the star over Bethlehem. It had appeared, the king's astrologers had confirmed, in that year when Jupiter was in conjunction with Saturn, and Herod Antipas had been close to his eighth birthday. Such a conjunction, the astronomers added, normally only came every eight hundred years. His father, so the story developed, had questioned them relentlessly, finally getting them reluctantly to admit that the star might be the long-awaited portent for the birth of the Messiah—that indeed he might have already arrived on earth.

His grandparents, their voices very likely as hushed as the heavens above Masada, had explained how his father had asked: where and when might the Expected One have been born? The astronomers had been unable to answer exactly but had suggested that Bethlehem was the most likely place—which would account for the overhead presence of the star. They had reminded their master of the old biblical prophecy: "A star shall rise out of Jacob and a scepter shall spring up from Israel."

Shortly afterwards three visitors had arrived at his father's court. They said they were astronomers from the East, members of the ancient cult of the Magi. The elderly couple had told the boy—and in doing so gave further luster to a story he already found fascinating that the Magi were really Melchior, king of the Persians, Gaspur, ruler of all the Indian and Balthazar, leader of the Arabian nations. Later, in another retelling, they had confided that the trio were really Japhet, Shem and Ham, descendants from Noah. The young Herod Antipas had not paused to wonder why leaders of pagan nations would come all the way to Judea to celebrate the birth of a Jewish baby. Instead, he had continued to be gripped by the unfolding tale.

The Magi had traveled over mountains, rivers and deserts to be present when the star had suddenly twinkled, brighter than all the others in the night sky, over Bethlehem. Then it had vanished. They had come on up to Jerusalem to seek the help of the Temple priests in solving the mystery. The high priest had quickly referred them to King Herod. The men had crossed the city to his palace, where he sat racked with uncertainty over what his own astrologers had said. Their arrival, according to the account passed down to his son, had galvanized the king. Their first question had stunned him. "Where is the newborn king of the Jews?" Herod the Great had suppressed his natural instinct to torture his visitors for information. Instead, he had questioned them politely. They told him of their thousand-mile odyssey, and of their fear that they had arrived too late: that the Messiah was already born.

Tormented by such news, his father had suggested they rest before speaking again. Then he had summoned the high priest and all the leading scriptural scholars in the city, even the hated Pharisees and the diffident Essenes. They had consulted their holy books and concluded that, according to the fifth chapter of their scroll of Micah, the Messiah would, when he came, be born in Bethlehem. King Herod had sat transfixed while the high priest read: "But thou Bethlehem Ephratah, though thou be little among the thousands of Judah, yet out of thee shall he come forth unto me, that is to be ruler of Israel, whose goings forth have been from of old, from everlasting." Bethlehem, the city of David, was then clearly the designated Savior's birthplace.

An already exciting story had taken yet another twist. While the king consulted with his seers, the Magi had slipped away from the palace—heading back for Bethlehem. It was again nightfall when they reached the small hillside city ten miles from Jerusalem. There the star had once more appeared. They had followed its rays as it led them across fields, where shepherds kept watch over their flocks on a late summer's night. Finally the star had brought them to a cave. Inside, the trio had found a man, a woman and a baby. Their quest was over.

Kneeling, they paid their respects to the Holy Family, and then presented the Boy Child with gifts usually given to newborn royalty in the Orient: gold, the symbol of divinity; frankincense, the potent incense used solely on religious occasions; myrrh, a spice used to embalm the dead. Herod Antipas was too young to know that myrrh was also sometimes given to those men and women his father ordered to be crucified. The Magi had explained to the Holy Family that they had left Herod's palace after a divine intervention ordered them to return to Bethlehem and warn Mary and Joseph that the king intended to kill the Boy Child. His grandparents had not explained how they could possibly have known all this.

But in answer to his questions, they had told Herod Antipas that the Magi had somehow escaped back to the east, before his father's troops had slaughtered every male child in Bethlehem under the age of two years. To a Herodian prince raised in an atmosphere of continuous bloodletting, that was a satisfying end.

He had subsequently never been able fully to convince himself all this had really happened—that it was no more than a fable. His father had steadfastly refused to discuss it right up to his death. Now there was nobody willing in Bethlehem or among his courtiers who could have confirmed the veracity or otherwise of the story that all these years later had returned to haunt the tetrarch. According to rumor, in spite of the wholesale killing, the Holy Family had somehow escaped into Egypt. What troubled Herod Antipas now was whether they had later secretly returned to Judea and their child had grown up to be Jesus.

Approaching Jerusalem in a great cloud of dust Herod Antipas' caravan—a procession of hundreds of horses, camels, donkeys and flocks of lambs to be slaughtered—passed workmen repairing bridges and roads and whitewashing tombs so that the devout would avoid them and not be contaminated before Passover. In an enclosed litter sat Herodias and Salome. The court flunkeys, slaves and eunuchs had made the entire journey on foot. All were protected by the tetrarch's personal bodyguard of nomad horsemen and three thousand Thracian, Germanic and Gallic troops, the mercenary army Rome permitted him.

At the Golden Gate, Herod Antipas dismounted, leading his stallion into the city and past the Temple. It was his token of respect for the forthcoming festival.

On foot, in his protective armor and headgear, Herod Antipas appeared more than ever as a squat, powerfully muscled figure with protruding eyes darting constantly from side to side. He knew moments like these were the most dangerous for him in this city which he hated—and whose people regarded him with similar loathing. Its population saw him as paramount among collaborators. In the wake of his father's death, when the people had risen against the hated Romans, the insurrection had been contained long enough for the legions to arrive from Syria and Egypt, Herod Antipas in the meantime having used his forces to defend the beleaguered garrison in the Antonia Fortress. That had been the terrible week in which Jew killed Jew on behalf of the pagans—a crime the people of Jerusalem would neither forgive nor forget. Even now somewhere in the milling crowd could be an assassin, a man or woman prepared to plunge under the flanks of his escort's horses and attempt to drive a weapon into the tetrarch's body. He could have thought of a thousand or more persons who would die happily knowing they had killed him. They were the relatives and friends of his victims. He had lost count of how many he had ordered to be put to death. Winding his way through the narrow streets, into the Upper City, he knew that waiting in the dungeons of his palace were more prisoners. It was not difficult to imagine their fear at the sound of his approach.

The palace loomed over the Upper City, forming part of its boundary walls. His father had told him it was built on the exact spot where King David had sung his psalms, and spies of Herod Antipas had reported that some of Jesus' followers claimed he was descended from the royal family.

The tetrarch would have known that in Judaism the use of the word "Messiah" did not automatically bestow divinity. Though he had not chosen to do so, he could have used the title from the day he was appointed tetrarch. Caiaphas had claimed the ancient right of all high priests to attach the word after his name; it meant "anointed," a reminder that his inauguration had been blessed with holy oil. The ritual had been introduced by King David, who was first to be known as Messiah or, in Greek, "Christos," Christ. Equally, Messiah also held another and far deeper significance to all devout Jews: the concept of a divine deliverer who would rescue them from centuries of subjection which had culminated in the horrendous oppression of Rome. Descending from David, would one day assuredly come, with the miraculous help of God, a very different Messiah than the title cheapened by Caiaphas. It was popular belief that the Expected One would liberate and return the Chosen People to their rightful place as the proud unfettered descendants of the most beloved of all biblical dynasties, the Davidic one, which had ended six hundred years before. The Scriptures contained numerous prophecies that the Messiah would be heralded by a precursor. John the Baptist had repeatedly claimed that role.

Often on those balmy desert nights, in Machaerus at the onset of the Baptist's incarceration, Herod Antipas had crept away from the bed of Herodias and ordered the guards to unchain the strange man in the dungeon and bring him to the tetrarch. Squatting on the floor before piles of sweetmeats, nibbling as he spoke, Herod Antipas would recount the first reports of the ministry of Jesus: Cana, exorcising the demons and even the unlikeliest claim—the healing of the son of a Roman centurion at long distance. The child had been dying and his distraught father had sought out Jesus, reaching him after a lengthy walk around Galilee. He had begged Jesus to return with him to help his firstborn. Jesus had told the soldier there was no need for him to come, that when the Roman went home he would find his son cured. The officer had indeed found his child out of bed and playing. The tetrarch would ask John why a Roman had behaved like that. The Baptist had confined himself to repeating that the Messiah would one day rule as David had done as the unchallenged King of the Jews, except that he would not only be a human figure, but would exercise power as God himself and all people would accept him and his Temple in Jerusalem.

For all their support for Jesus, the Pharisees were essentially opposed to the prospect of a Messiah. He would be a stumbling block in their republican ambitions to abolish completely the Jewish monarchy. Part of their religious philosophy was based upon the timeless words of Isaiah that the day must come when swords would be beaten into plowshares and the wolf would dwell with the lamb. It was enough for them to live by the old scriptural adage that God was "already" their ruler and Lord. There was no need for him to appear before them to reinforce this clear-cut understanding.

Nevertheless they would still support anybody who could trace his lineage back to David and unite the Jewish forces into a single army. To achieve victory the Pharisees would willingly grant such a person the right to assume the full glory of David's original title. Scriptural belief insisted that the Expected One would be recognized because he would possess prophetic powers not seen since Solomon's reign. He would perform miracles unequaled since Moses had fed the people in the Wilderness. He would, like Elisha and Elijah, be able to bring the dead back to life. Jesus fit all these expectations.

The tetrarch's palace was the most magnificent of all Jerusalem's dwellings. It was twice the size of the Antonia Fortress and dominated by four massive towers, huge enough for a hundred spearmen to stand on each of their ramparts. Three of the towers bore the names of the few people Herod the Great had really loved. The one overlooking the Serpent's Pool was dedicated to his friend, Hippicus. The adjoining tower, with a clear view across the roofs of the Lower City, was named after Phagael, an uncle of Herod Antipas, who had perished fighting the Parthians. Facing Herodium, the monolithic fortress-tomb his father had built in the prime of life to house his remains, was a tower higher than the others, rising a full one hundred feet above the battlements. King Herod had erected it in memory of his wife, Mariamne. He had put her to death when he believed she, too, was plotting against him. A perpetual flame burnt on top of the tower in her memory.

Far below in the dungeons other fires were kept constantly alight to heat the variety of rods and branding irons used on prisoners. The tetrarch would spend hours watching men and women being not only branded, but also scourged by whips or suspended from hooks with weights attached to their feet, soles barely clear of the ground.

Like Pontius Pilate, the tetrarch had come reluctantly to Jerusalem for Passover. Herod Antipas possessed a desert dweller's dislike for its crowded alleys and their unpleasant smells, enjoying instead the windswept landscapes, broken by chalky hills whose reflections dazzled the eyes and the narrow *wadian*, valleys which after a while broke the spirit of anyone but a nomad used to traversing them. His spies had reported that Jesus, born and bred in the verdancy of Galilee, had once spent forty days and nights testing himself in the Wilderness. It seemed a supernatural feat.

The Wilderness stretched, total and defeating, from the banks of the Dead Sea to the mountain chain in the far distance. Between lay the burning sand. The heat would have risen through the soles of Jesus' sandals, first blistering the skin, then forming callouses. After a while the sand would have become bearable. The further he penetrated into the desert, the sparser grew the vegetation. Finally, nothing, not so much as a blade of grass, was visible in this area where once the people of Sodom and Gomorrah had lived before the fire and brimstone of Yahweh had engulfed their immoral souls. Here, a man could indeed commune with God, trudging over the salt-encrusted earth, the silent dark desolation broken only by a jackal howling in the mountains, or from the Dead Sea the sudden unnerving sound of a massive chunk of asphalt breaking free from the lake bed and shooting to the surface.

From remembered times prophets had gone to the Wilderness to purify their bodies. Desolate and terrifying though the vast empty quarter was, a person could still survive there. Beneath the subsoil were edible roots and also wild honey was to be found.

When Jesus had come close to the mountains, his followers said he had met Satan. The devil had asked him to turn lumps of rock into loaves of bread to prove he was the Messiah. He had also invited Jesus to climb to the top of a mountain peak and hurl himself into space in the belief that his angels would stop him crashing to the ground. Jesus had rejected the challenge.

For the tetrarch any claim that Jesus had outmaneuvered Satan would be important evidence that he believed himself so exalted he could confer without fear with the devil. The holy books taught that only God could do that. Such a blasphemy would bring Jesus to the notice of the Temple. Then it would be up to the religious authorities to deal with the matter.

5

THE HIGH PRIEST

All things are delivered unto me of my Father and no man knoweth the Son, but the Father.

Matthew 11: 27

Each day for fifteen years Joseph Caiaphas had made his way from deep within the Temple towards the most famous of all its inner barriers, the towering Nicanor Gate. Ninety feet high, double-doored, each a foot thick, fashioned from pure silver and gold, it was so heavy that to open and close it required the efforts of twenty guards. They would be already waiting, Jonathan, the captain of the Guard, towering over them, ready to obey any order of the high priest. Behind his sanguine blessings Caiaphas was a man of whiplash power, driven by some inner force to keep the great machine—the Temple—grinding relentlessly forward on its ponderous way. There was a hard-rim interior to the man that matched his commanding look and the authority in his voice. It would make him all that Scripture intimates.

Once the high priest positively identified a crime of blasphemy—or adultery—it was crushed by the ancient capital punishment of stoning. The condemned would be led to the place of execution, a cliff beyond the city walls, specified in a tractate to be "the height of two men." There the doomed person was forced to the edge and suddenly hurled backwards, so that the fall either stunned the victim or broke his or her back. Caiaphas often threw the first boulder, aiming it at the heart. He then motioned the crowd to continue stoning until he was satisfied life was extinct. The mangled remains were left for birds to pick over, as it had been first ordained in Deuteronomy. The exact interpretation of Scripture was something the high priest cherished.

In the turbulent closing years of Herod the Great's reign, Caiaphas had also learned where to be servile, and how to appear accommodating—when he was at his most dangerous. Under the tutelage of his father-in-law, Annas—high priest for nine years—he had learned the most valuable asset of all: never to make a move without being certain of victory. Almost certainly Annas had only retired to live in his palace adjoining the Temple when he was absolutely certain all these lessons had been fully absorbed, and that his son-in-law, his anointed successor, would continue to protect the greatness of the Temple.

Not for a moment would Caiaphas have forgotten that one sacred and paramount responsibility. In all his decision-making would be one overriding consideration: that God's Chosen People would once more be divested of their position if anything threatened what the Temple ultimately represented—the miracle of faith for millions, down to the poorest Jew in the farthest corner of the Diaspora. He had promised to sacrifice anybody and anything to maintain this solidity. A hundred high priests before had made a similar pledge on taking office. That was why Caiaphas paid Pilate bribe money. It was a small price to remain in God's highest office. That was why he had also done nothing about those reports of his agents that placed Claudia Procula on the edge of the crowds Jesus attracted in Galilee. She was no threat; she was a despised Roman who would one day leave Judea with her husband. Nor had Jesus been a threat at first.

But at some stage the high priest's other highly attuned quality had surfaced. He could sense trouble the way animals smell prey. There was much he still did not understand or believe about Jesus, but the scent was there from the last Feast of Tabernacles. Caiaphas had been in his office when a commotion from the Court of the Gentiles had interrupted him. From the shelter of a colonnade he had watched Jesus addressing a crowd. Every word he had shouted remained engraved upon Caiaphas' mind from that moment when one of his own rabbis had challenged Jesus to explain how he dared to say he had more knowledge than the scholars of the Temple. Caiaphas knew the question was meant to unsettle Jesus, to mock and cow him and make him look foolish in the eyes of the crowd; his priests were expert at such tactics—it kept lunatic preachers at bay. Jesus had rounded on the rabbi. "My doctrine is not mine but his that sent me. If any man will do his will, he shall know of the doctrine, whether it be of God, or whether I speak of myself." Other rabbis, drawn by the excitement, had shouted threateningly at Jesus to explain. The demand had provoked a further outburst. "Ye both know me, and ye know whence I am: and I am not come of myself, but he that sent me is true, whom ye know not."

No word had come from Caiaphas: if he had felt some private humiliation it had never been allowed to surface. Only when Jesus was out of sight had he moved. The high priest had turned on his heel and walked back to his office, as if nothing had disturbed the unique balance of obedience and authority through which he ruled.

He could no doubt have rationalized his behavior: to apprehend Jesus in such a throng could have provoked a violent response; no one knew how many supporters Jesus had in the Temple that day.

The high priest and his escort crossed another courtyard. The darkness hid the colonnades, and the Temple's outer gates: the Water Gate, through which the flagon of blessed liquid was carried for the libation at the Feast of Tabernacles; the Mourner's Gate, restricted to the recently bereaved to come and worship; the Bridegroom's Gate, reserved for the newly wed; the Eastern Gate, through which the ark had first come into the Holy of Holies. That most sacred of all the divine places in Judaism—a sanctuary of which it was said "wherever it is written in the Bible 'before God'"—was protected by the Nicanor Gate. In daylight its appearance would have been overwhelming except for proportions in such perfect symmetry. Beyond where the money changers and purveyors of sacrifices traded, were the courtyards for the women and the Gentiles and a clerical bureaucracy. There was no way for anyone confined to those outer limits to begin to imagine what high responsibilities and cruel tensions existed within the Nicanor Gate.

It was in this inner keep that Caiaphas had deliberated upon the words of Jesus and begun to prepare the legal groundwork, shaping the questions which would entrap him: about his parents and ancestry; about his meaning of calling himself "the Son of man"; about the deeper significance of the curing of the paralyzed and the resuscitation of the dying. Caiaphas was not a man in a hurry. Speed was not the road to a guaranteed conviction, but slow and careful deliberation, with each question tested in the light of Scripture. That was the only way.

The high priesthood had always been in the gift of a few Sadducean aristocratic families whose private fortunes could meet its high costs: each encumbent purchased his personal religious vessels, tableware of silver and gold, and made generous donations to the Temple. This created a natural social barrier with the masses, further emphasized by sheer numerical size: Caiaphas ruled over almost twenty thousand men. Immediately beneath him were over a hundred chief priests who held equal status with the three treasurers who administered the Temple finances. Below them came seven thousand two hundred ordinary consecrated priests. Next came the Levites, who helped with the sacrifices, baked the shewbread and had general custody of the Temple, acting as clerks and administrators and ushers to the

Sanhedrin. There were over ten thousand Levites. Jonathan had a force of five hundred guards. There were almost a thousand singers and musicians.

There was a separate group, about six hundred in number, who also worked for God—but in a very specialized role. They were the doctors of the law, the scribes, who devoted their days exclusively to studying and explaining the many complex questions of religion. They traced their authority back to the book of Nehemiah, when Ezra established himself as the first scribe. Five hundred years later the scribes were accepted without demur as the arbitrators of sacred dogma. Proud of their position, they generally distanced themselves from priestly intrigues and saw themselves as the authentic intellectual power of the Temple. There were a number still alive from that day when Jesus, on the verge of manhood, had debated and often challenged them to the point where they had gone to their books and found his interpretations were both new and strikingly original.

Even Caiaphas' most careful questioning of these scribes had been frustrating. The incident had happened a long time ago, and all that they could recall with certainty was that the boy had been exceptional in his command of Scripture, and clearly his knowledge had been based on a strong and devout upbringing. Inquiries in Nazareth had produced no more. Jesus' teacher was long dead and his mother, brothers and sisters had instinctively drawn away from any probing stranger except to admit that Jesus had worked as a young man in his father's carpentry shop and upon Joseph's death had become the family breadwinner until the other children came of age.

Jesus and his four younger brothers were in Nazareth when Judas of Gamala had marched through the town on his way to capture Sepphoris, four miles to the northwest, and make it the Zealot capital of Galilee. The rebel had urged every able-bodied Galilean to join him. Scores had, only to die under the swords of the Roman legion which had routed Judas. The Romans had crucified all the insurgents who surrendered and razed Sepphoris to the ground.

Herod Antipas had persuaded Tiberius to allow him to rebuild the ruined town. The tetrarch had constructed within its keep an open-air theater, a massive semicircular building with seating capacity for over four thousand, a stage a hundred feet wide, an orchestra pit for sixty musicians and a resident company of players. When Herod Antipas began to spend most of his time at Machaerus and Masada the stage had become a forum for criticizing religious and political leaders; the continual lampooning of authority was reluctantly tolerated by the authorities as a safety valve for the oppressed—providing it stayed within limits.

There can be little question that the destruction of Sepphoris and its emergence as a platform for political protest had a powerful effect on Jesus.

The sight of men and women, among them no doubt his friends and neighbors, suffering excruciating pain on crosses lining the roadside from Nazareth to Sepphoris could only have increased Jesus' yearning to see his people liberated. Later, his own ministry, as well as increasingly placing him in direct confrontation with the Temple, was firmly set in the radical tradition of the Sepphoris theater. Assembling his case, Caiaphas may at least have considered whether the success of Jesus as a public orator was based on time spent with those professional actors and actresses who baited the high priesthood. If his parables and stories could be exposed as deriving from Sepphoris it would be another way to discredit Jesus, to place him firmly in the role of political agitator.

Joseph Caiaphas would never forget when he had been set apart from other men and received into the priesthood. The day had begun with a ritual bath in perfumed water. Afterwards he had dressed in white linen and was led by the high priest to make three animal sacrifices: a bull and two rams. Before slitting their throats Caiaphas had placed his hands upon the beasts and asked Yahweh to accept them. Their blood was mingled with holy oil. The high priest had used the mixture to anoint Caiaphas, receiving him into religious life with prayers that went back to the days of Moses. Intoning them, he had daubed the solution on Caiaphas' right ear, right thumb and right foot; ram's fat, unleavened bread and a cake baked from flour and oil had been carefully placed on his open palms and exposed thighs. These offerings were afterwards consumed in the altar fire.

When he became high priest, the ceremonies were even more solemn. Annas had anointed him with the most costly scents; the ritual sacrifices were spread over seven days—each killing accompanied by a reminder that in embarking upon supreme religious office Caiaphas must continue to conform to strict rules. He must never eat game or drink wine before services or trim the corners of his beard. He accepted these restrictions and the sacred robes in his fifty-first year after a long rabbinical apprenticeship which had taught him how to balance the affairs of religion and state. No one, least of all Jesus, would be allowed to disturb things, in any way to weaken the authority of the Temple and so divest Joseph Caiaphas of his position as the personal representative of God on earth, ruling in Yahweh's name over a vast cluster of buildings that made Jerusalem greater than all other cities in the eyes of devout Jews.

This spring morning marked one of the most important occasions in the Temple: the approach of Passover, the *Pesah*. It was the holiest, most fervent and ancient feast in the religious calendar, an occasion which combined gratitude for escaping from Egyptian bondage with a reminder that there was only one God. The rites of celebration were laid down in the twelfth chapter of Exodus where it is recounted that Moses instructed his people on how they must behave if they were to avoid the angel of death who had come into their midst to destroy their enemies. Once more, the paschal lambs—countless thousands of them—would be sacrificed and the blood from each animal daubed with a branch of hyssop upon the lintel and frame of every outside door. The Law prescribed that all who possibly could must come to the Temple to have their animals sacrificed. Each family brought an unblemished yearling lamb for the ritual meal that was one of the high points of Passover.

His feet encased in hand-tooled sandals, Caiaphas walked through the final narrow covered courtyard leading to the Nicanor Gate, carried forward by the unshakeable sense of destiny he had never lost and that men like Pontius Pilate and Herod Antipas would never possess, let alone understand. The high priest was as certain of that as he was that God had chosen Jerusalem to be the sanctuary for all spiritual life and that from here his voice would be heard "till the ends of the earth." It was foretold that three days before the Day of Judgment God would return to redeem Israel, appearing as the Messiah, and Elijah the prophet would appear on Mount Hebron.

That could be the logical explanation of why Caiaphas had been so dismissive of those first accounts of the sermon Jesus had preached on Mount Hattin. Some of what he had said brooked no argument; it was rooted in the best tradition of Judaism. But to imply as Jesus had that redemption was at hand was to arouse expectations cruelly. Then there had been his revaluation of the Mosaic Decalogue—the commandments which ruled all decision-making in the Temple—over such clear-cut matters as murder and adultery. Jesus had taught that not only killing but also an angry outburst must be punished. But what scale of retribution was to be applied? What kind of angry words merited a greater punishment than others? Jesus had not explained. Instead he had delivered further maxims which, under existing Jewish laws, were impossible to follow: "Judge not and ye shall not be judged"; "condemn not and ye shall not be condemned." But society could not survive without judgments being made and condemnations being delivered. In the high priest's world, the holy tractates already formed the bases from which a systematic and orderly code of civil law had grown. Rabbinical teaching provided commentaries and explanations of the biblical texts. These were embraced in almost two score scrolls; a precise listing of crimes and misdemeanors, ranging from the rape of a betrothed girl or the public cursing by a son of his father, to the removal of route-marking stones and using rigged weights. The punishment for all those offenses was death. Stoning was also prescribed for many other crimes: a man convicted of masturbation or sleeping with a menstruating woman; a priest's daughter who became a whore or a bride who concealed previous sexual experience. Taken to its ultimate folly, Jesus seemed to want to do away with the existing legal framework.

To a high priest nurtured in rabbinical literature, as well as in the rich oral tradition of ethical casuistry, a combined corpus of received ethical, devotional and legal precepts, Jesus' message seemed contradictory: on the one hand he was careful to distance himself from violent action, on the other he insisted the new life he proclaimed could only come through suffering. But who would suffer most in the world Jesus foresaw? To Caiaphas the answer may have become increasingly self-evident: the established order he headed. He could be forgiven for wondering if Jesus was cleverly encouraging others to launch a violent liberation movement, and, if it succeeded, he would proclaim himself its leader. Was that what lay behind his repeated statement that man could not live by bread alone? Judea was filled with its starving. The words could be a signal to them to appease their hunger by overthrowing the present system. Again Jesus had consistently preached that for those who accepted the kingdom he envisaged there would be protection. Was that another subtle call to insurrection? There were thousands of young Jews who might see it as such.

Educated in a quasi-systematic tradition of scriptural commentary, and elaborate and meticulous oral jurisprudence, the high priest could only have been horrified at some of Jesus' proposals—such as giving a litigant even more than he asked: "And if any man will sue thee at the law, and take away thy coat, let him have thy cloak too." But rabbinical lawyers in the Temple had used scrupulous care in formulating the rules for assessing damages. There was a vast library of scrolls, going back to Solomon, which covered such important issues as property ownership, loans and debts.

If only because he had taken no immediate action against Jesus it seems most likely that Caiaphas had initially regarded his teachings as the foolish, but harmless, idealism of someone who had no grasp of the practicalities of life. Israel had seen more than its share of those men during the high priest's reign. They peaked for a while, then faded as their followers drifted to a new claimant for religious immortality. Caiaphas' policy had been to ignore them; to take action would only have prolonged their presence and enhanced their reputation. But something had urged Caiaphas to keep his agents on Jesus' trail. In the past months the reports had grown more alarming, culminating in the one which described in detail the paralytic rising and walking out of that almost roofless house in Capernaum. That may well have been the moment when Caiaphas realized he could no longer dismiss Jesus as another harmless religious fanatic; if there was truth in what was being claimed for him, the matter must be handled with the greatest of care. To hurry unprepared against such a man would be to face a public outcry and certain defeat.

A complicating factor was the uncertainty about how great Jesus' influence was within three of the four main Jewish religious groups. Caiaphas' own party, the Sadducees, would continue automatically to oppose him. The position of the Pharisees was more difficult to judge. Recently they had shown signs of dissent over Jesus' attitude towards religious observances; for his part he had made some stinging references to Pharisee doctrine. Yet Jesus shared with the rank-and-file Pharisee a working-class background; Caiaphas knew that, for all their religious purity, they could still rise in his defense. Even more difficult for him to establish was the position of the Essenes. Numbering only a few thousand, and living in strict isolation on the edge of the Wilderness, they, too, believed that God would overthrow the powers of evil and inaugurate a new kingdom. Jesus had visited them on a number of occasions. The high priest had sent his most skilled rabbis to the Essene community beside the Dead Sea only to have them turned away by the sect's leaders. They would not openly commit themselves either way on Jesus—at least so far. But if they felt he had been unfairly treated they might march to Jerusalem and, magnificent debaters that they were, cause havoc within the Temple. Finally, there were the Zealots. Battered and bruised by repeated encounters with Roman troops, the Zealots were no longer the force they once were. But they still posed a threat. Suicidal though it would be, they could be driven to launch an uprising to save Jesus. All these factors required the most careful consideration.

Then, on a recent sabbath, Jesus had once more slipped unexpectedly into Jerusalem with the disciples. Instead of going to the Temple they had walked through the twisting streets in the Lower City. Near the Square of the Butchers, Temple agents had spotted Jesus. Preaching as he walked, unfolding once more his vision of salvation. Under cover of the growing crowd—word always spread swiftly when he was among them—the agents had worked their way close to Jesus.

A blind man had stumbled from an alley into his path. One of the disciples had posed a question. "Master, who did sin, this man, or his parents, that he was born blind?"

Jesus' response had been to say: "The works of God should be made manifest in him." Then he knelt and spat on the dust from which he kneaded two pellets. Rising, he placed these upon the sightless eyes and ordered the man to go to the Pool of Siloam and wash off the mud. Since King David's days Siloam had provided the sacred water used in Temple ceremonies; no one could use it without prior permission from the high priest.

One of the agents had followed the man; others had remained with Jesus to memorize any further extraordinary statements.

Shortly afterwards, incredulous cries came from the pool's direction, then into view, running unaided, came the man. "I can see," he kept shouting, "I can see."

The agents had hurried to the Temple. Jesus had not only broken the sabbath once more by working, but had almost certainly been party to trickery. The wretch had feigned blindness; beggars did it all the time. This single episode in the hands of someone as skillful as Caiaphas could be fashioned into an unchallengeable case of sustained blasphemy.

When they reached the end of the final courtyard leading to the Nicanor Gate, Caiaphas' escort stopped, watching as he climbed the three steps to a dais rimmed by a thin balustrade of solid gold. Like everyone else, he stared up towards the very tallest of the Temple towers, a cone-shaped minaret with a doorway leading to a tiny balcony, his thin hands gripping the rail, the style of his vestments unchanged since Joshua had led the first high priest into Canaan.

Caiaphas wore puffed-out pantaloons and a tunic made from a single piece of linen, open at the neck and held in place with silk shoulder strings. Over this was a sleeveless violet surplice, the lower half embroidered with pomegranates. Between each fruit were suspended bells made of pure gold and designed to repel devils. The sacred stole, unlike any other in the world, cut from silk dyed crimson and sewn with gold thread, was draped around his shoulders. This was held in place by ties made from onyx engraved with the names of the twelve tribes. On his breast attached to the stole by rings of gold was the pectoral, a box inlaid with twelve precious stones on the outside and containing the holy relics of the high priesthood: dice-shaped badges embossed with hallowed engravings. His head was covered with a cone-shaped turban; attached to it were two wide ribbons, scarlet like his stole. Wound round his waist was a wide purple sash. Caiaphas had once more collected this regalia from the Antonia Fortress to wear for Passover. How the high priest felt about this demeaning control over his office was also something he shared with no one.

In time to come, just as the physical appearance of Jesus and Pontius Pilate would be described—and disputed—so Caiaphas, who might otherwise have disappeared through the trapdoor of history, would be remembered as the high priest whose splendid robes did little to enhance his appearance. There was a serpent-like quality about his puny body and narrow head. The years had ravaged his skin, leaving it slack at the jowls and neck. But as the light lifted, bringing with it the first warming wisps of spring wind, it was the look in the high priest's eyes which would also have made it easy to misjudge the man; their watery appearance suggested weakness; the rheumy look of a man who knew that long ago he had lost the universal regard his office demanded; that his simonistic behavior allowed

Pilate to squeeze the nerve ganglion of Jewish religious independence. To all suffering Jews he was another collaborationist who had sold out. They failed to see his more deadly qualities.

Rejection did not trouble him. Caiaphas possessed an intellectual's belief—or contempt—that the masses had no real interest in the subtleties of religious dogma. Within the Temple, Pharisee scholars and Sadducee priests worked side by side, if not always in scriptural harmony, at least bound by a common understanding of the necessity to show a united front to the Romans. The sophisticated Temple Pharisees understood the meaning of self-interest and were far removed from their country cousins with their wild talk and aspirations. If it came to the crunch Caiaphas could have felt confident that these scholars would yet curb their Galilean brethren from protesting at any move against Jesus.

Nevertheless, there would still be another formidable barrier persuading the Great Sanhedrin that it should put Jesus on trial. Though the supreme court was the ultimate legal authority—responsible for the interpretation of all Jewish civil and criminal law—and, as high priest, Joseph Caiaphas was its president, it rarely involved itself in trials except those of national concern. While the Great Sanhedrin had total autonomy and authority in all cases which came before it, and the Romans would not break with precedent and become involved, the court was protective of its position; it would not wish to see its authority diminished by conducting a trial that in the end could turn out to be of little importance; nor had it previously been asked to judge an itinerant preacher like Jesus. The daily jurisdiction in such matters was in the hands of the Small Sanhedrin; these lower courts were established in all the major towns in the country. But to bring Jesus before a Small Sanhedrin in Jerusalem was a risk. That court could decide that any charges against him were not only offenses against religion but crimes under the Roman code. He would then have to be sent to the imperial tribunal presided over by Pilate. The problem that created would be manifestly clear to the high priest. The Romans would inevitably condemn Jesus to death. He would then become the martyr the oppressed masses needed.

Yet if the Great Sanhedrin could be persuaded to hear the case and if Jesus was convicted purely for offenses against Scripture the people could be convinced of the justice of the verdict. Nevertheless, to bring the case before the Great Sanhedrin would require a great deal of skill on the part of the president. While Caiaphas could count on the votes of the Sadducee judges, he could not be absolutely certain how Pharisee members would vote; at the end of the day, they might still be unconvinced of the gravity of the charges. Without their support not only was an overwhelming conviction impossible but the chances of convincing the people of its righteousness would be totally lost. Once they realized there had been an unsuccessful attempt to kill Jesus the population could easily be aroused into action by his enraged followers. Then the Romans would step in. Jesus would have brought about the situation that Caiaphas, like the tetrarch, feared the most.

On the minaret balcony a dark shape had appeared. At the first sign of daybreak, a priest-trumpeter raised his long-stemmed silver instrument and blew through its fluted opening three distinctive blasts. As the first one, the ear-piercing *thekiah*, broke the silence, Jonathan, the captain of the guard, ordered his men to remove the beam that barricaded the gate. Then came the *theruah*, a series of long blasts from the musician, so clear that the holy books record that when the Israelites captured Jericho—until then one of the oldest seats of moon worship—similar blasts had carried thirty miles eastward from Jerusalem and bounced against the walls of that pagan city, causing them to crack. Jonathan's men opened first one, then the other half of the gate. They completed the task as the trumpeter delivered a final *thekiah*.

Beyond, Caiaphas could see the first supplicants and animals entering the Temple. Another day had begun. As he did every morning, stepping down from the dais, he was led by Jonathan and his guards and his priest escort, to make his way through the Nicanor Gate to show himself to the people, to remind them again that he personified the living God and the Temple was his home on earth. All he surveyed was proof of that—the filigree on the gleaming marble around the roof into which were mounted spikes gilded with gold, designed to prevent birds from perching; the interlocking courts with their colonnades sculpted in the style found in Babylon and Athens; the massive outer walls, with their sheltered porticoes roofed in cedar and floored in colored stone; the religious courts where the doctors of the law debated and pronounced. The ritual over, the procession returned into the inner courts leaving behind the din of pilgrims bargaining with the money changers and sellers of sacrifices. At the Nicanor Gate priests waited to receive the animals.

Within the gate, beyond the narrow courtyard which Herod the Great had erected, was another large enclosure, almost three hundred feet in length and two hundred feet wide. Around it were various sanctums, including the chamber where the Great Sanhedrin met. In the center of the square stood the altar dedicated to burnt offerings, a block of unhewn granite, each side forty-seven feet long and rising to a height of thirteen feet, its four corners formed in the shape of horns, symbolizing the *shofar*. Cut into the block were a series of gutters which carried the blood underground to the Kidron.

The lambs to be slaughtered were tethered to one of the rings set in the ground before the altar. When their turn came to die they were pushed up a ramp to where the sacrificers waited with their sharp knives. The air was already beginning to reek with the stench of burning entrails and fat thrown onto the altar fire.

Beyond this scene of ritual butchery stood the actual Temple, reached by the twelve steps, each one representing a tribe of Israel. The colonnade which embraced the main building was a full ninety-eight feet high and a hundred and forty-seven feet wide. Rising above this were the unbroken walls of the building and its roof covered with gold.

At this point Jonathan and the escort halted, allowing Caiaphas to continue alone into the Temple within which Jews everywhere evoked Solomon's prayer: "Yahweh, thou should ever be watching, night and day over this place of thine, the chosen sanctuary of thy name. Be this the meeting-place where thou wilt listen to thy servant's prayer. Whatever requests I, or thy people make shall find audience here; thou wilt listen from thy dwelling-place in heaven, and listening will forgive."

The focal point of these preparations was the high priest's small office. It guarded access to the *debir*, the Holy of Holies, the most sanctified of all places in the Temple. There was no door to the *debir*, only an opening screened by two heavy curtains. No natural light ever penetrated this sanctum; illumination was provided by the soft glow from a seven-branched candelabrum. Only Caiaphas could replace the tall tallow sticks in the *debir*, which was strikingly different from all others throughout the Diaspora. Apart from their candelabra they were empty. But the *debir* of Jerusalem had in its center a large rock precisely placed to cover the mouth of the abyss out of which the world had grown. This was the Foundation Stone upon which King David had discerned the name of Jehovah. The letters had disappeared before his gaze—and since then it had been accepted that anyone who stood before the stone and "pronounces the Name letter by letter will destroy the world."

Caiaphas had a lawyer's mind, but he was not a stubborn and inflexible legalist. Only too clearly he saw that some of the evidence which his agents had thought so damning would almost certainly fail to impress the Great Sanhedrin. There was the accusation that Jesus had transgressed normal custom and often did not wash his hands before eating. While that could be certainly construed as antisocial behavior, equally Jesus could also argue that with the shortage of water often acute, especially in Jerusalem, it was a crime to waste it on such a small matter as handwashing. More important, there was nowhere in Scripture that made it obligatory to do so before dining. Again, the often reported charge he had leveled against many rabbis of being hypocritical could be defended. Caiaphas could well imagine that Jesus' judges, being men of the world, might be persuaded to see his accusation as no more than the overheated passion of someone who only wished further to improve the quality of religious life. There *were* priests who were tinged with hypocrisy; everyone knew that. No doubt Jesus had intended to be insulting—but what he had stated was hardly a capital offense. Again, on closer examination, much of what he preached, such as a need to banish evil and bring back the faithless from the edge of darkness, was unexceptionable.

There were difficulties in challenging claims Jesus made about his healing powers. Every Jew swore upon God's omnipotence—and therefore accepted his right to choose, however unfathomable, the instrument to carry out his will. Jesus could argue that he was only doing that; he could even make a case that it would—in scriptural terms—be blasphemous to *deny* God's right to help the incurable in this way on *any* day, even the sabbath. Jesus had also often said to the cured that their sins had been forgiven. But he could also vigorously defend such a potential blasphemy on the grounds that Scripture *did* contain indications that God forgave sins in many ways. The truth was that so much of what Jesus said could be argued as being no more than a warning that divine retribution would come unless there was an overall improvement in religious attitudes. That would almost certainly strike a sympathetic chord with the supreme court. Many of its members had repeatedly expressed concern that once more the Chosen People had forgotten the terms of the covenant. Nor did Scripture forbid prophesying; Jeremiah had done so centuries before.

The most promising avenue for the high priest to pursue would be the references Jesus had made to himself as the Son of man. It was a perplexing phrase—unless once more it was meant really to mean that Jesus saw himself as in some unique relationship with God. The high priest would have recognized that the key word was "son." It was an integral part of the covenant; it gave the Chosen People their sonship with Yahweh. In the book of Exodus was the sentence: "Thus saith the Lord, Israel is my son, even my firstborn." The book of Hosea contained the words: "when Israel was a child, then I loved him and called my son out of Egypt." In that sense the use of the word "son" meant somebody completely united with God in an exceptional manner. Was that why Jesus had been so careful always to refer to himself publicly as the Son of man to avoid the charge of blasphemy? Again, there was the way he used Father when referring to God. He used it in a personal sense, once more as if his relationship with God was very different from anyone else's. More recently Jesus had reportedly even begun to refer to "My Father" and "No one knoweth the Father except the Son"; and "I and the Father are one." That was, in the written Law of the Pentateuch, blasphemy. Yet to launch a prosecution on such grounds alone was no guarantee of success. Jesus had only to deny the allegation for the case to collapse.

Then came news that could only have given the high priest sudden and renewed hope. A Temple agent had rushed with it from Bethany. Jesus had a second home in the tiny village two miles to the west of Jerusalem. Whenever he came to the capital he invariably stayed with two unmarried sisters—Martha and Mary—and their brother, Lazarus. All three were among his earliest followers. More than one agent had spent time trying to establish the nature of his relationship with the sisters and the other young woman in Jesus' life, Mary Magdalene. For a while they had pursued the promising lead that Jesus had enjoyed a full sexual relationship with both Mary Magdalene and Mary of Bethany. If that could be shown it would be possible to convict him of licentiousness—punishable by stoning. But no satisfactory proof had been forthcoming. It appeared that Lazarus, never very robust, had been struck down with a sudden severe illness. Mary and Martha had nursed him, praying that Jesus would soon return. When Lazarus showed marked signs of deterioration the worried sisters had sent a trusted man friend to ask Jesus to help their brother. After days of searching, the man had found Jesus and the apostles on the outskirts of Emmaus, a small town deep in western Galilee. They hurried to Bethany. Well before reaching the village Jesus suddenly stopped: "Our friend Lazarus sleepeth; but I go that I may wake him out of sleep."

The disciples had looked puzzled. One said: "Lord, if he sleep, he shall do well."

Jesus' reply had stunned them. Lazarus was dead. Then he delivered a further pronouncement equally astounding: "And I am glad for your sakes that I was not there, to the intent ye may believe." With that, he had turned on his heel and strode ahead of them, without saying another word.

Approaching Bethany they had been met by Martha and her equally grief-stricken neighbors; Lazarus had been a popular figure in the community. Through her tears, Martha said her brother had been dead for four days. Mingling with the mourners, the agent heard Martha upbraid Jesus for not coming sooner. Jesus had gently taken her arm and said that Lazarus would rise again. His sister, her face ravaged by grief, had nodded numbly. Finally, she had forced herself to speak. "I know that he shall rise again in the resurrection at the last day."

Jesus had held both her hands, willing her to look at him, forcing her to raise her eyes and stop crying. When he had succeeded he delivered a shattering statement. "I am the resurrection and the life: he that believeth in me, though he were dead, yet shall he live." Silence, sudden and total, greeted the words. Eyes still intent on Martha, Jesus raised his voice so that everybody could hear. "Whosoever liveth and believeth in me shall never die. Believest thou this?"

Filled with sudden hope, Martha had responded: "Yes, Lord. I believe that thou art the Christ, the Son of God, which should come into the world."

Jesus told her to fetch her sister. Mary came running out of the house, and fell at his feet, weeping that Jesus had come too late. He gently lifted her up. He asked where Lazarus was buried. Mary and Martha led the way to the tomb, Jesus walking between them, murmuring words of comfort, his eyes filled with tears. Behind came the apostles, villagers and the Temple agent. All around him, between the sobbing, the spy heard the questions—asked but never answered. Why had Jesus, who had cured others, not done so in the case of Lazarus? Were his own tears from grief or guilt? Why were they going to the grave?

Lazarus had been laid to rest in a cave set in a hillside beyond the village, and a boulder covered the cavern entrance. Jesus told Martha to roll away the stone. She protested. "Lord, by this time he stinketh."

Once more, Jesus gently reminded her. "Said I not unto thee, that, if thou wouldst believe, thou wouldst see the glory of God?"

On Martha's command some of the village men reluctantly rolled back the boulder. Then fearful of what they had done, for no one tampered with the resting place of the dead, they withdrew down the hillside. Even the apostles backed away.

Jesus walked to the mouth of the tomb. Then he raised his head to the heavens and cried out: "Father, I thank thee that thou hast heard me. And I knew that thou hearest me always: but because of the people which stand by, I said it, that they may believe that thou hast sent me."

There was a long moment of silence. The first breeze of evening sighed, carrying the odor of the sepulchre in the air. Then, in a thunderous voice Jesus shouted into the cave: "Lazarus, come forth." There was another long moment. Then a movement came from within the cavern. Slowly, bound in his shroud, unfolding it as he emerged, and removing the burial cloth which had covered his face, Lazarus walked into the daylight. Jesus turned to the openmouthed crowd: "Loose him and let him go."

As Lazarus embraced his sisters, the agent began to run to Jerusalem to tell Caiaphas what had happened.

The high priest knew there was now no time to ponder the finer points of evidence to hand. By raising Lazarus from the dead, Jesus would have finally proven himself in the eyes of the great majority who would come to hear of the story.

Throughout the Diaspora was the spreading expectation that the Messiah was imminent. Millions *could* be aroused by the followers of Jesus, and even himself, to march on the Temple and demand his recognition as the Expected One. They could bring Lazarus with them as proof of his divinity; Jesus could perform further feats to support that claim. And if they were then still refused they could take matters into their own hands. Jonathan's guards would be trampled out of the way. The forces of Herod Antipas would be no real opposition for such an aroused mass. Even Pontius Pilate's legions might not be able to contain the fury of the mob.

Recognizing the full peril, the high priest saw only too clearly that he, and he alone, would have to move swiftly. The slightest show of panic or uncertainty on his part would be disastrous. In the action he planned, Joseph Caiaphas, with the connivance of a few others, was condemning untold future generations of Jews to unparalleled hatred.

THE PASSOVER PLOT

My soul, sit thou a patient looker-on;
judge not the play before the play is done.
Her plot hath many changes:
every day speaks a new scene:
the last act crowns the play.

Francis Quarles, *Epigram: Respice Finem*

6

WITH INTENT TO MURDER

Ye are my friends if ye do whatsoever I command you.
John 15:14

Jesus and the apostles continued to pick their way over scree and down the sides of ravines before climbing again. Ahead was the Mount of Olives, adjoining it their next landmark, the massive outcrop of *Ha-Zoafim*, Hebrew for the Overlooker. The hill dominated the landscape to the east of Jerusalem. In choosing this escape route from Bethany, Simon the Canaanite knew that no one would expect them to come so close to the city walls. He had led them past the place where Joab had first found a way into Jerusalem, allowing King David's army to capture it. Almost ten centuries later, Jesus, his descendant, edged past the site of the royal tomb towards the ground where, in the wake of David's death, another Jewish king, Manasseh, had sacrificed children to appease the pagan god, Moloch. Few pilgrims encroached into the Valley of the Slain. Simon led them round the isolated pocket of land before they were once more engulfed in the crowd.

Redolent with animal and human odors the air was also awash in noise: a confused din of peddlers and public criers, herders and tradesmen, animals being driven in and out of pens and the rhythmic hammering of construction vying with repetitive psalmodic choruses. It was an unbelievably crowded atmosphere where the hurly-burly of commerce mingled with religious piety. Both the Temple guards and the tetrarch's troops recognized the futility of searching in this melee; the Romans would not be so foolhardy as even to consider entering the area. But for Jesus and the apostles to remain within the crowd's protective cover had meant climbing *Ha-Zoafim*, a test of stamina. Beyond lay another of Judea's desertscapes; a legion would not easily find anyone there.

They all knew that the threat of arrest had become very real after the resurrection of Lazarus. The action of restoring life only properly belonged to God. By demonstrating he had that power Jesus had opened a far more dangerous phase in his career. When word spread the Jewish people would flock to him. While he had made clear his sympathy for their desperate plight he also wanted them to realize his purpose was not to lead an apocalyptic movement, that his kingdom would not be fashioned from bloodshed—except the shedding of his own. That was the sole purpose of a life he must prolong a little longer. He had fled with the apostles from Bethany to gain further time to explain the realities of the plan he had first revealed on Mount Hattin: to show them that their grace would only come through participating in his; that the redemption he would win and the eternal life he offered were infinitely possible.

Yet, in spite of all his efforts, they continued to see him in human terms, identifying many of his responses with theirs. They could very easily have believed that he, like them, had been genuinely attracted to evil before taking the hard and worthwhile decision to reject it. Being young and healthy themselves, they had undoubtedly speculated whether he was sometimes sexually drawn to the women he seemed so often to go out of his way to attract, and whether he did so to show them it was possible to have control over the demands of the flesh. They still regarded Jesus as a man of God, not as the Son of God.

Judas, in particular, had displayed increasing signs of real misunderstanding. Culturally and politically more sophisticated than his fellow disciples, imbued with a high-minded thrift about money—the slightest expenditure had to be justified—he was above all a man of action and had become convinced that in any confrontation with the existing powers—whether Roman or Jewish—Jesus was certain to emerge victorious. Who can therefore doubt that the treasurer would have regarded Lazarus' resurrection as further proof that the Messiah was among them. The apostle's bewilderment would have been understandable when Jesus abruptly led the flight from Bethany. To Judas it must have seemed as if Jesus was once more avoiding his responsibilities to launch the kingdom. Finally, Jesus had delivered a gentle rebuke: "But of that day and that hour knoweth no man, no not the angels which are in heaven, neither the Son, but the Father." But the time was drawing close enough for Jesus to have realized he must take urgent action to show the disciples his very humanity was deliberately designed to lead them deeper into self-knowledge; through him they would learn their own new relationship with God: through them the world would savor salvation.

They made their way through another encampment. Tied to a stake outside each dwelling was a *mezuzah*, a cylinder holding replicas of the commandments God gave Moses. Women ground corn between millstones carried from distant parts of the Diaspora and pummeled the dough in wooden kneading troughs whose shape had remained unchanged since the exodus. The air was pungent with cooking, including the distinctive smell of locusts being fried in oil or boiled in brine. Yet, within a month, the last pilgrim would have departed and the ground cleaned of the carrion from the execution mound of Golgotha, where the birds picked at the crucified, extracting eyeballs and pecking away fleshier parts like lips and genitalia.

Jesus spoke often nowadays of his own fate. Again the disciples stared at him: in the eyes of Peter that familiar look of honest fear; Thomas perplexed; Judas' face a controlled mask; the others openly confused. Even James the Less, his blood brother, it was clear, had not fully realized that to bring forgiveness to the world Jesus must allow his earthly mission to end only in one way if he was to demonstrate God's full pardoning of man—through his death.

Yet, after almost three years of continuous teaching, during which he had consistently revealed himself as the creator of a new religious ideal, they saw him as earthbound as they were.

Their misapprehension was also understandable. In some ways Jesus' behavior fitted a popular concept that the Expected One would reveal himself in the guise of a brilliant strategist; that he would appear and strike unexpectedly, a dazzling figure who would consecrate anew the lives of all those on earth he touched. Nevertheless, outside a faithful coterie, mostly around the Sea of Galilee, few still even knew what Jesus looked like. The Temple agents and the other spies who dogged his footsteps, had, when pressed by their masters, no doubt found it hard to describe him as being different from other practicing male Jews: he had no distinguishing facial blemishes; his long hair, beard and curling side-locks, far from setting him apart, were typical, so were his clothes. At table, he behaved like any other man, using only his right hand to eat a staple diet of fish and bread washed down with goat's milk; roasted lamb never passed his lips from one Passover supper to another. Jesus' command of languages was not unusual: Aramaic for everyday conversation; Hebrew while preaching and interpreting the liturgical language of the Bible. That he understood Greek and Latin was no more than a mark of diligent days at school.

In the years preceding his ministry Jesus had spent time with a group of Pharisee teachers in Galilee; the sect was the only one which educated the poor. Under their tutelage he had become a superb preacher. But it had also become increasingly clear that in spite of the vividness of his teaching—which frequently drew upon such homely examples as sowing and harvesting to try to describe his concept—even the disciples failed fully to understand he was not in any sense a military leader.

Yet the strong anti-Roman feeling of the great majority of Jews could only be satisfied by the Expected One leading an armed insurrection. The death of John the Baptist had increasingly placed the onus for triggering that deliverance squarely upon Jesus. Like Judas, many of the Baptist's followers said Jesus must take *action* to support words which they interpreted as meaning he intended to fulfill the prophecies of Isaiah, Joel and Zachariah, who had envisaged a great climactic battle in which the Messiah would lead the nation to victory. The more Jesus tried to explain this was not his mission, the more the belief had spread that he would perform such a feat. A desperate people had cast him in the role of a very different type of deliverer than he intended to be. To convince them otherwise first required the disciples to understand that only his death would inaugurate the kingdom and bring a very different kind of victory.

As they followed him past one tented family after another, such ready examples of human life made it natural for them to put into a purely earthly context his views on such issues as sex, marriage, divorce, virginity and celibacy. Time and again, since delivering that manifesto on the slope of Mount Hattin, Jesus had returned to those topics, patiently answering their questions, reminding them, for example, that those whom God had joined together, no man should attempt to put asunder. Did that mean, they had pressed, that marriage was such a risk that it was better to remain celibate? Jesus offered a response meant to make each apostle think the matter through for himself. "There are some eunuchs which were so born from their mother's womb and there be eunuchs, which have made themselves eunuchs for the kingdom of heaven's sake. He that is able to receive it, let him receive it."

The linking of the forthcoming kingdom with such human functions as marital relationships and the problems of everyday living made it difficult for them to grasp the reality of his repeated and growing proclamation that he must sacrifice himself. Frequently struggling to understand their master's exact meaning of redemption, there was no scriptural precedent of a Messiah having to suffer for the salvation of the world.

In many ways the apostles were still conditioned by the Mosaic laws. Until Jesus had called them, those laws had provided a matrix which they accepted without equivocation. There was a religious commentary for everything: how they must dress, eat and work; how they should behave in every relationship, whether in the family or in the larger community. For them, despite having witnessed stunning examples of his power, the kingdom of heaven, when it came, would appear in surroundings with which they would be reassuringly familiar. Nowhere in the Torah or any other holy book was there one word which said the Messiah would come to die to ensure the birth of his prophecies. The apostles could still not fully grasp that this was the one fundamental factor which placed Jesus apart from all other religious authority: he saw his fate as a deliberate sign of contradiction—but never one of defeat.

The miracle of raising Lazarus had, in some ways, changed everything, yet on the other hand it had not. Bringing a person back from the dead was undoubtedly the most dramatic of all his feats—made all the more vivid by the event's proximity to the Temple and a direct affront to the stated dogma of its high priest that resurrection was an impossibility. But many Jews would not have been entirely overwhelmed by the happening because they no longer believed in the claim that when the angel of death put the "deep and bitter gall" upon the lips of the dying, the soul was carried away to some mysterious region that Scripture often called *Sheol*, identified by Job as that "place of darkness and of the shades of death." The Psalmist described it as "the dwelling of silence," located so far from earth that Job, again, had recorded that even "the anger of the Lord" could not penetrate into *Sheol*.

Jesus had explained to the apostles that his meaning of resurrection went far beyond what was essentially a Judaic belief in reincarnation. He was talking about a unique transcendent power—his—which would make his ministry so different from all other faiths. He had already spoken of that authority in his words to Martha: "I am the resurrection and the life."

He had meant them not only to comfort her but to provide another lesson for the disciples. He wanted them to absorb it as the core of the faith they would spread for him; only then could they be his witnesses. In raising Lazarus he had demonstrated the full hopelessness of the existing human situation he had come to save; he had to make the disciples understand that dying should hold no terror when contained within a belief in all he represented. Jesus had hurried from Bethany to continue to prepare them for his bitter fate—a prerequisite to launching his message. He had to make them all absolutely accept that, while by birth and upbringing he, too, was a son of the covenant; that while he was capable of loving and being aroused to anger as a man; that while he accepted his people had their own place and destiny in history; that while he supported all the Mosaic laws; that while all the touchstones of the faith he was born into were encompassed in his teaching, including a total and imperative acceptance there was only one God: that while all this, and a great deal more, he held to be absolutely true, he still had more, so much more, to offer to all those who wished to perfect their own way of knowing and seeing God. His apostles must be completely convinced that he was concerned with more than satisfying the longing of hundreds of years of Jewish expectation. The salvation he was bringing was for all humanity. Unless they understood that, they would never be able to go out into the world and properly continue his work. He would gladly pay for that clear understanding with his life.

The time of supreme sacrifice was not quite at hand. After Lazarus had embraced his sisters, Jesus saw it as the sensible precaution for them to leave the village before word spread of what had happened; the Temple agent racing off towards Jerusalem clearly forebode trouble. Mary and Martha, supporting their still dazed brother, headed south, probably to the safety of caves where Amos, the misogynous shepherd-prophet, had prepared his thunderous denunciation against rich women. The villagers would keep secret the route he and the apostles had taken.

Simon the Canaanite had shaded his eyes against the sun whenever there was a glimpse of the track which led from Jerusalem to Bethany after he spotted the column of guards racing from the Golden Gate towards the village. He switched direction several times, taking them through the larger camps, where in the turmoil people would be less likely to remember a group of men moving with unassuming purpose. From the crowded top of *Ha-Zoafim* Simon saw the guards trudging slowly back towards the city. For the moment Jesus and the apostles were safe. They continued to pick their way along yet another track, heading north, away from Jerusalem. Jesus led them as he had on that day when, hungry, thirsty and tired, a similar path had brought them into a small Judean village. It was a day Matthew would never forget.

Matthew, in spite of immediate acceptance by the others, found it hard at times to shake off his past. For years he had been a Roman tax gatherer, a Jew to be despised, whose circle of friends had been restricted to other outcasts: alcoholics, vagrants and prostitutes, the reviled and rejected. Then Jesus had passed his collector's booth in Capernaum and commanded Matthew to follow him. He had obeyed without hesitation, bringing to an end days spent counting coins and poring over schedules of tolls.

When previously Matthew entered this village to collect imperial dues, the children had tormented him with jeers that he was a paid thief. Now, at the end of another of Jesus' long and exhausting treks, these unhappy memories surfaced when a group of urchins raced towards them. Recognizing their old enemy behind the beard he had grown, they began to catcall. Matthew ran towards them, waving his fists, followed by Peter, who could be quick-tempered, and Philip, anxious to defend the dignity of his best friend. The children backed away, keeping out of reach of the dust-smeared trio. Jesus strode forward and stopped the pursuit with a firm rebuke. "Suffer little children and forbid them not to come unto me. For of such is the kingdom of heaven."

Watched by the shamefaced disciples Jesus walked over to the boys and asked their names. Then he beckoned the apostles to join him. When they gathered around, he addressed the children, reminding them of the proverb in Holy Writ which said everyone must keep to the course he had begun; even when he grew old he must not deviate from that chosen path in life. Jesus looked into the children's suddenly serious faces, smiling gently as he put the questions. Did any of them wish to depart from the rule their fathers had given them? The one about showing respect to their elders? Did they want to forget that was as important as all the other maxims of Holy Law? One by one the children shook their heads. Then they turned and bowed bravely towards Matthew.

That evening Jesus and the disciples were supper guests of the *hazzan*, the village schoolteacher who greeted them in turn, giving each the kiss of peace, and led them to an inner courtyard where the girls in his family waited with bowls of water to wash their feet. Afterwards Jesus motioned the apostles to stand and, wrapped in their prayer shawls, to face in the direction of Jerusalem, a reminder that the prophet Daniel had done so every time he had prayed throughout the long exile in Babylon. They knelt, outstretched their arms and recited the *Shema*, the ancient and uncompromising promise they would never forget they were the People of the Book, and other prayers, a haunting repetition of low chants which glorified God and this land of Abraham and Jacob. Finally, as they did before each meal, they repeated the "Our Father."

The guests stretched out on cushions, each supporting himself upon the left elbow, using the right hand to pick at the food. Jesus, as usual, had the place of honor—facing the gap in the dining area through which the women came and went from the kitchen. The *hazzan* served them in strict precedence, offering the dishes to Jesus first, then the apostle on his left, Judas: being at his elbow was deemed to be the safest place for the man who carried the money that paid their board and lodging. The host worked his way around the group until he finally returned to serve Peter, at Jesus' right elbow. Each apostle followed Jesus in taking a handful of food on to a tin plate; earthenware was ritually unclean. The host poured goat's milk for Jesus and wine for the others. The fare was simple: fish, locusts, fruit and bread. Passover was approaching and it was a time for frugality before the greatest of all celebrations.

Throughout the meal Jesus touched upon themes never far from his lips: those who suffered insults and persecution in his name would have a rich reward in heaven; those who followed him would be seen as the salt of the earth. They were familiar allusions to the problems they would face and the rewards for dispelling the gloom of a somber and uncertain world. During the discourse villagers had crowded into the courtyard to listen, including several of the boys who had earlier mocked Matthew. Jesus motioned one of them to come forward. He sat the child on his lap and began to speak again. "Whosoever shall humble himself as this little child, the same is greatest in the kingdom of heaven."

He waited, the pause of a natural storyteller, eyes no doubt sweeping the circle of apostles, drawing the boy closer, the way a father would hold his own son, the disciples staring at their master clasping this child clothed in rags, barefooted, constantly brushing flies from his eyes and skin, no different from all the others. Jesus emphasized that the only way people would understand the true meaning of his teaching would be to acquire the innocent mind of a child. This boy, he continued, had yet to assume his elders' selfish ambitions, privileges and position. Anyone who hoped to enter the kingdom of heaven must first relinquish them. He sent the child back to his friends.

Jesus returned to another familiar theme: social justice and the disparity between rich and poor. Staring at the intent faces before him, Jesus reached into their farming background to illustrate his meaning. "Which of you, having a servant plowing or feeding cattle, will say unto him by and by, when he is come from the field, Go and sit down to meat? And will not rather say unto him, Make ready wherewith I may sup, and gird myself, and serve me, till I have eaten and drunken; and afterward thou shalt eat and drink? Doth he thank that servant because he did the things that were commanded him? I trow not. So likewise ye, when ye shall have done all those things which are commanded you, say, We are unprofitable servants: we have done that which was our duty to do."

By such analogies Jesus tried to show the disciples how his message should be taught; that, when the time came, they must also explain to others that the choice being imposed was a deliberately hard one to accept. People could either let their lives remain as they were "make ready wherewith I may sup"—or they could make a clean break and hope for eternal salvation. There was no easy promise; to achieve redemption would demand a consistent application of new, hard-to-live-by standards.

Jesus had been about to embark upon further explanations—no doubt once more searching for an example with which his audience could identify—when into the courtyard came a stranger. He wore an expensive *chadlock*, a garment which signified his social position. Only a wealthy landowner could afford a coat of embroidered silk squares. Hands hooked into its belt, the man halted before Jesus.

"Good master, what good thing shall I do that I may inherit eternal life?"

Early on Matthew had noted that, almost more than any other precondition, Jesus made rejection of material possessions the prerequisite of salvation. Throughout the Sermon on the Mount, his commitment to social and economic equality had been clearly proclaimed; without it there was no redemption. Salvation was beyond anyone who did not realize that material wealth was potentially an instrument of corruption.

"Why callest thou me good?"

The man looked perplexed.

Jesus explained: "There is none good but one, that is God. Thou knowest the commandments . . ."

The man interrupted. He insisted he had kept the law, each tenet of it. What more could he do?

Jesus would not have needed a rueful smile to explain. "One thing thou lackest: go thy way, sell whatsoever thou hast, and give to the poor, and thou shalt have treasure in heaven: and come, take up the cross, and follow me."

Understandably, the wealthy man stared at him, his face working, his voice unquestionably filled with baffled regret: he could not possibly follow Jesus' advice. He *needed* to keep his possessions; they were an inheritance and an insurance for the future of his family. His wife and children depended on him. Motioning towards the crowd he said, his voice rising, that *his* money and *his* position ensured *their* future. He turned and walked out of the courtyard.

Matthew also noted the next words: "It is easier for a camel to go through the eye of a needle than for a rich man to enter into the kingdom of God."

Peter broke the silence. His intervention was also understandable. Indicating his companions he said that surely *they* would enter because of what they had already given up: their families, homes, their fishing boats and land. They had forsaken all, and gladly, to follow him. Could there be any doubt about their reward? Would they not have precedence over those who continued to enjoy worldly pleasures throughout their lives and only sought redemption at the very end?

Jesus, who had spent so much time trying to explain the real meaning of forgiveness, would have seen only too clearly the human concern and failing behind Peter's question.

Caiaphas waited for the return of Jonathan's men from Bethany. Their orders were to arrest and bring Jesus to the Temple before word of Lazarus' resurrection spread. The immediate threat he posed would then be reduced. In the meantime, Annas was discussing the *prima facie* grounds for a trial with the court's seventy-one judges, arguing that Jesus had set himself up as a direct opponent to God's delegate, the high priest, and Moses and his laws. Therefore, Jesus opposed Yahweh himself, the Ten Commandments and all their attendant corollaries, the 613 obligations, 365 of them negative and 248 positive, that guided the behavior of the Chosen People. Caiaphas could have been well satisfied with such a strong holding charge pending the formation of even greater accusations.

The guards had returned empty-handed. No amount of threatening on their part could persuade the villagers to talk. A proposal from Jonathan to send his patrols into the crowded hills would have been a logical response; its rejection in keeping with the high priest's pragmatism: even if the guards were able to pick up his trail, bringing him through the pilgrims was now fraught with risk. As word spread about Lazarus any move against Jesus and his followers would certainly attract attention and very likely provoke resistance. An insurrection could flare in sight of the city and precipitate a Roman involvement.

However, with Lazarus and his sisters gone from Bethany, the danger seemed somewhat reduced; without the physical presence of a body returned to life the story would be that much harder to believe.

Jesus and the apostles found that beyond *Ha-Zoafim* the crowds began to thin. For the moment the crenellated walls of Jerusalem were out of sight. Below was the road that led northwards into Galilee, the oldest of all the caravan routes, following the backbone of the land. In the distance was a ring of hills. To reach them meant crossing a desolate landscape broken by dried-out beds of streams and *wadim* plunging a hundred feet, and more, to their boulder-strewn floors. They made their way into the desert, moving under the cover of one gulch to another. They finally reached the hills with the sun setting behind them. There was no sign of pursuit.

They continued past shepherds tending their flocks, to the tiny village of Ephraim: no more than a handful of houses grouped in pairs around a common courtyard, each yard with its mill for grinding corn, a clay oven for baking bread and a fig tree providing shade against the fierce noonday heat of summer. In the center of the village stood its most imposing building, rectangular-shaped, with stone ashlars and an open staircase along one wall that led to a gallery. Its facade was faced with a double row of Corinthian pillars, and the lintels above the entrance and window were decorated with various religious motifs. Everything about the building proclaimed its importance in the life of the community. It was the village synagogue.

Jesus led them towards the entrance, the door surmounted by a window designed according to Scripture to face the source of all light and wisdom—Jerusalem. In every synagogue throughout the Diaspora there was an identical opening. In contrast with its ornate, almost flamboyant facade, the interior was surprisingly bare; the floor of plain flagstones; columns supporting the gallery where the women worshipped. When their eyes adjusted to the light Jesus and the apostles saw the familiar frieze, with its images and symbols set within medallions.

In size and shape the synagogue was similar to the one in Nazareth. None of the disciples would forget that first and only occasion when Jesus had brought them there; his reputation was already beginning to be established around the Sea of Galilee and he had told them he wanted to carry the good tidings to where, as a child, he grew up with his brothers and sisters, watching their father work with wood, and the tanners and potters cut and mold objects of lasting beauty.

Jesus had been the first of Mary's children to go to school, and sit in a circle and repeat after the *hazzan* in a loud chorus the scriptural verses to be learned by heart. When his brothers and sisters came of age they had squatted beside him; if they stumbled he had corrected and encouraged them, the way any older brother would. Their mother had thoroughly indoctrinated each of them about the role of religion in the home. Everything was sacred; the smallest and most insignificant act required thanks to be given to God. Every morning they recited the first *beraka*, a blessing for the day; another for the clothes they wore; the sandals they laced; the food they ate. They even learned to repeat blessings for natural bodily functions. "Blessed art thou, O Lord, who has fashioned men with wisdom and hast created in him apertures and outlets." After school they had gone into the countryside to watch the women tilling, planting and harvesting and discovering how to distinguish the differing calls of the shepherds. All this most definitely had influenced his approach to his ministry. It had to be clear-cut enough to reach the uncomplicated minds of his people.

On their memorable visit the disciples with Jesus had reached Nazareth before sundown on the eve of another sabbath, and had gone to his mother's home to wash. Mary and her daughters were completing the preparation of food to last for the duration of the holy day, during which no fire could be lit or cooking done. As dusk approached she had lit the oil lamps which would burn continuously, untouched by hand, for the next twenty-four hours; his sisters had drawn enough water from the village well for domestic needs. Then, while his mother and sisters went to the women's gallery, Jesus led the apostles through the main entrance of the synagogue.

Its flagstoned floor was crowded with men and boys. They stared attentively at the *tebah*, a simple platform lit by a single oil lamp standing close to a lectern. A legend was to grow that before he died Joseph carved the ambo. On it rested the holiest object in the synagogue, a copy of the *Sefer Torah*. The handwritten parchment scrolls had been removed from the wooden ark kept in a small room behind the *tebah*, and placed on the lectern. It was dressed in the garments appropriate for the rites: a mantle protected the scrolls from public view; finials, decorated knobs, had been mounted on to the staves around which the parchment was rolled.

With the villagers Jesus and the disciples watched two figures standing before the ambo. One was the *hazzan*, the other a boy, limbs still developing, voice unbroken, eyes respectfully following the *yad*, the pointer, in the *hazzan*'s hand; during the reading of the Torah it is forbidden to touch the parchment. The boy repeated each sacred line in a high-pitched voice, demonstrating that when the time came he would be able to read the *Parashah*, the first public profession of his faith, the audible proof that he was fully prepared to partake in the greatness and the fate of the Chosen People. Every Friday night in synagogues throughout the Diaspora boys stood before their elders and chanted the blessings and readings of the law.

(On the threshold of his thirteenth birthday, shortly before his trip to Jerusalem where he bemused and startled the scholars of the Temple, Jesus stood on this same *tebah* repeating every gesture and intonation of his teacher, showing his proud family he was capable of officiating and praying in public.)

When the boy's instruction ended and the Friday evening service began, Jesus and the apostles recited the blessings designed to concentrate minds upon the timeless world of the sabbath. Afterwards they all walked home to his mother's house, built by Joseph on a shoulder of a hill and with a magnificent view towards the distant plain where Elijah slew the prophets of Baal. The dwelling had changed little since Jesus lived there: the thick interior walls of mountain stone that much blacker with smoke; the number of sheep, goats and chickens penned near the front door that fewer now with the children growing up and moving out. But otherwise the house would be as he always remembered it: an earthen ground floor leading to a platform at the rear, supported on stone pillars and reached by a wooden staircase. This was the heart of the household, a spacious area of bare floorboards where the family ate and slept. An opening led to the flat roof, itself designed to slope to one corner so that rain drained into a covered stone trough for those long summers when water was scarce. Jesus and the apostles slept on the roof beneath the stars.

On Saturday morning they had returned to the synagogue. The main service of the week began with prayers that brought together the truths of Abraham's religion: respect for the Creator, a full understanding of the law and the role of the Chosen People as the true representatives of the entire human race.

The rabbi then invited a member of the congregation to read the first of the one hundred and seventy-five verses of the *Parashoth*, the portions of Holy Writ. Jesus strode to the lectern where the rabbi handed him the yad. The parchment was open at the book of Isaiah. Jesus began to quote: "'The Spirit of the Lord is upon me, because he hath anointed me to preach the gospel to the poor; he hath sent me to heal the brokenhearted, to preach deliverance to the captives and recovering of sight to the blind, to set at liberty them that are bruised. To preach the acceptable year of the Lord.'"

His voice ringing with certainty, Jesus uttered the first prophetic words of commentary. "This day is this scripture fulfilled in your ears."

It was not difficult to comprehend the shocked murmur which swept the congregation, or that men began to murmur to one another. Matthew would remember voice after voice joining the chorus of accusations and hands perhaps gesticulating first at Mary and her daughters, and then where Jesus' brothers stood in embarrassed silence. A worshipper turned to a neighbor and demanded: "Is not this the carpenter's son? Is not his mother called Mary?" Another voice shouted that Jesus could not possibly claim any right to fulfill Scripture; God alone did that.

Jesus' exasperation survived along with the angry grumbling. "Ye will surely say unto me this proverb. Physician heal thyself: whatsoever we have heard done in Capernaum do also here in thy country."

Tumult broke out. Men and women yelled in fury. How dare he come here with such blasphemy? They all remembered him as a boy who had worked alongside his father, who had prayed here with them, a devout Jew linked in a special way to the faith of his forefathers. What gave him the right, the madness, to pretend he was now endowed with gifts from God? They had heard the stories about how he had supposedly given a cripple back the power to walk and a blind man sight; that he had driven out demons and sent life coursing through those mentally stricken. They had heard, they shouted, and they didn't believe. Let him show *them*! There was a man newly blinded in the town. They would fetch him—and he would show *them* if he could restore sight! There was a woman dying—show *them* how he could cure her! The taunting challenges came from all sides. "Show us! Son of Mary—show us! Show us—son of Joseph! Show us—and your brothers and sisters!" Jesus raised his hands to silence them.

"Verily I say unto you, no prophet is accepted in his own country!"

He reminded them of the fate of those in the past who had refused to believe: women who became suddenly widowed; lepers who had been left uncleansed. God had himself momentarily withdrawn from his people in the face of their religious intolerance and prejudice.

The full fury of mob violence swept the building, and before Simon the Canaanite, Peter, Andrew, Philip and even the puny Judas could make their way to their master a core of men bundled Jesus from the platform and dragged him through a side door, screaming and shouting that he must die for such heresy. His mother, brothers and sisters were swept aside as they struggled to reach him; Thomas and Thaddaeus paused to help them while the other apostles fought their way through the crowd, urged on by James the Less who knew where they were taking his brother: the sheer cliff face at the northern end of the town, where as boys they had looked out towards Mount Hattin. James knew what the mob intended to do: hurl Jesus headlong to the rocks far below. Of the disciples he was the closest to Jesus as the crowd reached the cliff. Then, before their eyes, he was gone. No one could say how. The stupefied onlookers stared at one another in disbelief. They veered away from the disciples as if they, too, were charged with paranormal capabilities. But all the apostles could say to a relieved Mary was that Jesus "passing through the midst of them went his way."

The disciples had found him the next day on the far side of the Sea of Galilee. Jesus never explained how he reached there. His very lack of discourse and elaboration would reinforce the authenticity of a happening beyond all human capability. It had been an event of divine intervention, defying any earthly criteria.

In Jerusalem after the evening offering, during which the priests had led the faithful in reciting the *Shema*, a procession emerged from the Temple. Led by Jonathan, a contingent of his guards formed a phalanx of shields and swords forcing people and animals to one side. Next came a group of robed chief priests creating a circle around Caiaphas. In preparation for Passover he had undergone a seven-day period of purification, during which he had given up all physical contact with his wife and moved into bachelor quarters in the Temple. The priests were there to ensure that Caiaphas particularly avoided any risk of defilement through contact with the dead; the route across the city had been checked to ensure they did not pass a house where a corpse awaited burial.

Nobody could remember when a high priest had last ventured forth into the filthy winding streets of Jerusalem before a festival and, to emphasize the importance of the occasion, Caiaphas had exchanged his turban for a golden diadem engraved with the Hebrew words: "Glory to God." Jonathan led them down a long flight of steps which divided the Upper from the Lower City, and on past the royal palace of the Hasmonean dynasty which had been ruthlessly destroyed by the father of the man upon whom Caiaphas was calling. A detachment of Herod Antipas' soldiers waited to escort the procession into a heavily fortified enclave. There were two main palaces and a score of lesser buildings, banquet halls, baths and accommodation for a thousand guests as well as extensive servants' quarters above the notorious dungeons. Groves of trees stood between canals and small lakes studded with bronze fountains. The tetrarch's private quarters were in the Hippicus Tower, the most secure site in the complex. Herodias and Salome lived in the tower his father had dedicated to Mariamne—the wife the old tyrant had executed.

Drawn up in a courtyard was a contingent of the household bodyguard, caped and armed in Roman style, each man a slave who had been given his freedom after pledging undying loyalty to Herod Antipas. With them were several black-garbed chamberlains holding lanterns to show the way. They brought the Temple entourage to a reception hall where courtiers were grouped around the tetrarch's secretary. Caiaphas advanced to receive the reverential welcome from the official, who then conducted the high priest through several smaller reception rooms and across courtyards surrounded by colonnades, a watchful soldier before each pillar, a brazier beside him to lessen the chill of guard duty.

The tetrarch's audience chamber was a perfectly square salon reached through double doors with a throne at the opposite end that Herod the Great had installed. His son preferred to receive visitors while seated on cushions on the floor. The room was lit by oil lamps on low tables. Outside the doors the high chamberlain greeted Caiaphas and escorted him across the marble floor to where the tetrarch had risen and stood waiting. Courtesies over, they settled themselves cross-legged on the floor and sipped from tiny cups of mint tea served by Chuza. The two most powerful Jews in the world began discussing plans to murder Jesus.

After sleeping out in the hills around Ephraim, a precaution to reduce the risk of discovery, Jesus continued to demonstrate he would be forever remembered as the greatest of all teachers. From the beginning of his ministry he had shown that his message must be permanently memorable to all those who could neither read nor write, which included the majority of the apostles. Just as Jesus had been educated by rote and example, he used the same approach to lodge in their minds sayings which bore the mark of blinding reality. Seated in the cool morning air—the sun rising over Jerusalem in the distance, its rays reflected against the gold roof of the Temple and radiating off its snow-white walls—he reminded them again of epigrams which held a very different kind of truth than taught at Judaism's prime religious center. They repeated after him words of a supreme quality. He asked them: "What shall it profit a man if he shall gain the whole world and lose his own soul?" And when their voices had chorused the words he had put the next question. "Or what shall a man give in return for his soul?" Phrase by phrase, as Jesus did every morning, he reinforced in them the principles he held so dear. "Whosoever exalts himself shall be abased, and he that shall humble himself be exalted"; "a man's life consisteth not in the abundance of the things which he possesseth"; "he that findeth his life shall lose it, and he that loseth his life for my sake shall find it."

He demonstrated that worldly standards of greatness and power could be destroyed in a sentence; that in a few words values could be forever redefined; that what may sound incredible and unreal, on reflection, could not be denied; that to succeed in spreading the Word they must be willing to unshackle their listeners from their religious roots by every available means: hyperbole, the overdrawn language of poetry, the use of metaphors and humor—anything which would jerk people bolt upright, forcing them, even against their will, to see the new truth. They had, he continued, traveled a long and difficult spiritual road. Now there must be soon a physical parting of the ways. Once more Jesus had looked at them and added that they must take comfort from the ever more rapidly approaching kingdom. Then staring deeply into each face he added: "There be some standing here which shall not taste of death till they see the kingdom of God."

Jesus had first spoken those words when he was only too aware of the hostility he was attracting and he knew that, in human terms, his enemies must take away his life. Even then, in the second year of his ministry, the certainty of the cross was inevitable. To earn a temporary respite from the pressures, he had taken the apostles far to the north of the country, to the mountain citadel of Caesarea Philippi, where the Greeks believed their gods once lived and from where, in a cavern, the Jordan began its long journey south. Towering over the city was a gleaming white marble temple, erected by Herod the Great in memory of Julius Caesar.

In its sight Jesus had told Peter, in Matthew's hearing, that his first apostle would have "the keys of the kingdom of heaven." As a reward for being the first apostle to have recognized Jesus as the Messiah he had been promised the post of a faithful steward who would symbolically open the door of the kingdom by being the founder of its Church. Jesus had once more spoken bluntly of the suffering that lay ahead for him. Peter had reacted violently, shouting this would never be allowed to happen. The apostle's response was, for Jesus, no doubt deeply touching. But it was also a further reminder of the problems he faced in trying to convince the disciples that his going to the cross was essential. He had not wasted words soothing the distraught Peter. Matthew caught the anger in Jesus' words. "Get thee behind me, Satan, thou art an offense unto me; for thou savorest not the things that be of God, but those that be of men." Peter had confronted Jesus with a temptation similar to the one he had faced in the

Wilderness: the easy road to power. Peter out of love had tried to weaken Jesus' resolve.

Now, on the hillside overlooking Ephraim, Jesus had the joy of knowing his ministry was secured because at least Peter, John and James the Less finally understood. The realization came through an event on Mount Hebron regarded as ultimate proof of God's approval for Jesus' work.

After his appointment of Peter, Jesus had led the apostles still further north from Caesarea Philippi to the foothills of Mount Hebron, the only mountain in Judea coated with deep layers of ice all year round. Near one of the ruined villages of the Hittites, the tribe Joshua had overcome to complete the conquest of Canaan, Jesus ordered the others to make camp while he took his brother, Peter and John on up towards the summit.

Several of the disciples had been concerned by their flight from Caesarea Philippi; they may indeed have thought his ministry effectively over. However, after his transfiguration they must have seen that Jesus was revitalized, filled with renewed zeal, purpose and a certainty that the course he was embarked upon *was* fulfilling the will of God. The apostles felt a renewed and deeper loyalty to him and to each other. He had promised them that when he descended from the mountain they would journey together to Jerusalem to hasten the coming of the kingdom.

Let there be confrontation, Judas had cried in his guttural desert patois; the enemies would be swept aside. In his voice could still be heard the authentic longings of Jewish messianic hopes, dreams and expectations. He still clung to the dangerously misguided idea that Jesus was the all-conquering hero—and never destined to face the lonely agony of the cross.

Watching the master he adored disappearing up the mountain the first seeds of what he must do had been planted in the deluded treasurer's mind.

The three men following Jesus had an easy climb. In spite of its height, about ten thousand feet above sea level, the Hebron slopes are gentle. The ascent began in midafternoon. By the time they reached the halfway stage the sun was sinking. They paused by one of the many streams tumbling icy water from the snow level, and joined Jesus in once more kneeling on the grassy stubble beside the brook to pray. When they opened their eyes Jesus was already a few yards away. He turned and faced them. Not only did his face assume an ethereal appearance, but his robe glowed with a light so white and intense that they had to shade their eyes. Then, as they remained kneeling, too awed to move, two figures appeared on either side of Jesus. They were Moses and Elijah.

Peter, clutching to something he could understand, stammered: "Lord, it is good for us to be here; if thou wilt, let us make here three tabernacles, one for thee and one for Moses and one for Elias."

Jesus made no response. As they watched, the apostles were convinced the two figures spoke to him. A cloud rolled down over the mountain obscuring Jesus and his companions. Throughout the history of the Chosen People the concept of the *Schechinah*, Hebraic for "the Glory of God," had often been expressed in the form of a cloud. During their forty years in the Wilderness a cloud, in the shape of a pillar, had led them to safety. God had emerged to give Moses the law from a similar cloud; it was present at the dedication of Solomon's Temple. The glorious cloud had always been at hand on the most significant occasions. When it dispersed the disciples saw that Moses and Elijah had vanished. Then came a mysterious voice, the one Peter and John had heard after Jesus was baptized. Once more it boomed out, its rich timbre bouncing off the rock, filling the apostles with understandable awe as it proclaimed: "This is my beloved Son, in whom I am well pleased; hear ye him."

Prostrate on the ground, hands over their ears to keep out the unearthly voice they believed was God, the disciples felt Jesus gently shake them, telling them to rise. When they did so he stood among them, putting his arms around their shoulders, calming and reassuring them with his words. When they recovered, he cautioned that what they had seen and heard must be divulged to no one until a certain condition was met. Jesus, by their own account, administered the oath of silence in words which once more could only have reawakened an old anxiety. "Tell the vision to no man until the Son of man be risen again from the dead."

He said that those who were supposed to teach the old prophecies, the Temple scholars, had not recognized that the spirit of Elijah was the guiding force behind the ministry of John the Baptist. Jesus added, somewhat cryptically, that John had died violently to fulfill part of those prophecies which the scribes taught but had not grasped and that his own death would complete a sacred prediction.

Coming down the mountain, united by the so far most important advance in the history of Jesus, the apostles were convinced that in that one dazzling incident they had, through him, witnessed the greatness of the Jewish past uniting him with the even greater challenges of the future. They had been asked to accept there was a direct line which led from Mary's annunciation to the transfiguration they had just witnessed of the Son of God she had been chosen to bear.

In his office Caiaphas, Annas and a number of other Sadducee judges listened carefully as the Temple crier read aloud from a parchment scroll.

He would repeat the words throughout the streets of Jerusalem and at every encampment on the surrounding hills.

> Anyone who has information on one Jeshu Hannosri, especially his whereabouts, let him declare it to the Great Sanhedrin. Anyone who can speak let him come forth and do so to the same body."

Jeshu Hannosri was Hebrew for Jesus the Nazarene.

Because he would be facing criminal charges, prosecution witnesses must be found. There was every possibility that among those who would come forward there could be someone Jesus had offended or disappointed. In the hands of Caiaphas they could be tutored to carry off a role which otherwise held its own special risks. An accuser was invariably stoned if his evidence was false. Yet until persons were found who were willing to testify before the supreme court there was no legal way of proceeding against Jesus.

7

HOSANNA

Sufficient unto the day is the evil thereof.
Matthew 6:34

Puzzling though some of the apostles must have found the lack of pursuit after their headlong rush from Bethany, they raised no recorded objection when Jesus announced they would leave Ephraim and return there. It was on Simon's advice that they would head for Zorah, where Samson was born, bringing them south of Jerusalem before they would turn east towards Bethany. The route was across rugged terrain barely patrolled by either Roman or the tetrarch's troops. To reach Bethany would be a day's hard walking; if it was safe, they would stay in the village which had become their traditional base for the past three years before going on up to the festivals in Jerusalem. Their hope was that Martha, Mary and Lazarus would have by then returned home. There was the usual good-natured grumbling about once more having to live with Martha's domestic routine. Her sister was dreamy and easygoing, content to hover around Jesus, a born listener.

Further discussion ended with Jesus preaching one of his longest sermons since Mount Hattin. He began with the story of the rich man who gave his servants money, and how all but one, through hard work, multiplied the coins. The message was clear: common sense and effort were prerequisites for the new life. The parable was an immediate and arresting way to get attention for the *euaggelion*, the gospel of good news, Jesus was intent on bringing. He wanted them to understand that to remove injustice and help the underprivileged was a continuous challenge: hardship, opposition and the utter rottenness of so much of human behavior had to be dealt with unflinchingly. To follow in his footsteps, he kept on reminding them, needed not only a total devotion to God but also having to conquer temptation within themselves. Until they could achieve that they would not be fully committed. Becoming like him meant not only being able to serve others but also being of service in God's name.

The five who had stood on the bank of the Jordan listening to John on the day Jesus was baptized could only have been struck by how different his approach had become to the Baptist's. To the end, John's ministry was based on perpetual threat: fires consuming nonbelievers; the axe hovering over their heads; wholesale destruction of all kinds. For all the *qadosh*, holiness, of John's teaching, there was an unapproachability about the God he perceived. Jesus, on the other hand, spoke continuously of a self-revealing God, whose paramount desire was to be known by everyone, and whose message was based on love.

They had all recognized his teaching ministry and healing miracles were often at their most powerful after He had spent prolonged periods praying. Those who had been with him from that day when they were convinced they had heard the words of God—"This is my beloved Son in whom I am well pleased"—had accepted that his sense of intimacy with the Almighty remained unique. For his part, he continuously promised them they would all share in it, though there could be no shortcuts. Jesus had made that trenchantly clear.

As he spoke about clothing the naked, visiting the imprisoned, nursing the sick and feeding the hungry, he was really describing a God committed to help every human situation, a selfless God who wanted to share himself with all humanity in a totally different way from what they had known before. He was saying that the love of God could forgive any sin providing there was genuine repentance. He reminded them he was again describing a God who was not only inviting and forgiving, but also more meaningful. The Temple scholars taught that a sinner who came on hands and knees to seek public forgiveness, who loudly proclaimed his contrition and remorse in the presence of priests, who made sacrifices and paid penalties, might be forgiven. But the God Jesus spoke of asked none of these things; his God did not wait for penitents to come to him, but went out in search of the fallen and openly appealed to them: "Come, follow me."

They listened, magnetized anew by the sheer brilliance of his concepts. There was a warmth and vitality about his words which matched the morning sun on their faces. The trio who had climbed Hebron with Jesus and witnessed the transfiguration particularly noticed the boundless energy which had sustained him from then on: they realized that plainly the event had been his coronation. Those words of God—"This is my beloved Son"—

had their echo in the ancient anthem chanted at the crowning of every Jewish ruler since Saul. An important feature of the ceremony was that it took place on a mountain and that the twelve tribes of Israel must be represented. Well could James the Less, Peter and John believe they had been chosen to fulfill that role. When they saw the transfiguration in that light they were understandably thrilled that among the Twelve they were still the only ones who knew how close Jesus was to launching his kingdom.

Here, on a hillside above Ephraim, he reminded them all of an earlier saying of his: no one could survive in isolation; that everyone needed someone to complete himself—and that God was the forging link. That was why God had created the world and populated it, so that they could love each other—and that was why God was willing to make any sacrifice to bring people to that realization.

Shortly, Passover would begin—and during it "The Son of man is betrayed to be crucified." Jesus reminded them of the glory which awaited him and them—life eternal. Unlike many of his parables—where the details were not meant to be closely examined and each line given its own significance—he wanted them to understand first the brutality of what lay ahead—and then the joy beyond. He impressed upon them they must never see him as a victim; rather, that he was ready to lay down his life; that from the beginning he was only a chosen instrument in a drama whose every twist had been under the direction of God—just as would be its culmination. They should not weep. They should rejoice.

Heading west across Judea towards Jerusalem the full impact of the words struck them. For the first time Jesus had indicated he would be betrayed. But how? Who would do such a thing? Clearly he or she would be motivated by Satan; Jesus never tired of saying that just as God had need of them, so the devil was looking for willing hands. Ultimately, it would not matter whether it had been left to Thomas or one of the others to synthesize the situation, no one could be used without cooperation, everyone could keep out the devil. The betrayer would have to be someone with a sufficient lack of faith to succumb to temptation. No doubt they were certain Jesus could not have meant any of them. They were now at last a close-knit unit, a fusing of very differing personalities. Thomas was noticeably less prickly; John, since coming down from Mount Hebron, more content to listen and not jostle for Jesus' attention. Bartholomew's last signs of reluctance over whether he should be tramping the countryside in the footsteps of Jesus had gone. Andrew and Thaddaeus, separated by a score of years, who had sometimes argued over trivialities, were inseparable. Simon the Canaanite, next to Peter, was the most amiable among them. No brother was more devoted than James the Less, and the behavior of Philip, Matthew and the portly James was also above reproach. While some of the apostles had found Judas' fanaticism a tiresome trait, clearly no one doubted his loyalty. Following Jesus over the broken ground, they had sensed a certainty which matched his stride—that his message would survive and that a world far beyond this parched landscape would come to know and accept it. In the past he had predicted so many other extraordinary events which, if they had not witnessed them, they might well have not believed. Matthew could certainly vividly remember a very different journey they undertook during that first year of Jesus' ministry.

The sun had been slipping across the sky when Jesus asked Peter to find a boat to ferry them from the small port of Dalmuntha to Kursi on the east shore of the Sea of Galilee. It had been another long day of preaching and healing, not made easier by the constant interruption from Temple agents, including a rabbinical lawyer. He had shown himself more skillful than Simon the Pharisee, his cultured Jerusalem accent posing questions which Jesus had answered in his broad country dialect. The attorney had joined the crowd at Dalmuntha, edging his way to the front, biding his time, waiting for Jesus to reach that now already mandatory point in his teaching: the promise of life everlasting. The lawyer asked how he could be granted such a privilege. Jesus calmly replied by asking the heckler how did he interpret the law. The lawyer ignored the riposte and the crowd had fallen silent sensing another theological battle was about to commence. The lawyer asked Jesus to remind them of the first commandment. Jesus had not hesitated. "Hear, O Israel; the Lord our God is one Lord, and thou shalt love the Lord thy God with all thy heart, and with all thy soul, and with all thy mind, and with all thy strength: this is the first commandment."

The lawyer asked Jesus to evaluate the various stages which had led to this definition. Matthew recognized that behind the exchange lay a deadly legal trap. The lawyer must have hoped Jesus would insist all the commandments had equal importance. That could have led to a complex discussion over the position of each of the prohibitions and positive amendments to the basic Mosaic tenets—a minefield of tractates in which the agent would have tried to ensnare Jesus. The subtleties of the law were not only rooted in the greatest antiquity but highly developed in every Jew; to misconstrue a point was a grave offense. No man entered adulthood without knowing that, while the Bible was at the root of all legal interpretation, it contained three distinct codes laid down in what was called the book of the covenant—chapters twenty to twenty-three of Exodus, five chapters of Deuteronomy and the book of Leviticus. During the previous five hundred years the Temple scribes and scholars had continually refined this already extensive jurisprudence, adding to and rewriting it so that the original commandments were hedged within a jungle of legal caveats. But, better than most, Jesus well understood the gulf between the ideal and application, and he dismissed the lawyer, saying the man had a contempt for the humanity of justice and was only interested in debating esoteric points.

When the crowd dispersed, Matthew saw how exhausted Jesus was. Though he was able physically and mentally to continue far beyond the limits of anyone the apostle had known, the strain did sometimes show. While it was clear to Matthew that it was already beyond anyone's power to eliminate him from all future history, the apostle knew that continuously preaching the Gospel of God was a draining process, even in Galilee, among people Jesus could speak to in their own way because he understood their character and temperament and shared their history and hopes. Though there was an intrinsic chivalry and politeness about Galileans, they could be persistent—especially when it came to a stunning message summed up for Matthew in one unforgettable sentence: "Repent ye, for the kingdom of heaven is at hand."

Jesus had asked for a boat to bring them across the lake to take a brief respite from the continuous demands on him. On board he had curled up and fallen asleep. The crossing to Kursi normally was a short one. But the Sea of Galilee, as Peter and the other fishermen knew, could be unpredictable. The lake bed was littered with wrecks and the caves in the surrounding hills filled with bodies of sailors who had been victims of sudden storms. Departing from Dalmuntha the forecast seemed fair: a prevailing southerly wind, barely strong enough to ripple the surface, one that would carry them smoothly and quickly to Kursi.

As they often did when Jesus slept, the disciples spoke quietly among themselves about such pressing issues as the disparity between the rich and the poor, a chasm which Jesus had attacked from the outset; about the way the priestly class deliberately separated itself from all others, and then, within itself, divided again so that there were only eight families with the privilege of filling the office of the high priest; about the fact that while slavery was officially frowned upon there were still wealthy Jews who kept them and how the law made a clear distinction between pagan and Hebrew slaves: the former had far less protection unless they agreed to be circumcised. These factors had contributed towards a society which, while outwardly unified, was internally riven. The hostility between the classes was a tangible matter. The rich and powerful gravitated towards the protection of Rome, becoming often paganized in the process. The desperately impoverished had only their faith to cling to. Integral to their belief was the conviction that rescue would come. Looking at the slumbering man in the stern, they realized what a huge responsibility Jesus carried. On his slim shoulders rested the hopes of the downtrodden, the despised and overlooked. It was upon these he had concentrated his ministry, and it had spread, rippling through the base of the economic strata, gnawing away at a crushing system of taxation, at the foundations of the Temple, at the Herodian dynasty, at Roman domination, above all at a narrow Jewish religious life that Jesus realized was no longer sufficient and which he, single-handedly, was determined to supplement with an altogether wider vision.

It was, the apostles agreed, one far removed from the two existing centers of worship: the Temple and the synagogues. Jesus had told them that before he would conquer the Temple he must first secure the synagogues. The Temple existed solely for sacrifice, prayer and music. Within its liturgy there was no room for him easily to spread his word. That had to be done through the synagogues. From the earliest time, when ten or more Jewish families had chosen a spot to settle, the law of Moses decreed a synagogue must be erected to deliver the word of God. Jesus had brilliantly exploited the well-established custom that at a certain point in the order of worship, the reading and interpreting of Scripture, anyone with a message from God could deliver it. He had begun to do so in the synagogue at Capernaum and, apart from that occasion in Nazareth, he had continued teaching and preaching in every synagogue without hamper. The following morning he intended to do so in the tiny one at Kursi.

At some point the discussions were interrupted by the stars vanishing behind scudding clouds and the wind direction veered and strengthened, sending the bow wave crashing into the boat. Peter ordered the sail to be reduced. It made no difference. The waves continued to wash over the sides. The apostles frantically bailed. Water slopped around their ankles. Jesus, still asleep at the stern, remained oblivious to the serious crisis developing. Repeatedly Peter tried to get the boat to run before the storm, but this stretch of water was among the most unpredictable in the world; the wind changing capriciously in all directions defeating even Peter's seamanship.

Judas, born and raised far from such a frightening sea, was the first to panic. He crawled on all fours to the stern and shouted at Jesus. "Master! Carest thou not that we perish?"

Jesus slept on. Another wave broke over the boat, sending water surging from prow to stern, settling the craft even lower. Peter stumbled past the man clinging to the mast and rigging and grabbed Jesus by the shoulder, shaking him violently. "Lord, save us! We perish!"

Jesus opened his eyes and stared about him sleepily. Peter shouted to make himself heard above the pounding seas. "Master, master, we perish!"

Jesus rose to his feet, somehow managing to stand unaided, something no one else in the now rapidly foundering boat could manage. He spread his hands towards the heavens and then the sea. But his words were for the men in the boat. "Why are ye fearful, O ye of little faith?" Then, in the same powerful voice that later would command Lazarus to emerge from his tomb, Jesus ordered the storm to abate. The wind and sea instantly dropped. The disciples bailed out the water, rigged the sail and reached Kursi under a moonlit sky, marveling at Jesus' miraculous intervention.

Not only had a storm been stilled on a lake but a more important one calmed in the hearts of the apostles. Jesus had restored belief in those closest to him. The fishermen among them were necessarily men of natural courage, used to confronting the elements and taking their lives in their hands. That required its own act of faith. They knew all about the business of surviving. That came also through faith. Yet, at the crucial moment, as Jesus had said, and Matthew would record, their faith in him had faltered. It had taken Matthew a long time to realize that, in rebuking them, Jesus had felt they had not enough faith in his mission; that they had failed to understand that his kingdom was not in some invisible heaven but here on earth—or out on that storm-tossed lake. If they had completely accepted that, his words implied, they would have felt no fear. It was a brilliant exposition of the glory and mercy of God being expressed to show his love for humanity.

Making his way to Bethany, Matthew had no doubt that whatever lay ahead his belief in Jesus would never again weaken. That was why he could be sure any betrayal must come from outside the group.

Along the arid path which would eventually bring them to Zorah, a small village on their route to Jerusalem, Jesus preached as they walked, his face reflecting the inward struggle and determination not to flinch from what must soon happen. Yet there was no pessimism, despair or hopelessness in his voice. Instead, his words sustained an abiding conviction that while man was a helpless sinner he was also capable of redemption which would bring him close to God. He reminded them—and it was one of the first lessons Matthew had noted—that they must be "perfect as your Father which is in heaven is perfect."

As they wound their way around hillsides, forded streams and passed through hamlets so tiny they would never appear on any Roman map, he taught that among the greatest challenges they faced was helping to remove sin from themselves and others. Jesus repeated—because that was his way—that, no matter what else a person lacked in life, he was equipped to cope with sin. Each one of them should remember that it was rooted in an absence of love, pity and respect, but they must never forget the infinite capacity in every person to fight temptation. Even more serious was the sin committed by anyone who set out to trap others through words and deeds and offered bribes and promises to gain his or her own ends. That was the path that eventually led to the worst of all sins—sinning against

God. In these past three years, if they had learned nothing else, he had given them repeated examples of those who insisted on doing this; men and women who could not recognize God's voice when they heard it—or his presence when faced with it. They were the ones who still failed to see he had been sent by God, come to fulfill far more than the ancient prophets had envisaged in their wildest dreams; that above all he was the harbinger of mercy: mercy for the spiritually captive; mercy for the spiritually poor; mercy for the spiritually blind. And, he reminded them, it was all being offered as a promise, without threat or inducement. Yet already they had seen, in his very hometown, how such an offer could be cruelly misunderstood by those who saw in him a terrible threat because he challenged their conformity and the prejudiced way they clung to the conventions of their upbringing. They hated him, he said, because they hated themselves: there was no room in their hearts for the grace and love of God. Not yet, anyway. That was why he was going to Jerusalem.

There had been that day, he also reminded them, even hotter than this one, when they had numbered only himself, his brother, Peter, Andrew, John, James and Philip. John the Baptist had just been arrested, leaving his followers in disarray. All along the Jordan there was talk that Herod Antipas, in the full fury of his madness, was about to round up every traveling preacher. To reach Galilee and the safety of its forests and caves Jesus elected to travel through Samaria, following a trail which passed near Shechem.

John for one would never forget how fearful his fellow apostles had been. Because they were men of human judgment, they had applied that quality to the route he had chosen. To them it had seemed as if he was taking an unnecessary risk. The feud between the Samaritans and the Galileans was old and particularly deep, going back over centuries when the Samaritans had first collaborated with occupiers long before the Romans arrived. Since then the other tribes had continued to look with contempt upon the people of Samaria and no self-respecting Jew would now willingly choose to pass through their midst.

Jesus led them to the well Jacob dug, and sat down in the shade of its stone walls telling the others to go into Shechem to purchase provisions. When they hesitated he assured them there was nothing to fear. On the way into town they passed a young woman balancing a large empty pitcher on her head. What Jesus described had happened between them remained for John highly significant. He had invested the encounter with a sense of pure drama.

Jacob's Well was rimmed with a wall twenty feet in circumference and a meter high. The woman looped a rope, fastened the jug and lowered it into the well. With the water drawn she glanced up—and found Jesus looking at her across the parapet.

He pointed to the brimming container: "Give me to drink."

She stared at him, stupefied. The words were enough to reveal he was not from Samaria. But what was a God-fearing Jew doing breaking the adage which said that anyone "who takes bread or water from a Samaritan, is like him who eats the flesh of swine"? She asked why Jesus would consider breaking the rule.

He smiled at her. Ever since he was old enough to understand, he had heard, in one form or another, prejudice expressed towards Samaritans. His mother had told him that, when she and Joseph went to Bethlehem for the census count shortly before his birth, they avoided Samaria just as they had done at each Passover. Later, in the streets of Nazareth, he had seen that when the boys momentarily tired of playing Zealots and Romans they switched to Galileans fighting Samaritans. Once more Jesus indicated the water.

"If thou knewest the gift of God, and who it is that saith to thee, 'Give me to drink,' thou wouldest have asked of him and he would have given thee living water."

The woman stared openmouthed, incredulous that she, with a full pitcher, would seek water from this stranger, and not just well water but something called "living water." She recognized his accent was unmistakably Galilean. Like all Samaritans she had been brought up to believe that her northern neighbors were often stricken with a form of madness arising from a determination never to marry outside their community. She looked around her; there was no help in sight. The sun was overhead; the women of Shechem had forsaken their work in the nearby fields and orchards. She decided to try to humor the stranger.

"Sir, thou hast nothing to draw with, and the well is deep. From whence then hast thou that living water?"

Jesus walked around the well and stood before her. Tapping the jug he pronounced: "Whosoever drinketh of this water shall thirst again. But whosoever drinketh of the water that I shall give him shall never thirst; but the water that I shall give him shall be in him a well of water springing up into everlasting life."

Trying to contain her growing alarm at words that made even less sense, she replied: "Sir, give me this water, that I thirst not, neither come hither again to draw."

Jesus peered into her face. Finally he made another astonishing request. "Go, call thy husband."

The woman clasped the jug to her body, flustered. Finally she stammered: "I have no husband."

Jesus brought his face close to hers, his voice was gentle but his words made her shiver. "Thou hast well said, I have no husband. For thou hast had five husbands: and he whom thou now hast is not thy husband."

The woman slumped against the parapet, her voice weak. "Sir, I perceive that thou art a prophet."

The silence between them stretched. Then Jesus spoke. "They that worship him must worship him in spirit and in truth."

She nodded, the first glimmer of realization on her face. She, too, had heard what John the Baptist had proclaimed. "I know that Messiah cometh, which is called Christ. When he is come he will tell us all things."

Jesus stepped back from her. "I that speak unto thee am he."

Not trusting herself to answer, the woman grabbed the pitcher and ran, sloshing water as she went.

The full significance of the encounter only came to John after the transfiguration.

Jesus chose to reveal his identity to the woman because even then he had been preparing the way for the fate awaiting him shortly in Jerusalem; he had chosen to announce himself to her, knowing she would never be able to keep secret their encounter, accepting that eventually word of it must reach the Temple. Yet on hearing of this encounter, John could no longer feel afraid—not after what he had witnessed on Mount Hebron. There Jesus had received God's double benediction: he was to wear a crown no other Jewish king had before worn and gladly go forward to his death.

At noon, like all highborn Roman women, Claudia Procula prepared for another of the several baths she took every day. Almost a quarter of her waking hours were spent in water. Dressed in a full-length white robe, the procurator's wife left her bedroom accompanied by her retinue of slave women and descended a wide marble-stepped staircase within the Antonia Fortress's east tower. The attendants carried jugs of oils and jars of spices and bath salts. One carried a *strigil*, a soft claw-like leather instrument with an ornately carved handle embossed with the crest of the Augustine dynasty. It was to massage her mistress's skin and remove dead epidermis.

Claudia Procula had never understood the attitude of Jewish women to personal cleanliness. While their menfolk bathed daily, many of the women simply doused themselves with scents and renewed the henna in their hair. For them a weekly bath often sufficed. On her visits to Galilee she found it unpleasant to be surrounded by women reeking of camphor, storax and the pungent aroma from the crushed horny operculum of shellfish. One of the decisions she made after her first visit to Jerusalem was to order an architect to be brought from Rome to design a new bathroom for her use in the fortress.

The staircase led to an enclosed passage, its fresco depicting Vesta and the Vestal Virgins guarding the undying fires, symbolism which played an important role in the mythology of Roman life. The passage ended in a tiled courtyard, open to the sky but designed so that it was not overlooked. Between the Corinthian columns rising from pedestals of solid marble stood the statues of Rome's gods, dominated by Romulus, founder of the city, and the triad of Jupiter, Mars and Quirinas. Guarding the arched entrance to the bathing area were the goddesses Juno and Minerva. Set in the wall above the arch was a large medallion depicting Janus, a handsome bearded figure with two identical heads joined at the neck, ever on the lookout instantly to aid any Roman.

The designer had spared nothing on cost or attention to detail in the bathing area. The room was almost forty feet long and thirty wide, with marbled floor and walls. At one end was a changing area, concealed by curtains made of gold threads; at the other were the warm and sweltering chambers, with baths rimmed in solid silver, their temperature regulated by floor vents and hypocausts. In the body of the room were five separate baths each of varying size. The one closest to the hot rooms was a cold douche. Next came a vapor bath, its oil of camphor strong enough to bring forth tears. In the center was a spacious circular pool with a pure bronze fountain in the middle providing an endless cascade of sparkling water. Close by was a massage block, a body-length sculpted slab of unblemished white marble. Two further baths were sunk into the floor. The water in one was slick with oil; the other perfumed with various salts. The walls of the salon were decorated with pure gold mosaics inlaid into the marble; they included Apollo wearing a radiate crown and driving a four-horse chariot through the sky and Dionysos, the god of fertility, embracing his consort, Libera.

Completely naked, surrounded by women soaping her body and rubbing it with ointments and spice water each time she moved from one bath to another, the procurator's wife was the epitome of a rich and pampered imperial woman.

She was the closest living female relative of the emperor Augustus who had laid the foundation of a dynasty that, through no fault of his, had been short-lived, but which now, in troubled Rome, was being recalled as the golden age of the empire. She was imbued with her grandfather's unrivaled relentlessness and cunning, and remained one of the most powerful voices in the imperial world in spite of her husband's relatively modest status. Yet, over the past year, her behavior would have appeared to any Roman as inexcusable and inexplicable. She had put Pilate's future, and perhaps her life, in jeopardy.

Claudia Procula had spent endless hours in her equally magnificent bathing salon in Caesarea, pretending and prevaricating, unable to understand what had first taken her to Galilee. Partly it was frustration with the petty, restricted and isolated life in Caesarea; partly no more than arrogance which originally drew her to stand on the shore of the Sea of Galilee and initially be filled with the overwhelming certainty that no man could offer more than Rome did.

But, as she had listened to Jesus, understanding almost nothing of what he said in Aramaic, let alone when he quoted Scripture in Hebrew, his compelling manner and the compassion in his voice had attracted her. She had returned with a servant who spoke his language. Standing at the back of the crowd, dressed like any wealthy Jewess, brightly bangled and beaded and her hair held in place with combs, the full and troubling import of his message reached her. Back in Caesarea she had tried to shake off the vivid images Jesus had created of a world so different to the one she knew—a place where love not violence was the ultimate weapon. Just as her husband continued to immerse himself in Jewish religious customs, so she had begun to study their beliefs. That could only have led to another startling discovery: the future Jesus proclaimed was so often at variance with Judaism; that he was indeed a new and tremendous force for good.

From then onwards Claudia Procula accepted that Jesus had entered her life and that he had begun to influence her outlook towards all that Rome held holy: its gods, rituals and customs, the very trappings she had been raised to believe were sacrosanct.

It has been suggested she had learned that a new threat had now emerged against Jesus, that she knew of the high priest's plan to bring him to trial, or that while the slaves kneaded and pummeled her body on the massage block, she was preoccupied with the question of what she could do to save him. Apocryphal or not, that possibility would be enough for her eventual veneration as a saint by the Greek Orthodox Church.

Jesus and the disciples reached the vicinity of Bethany without incident. Simon had gone ahead and returned with the reassuring news that the Temple guards had not returned, but Lazarus and his sisters were back home. Jesus led the way down the winding path which descended from the desert through a *wadi* into the village. Like many other Jewish settlements the hamlet was too small to have a protective wall and gates which could be closed at night with sentries posted on the battlements. Its workmen's houses and unpaved streets huddled round a couple of wells. The community numbered too few to warrant its own court of law and a judge; all crimes were referred to the Small Sanhedrin in Jerusalem. No one could remember when that had last happened; the people of Bethany were hardworking, God-fearing and law-abiding. Yet, despite its lack of size, it was still a noisy place from early morning to late at night; only in the heat of the day were the alleys and courtyards peaceful.

The arrival of Jesus was a matter of further excitement, following on the heels of the return of Mary, her sister and brother. Virtually the whole village followed Jesus to the house where they waited to greet him. He climbed the stairs to the flat roof, picked his way over Lazarus' tools, avoiding the washing spread out to dry. Many times these past years he had used a roof to emphasize a point. "That which ye have spoken in the ear in closets shall be proclaimed upon the housetops." Jesus thanked the villagers for the welcome and asked for their understanding; in the morning he must go to Jerusalem, tonight he wanted to be with his three friends in their home. The onlookers saw the emotional significance of the request; the word "home" had a strong biblical connotation; it was a reminder that the Chosen People had ceased their wandering and no longer lived in tents but had sent down permanent roots. Respecting his wish, the gathering dispersed.

Lazarus had built a house for his sisters and himself around a central courtyard with sleeping accommodation and other small rooms leading from it. During the evening Mary the mother of Jesus, and Mary Magdalene arrived. The women had walked from Galilee for another Passover; his mother had not seen him for months. Since that clash in the synagogue he had never returned to Nazareth. As they greeted each other, the recognition of the redemptive sacrifice he must make was already seared into her face. But there, too, was the realization that she must accept it—that the reality of what he must soon experience was, in part, designed as a test of her faith in his messianic mission. What passed between them was more than words: it was an understanding that he would not be able to help her struggle between her feelings as a mother and accepting that she had borne him for this one purpose.

Apart from his mother one other woman enjoyed a special intimacy with him. Mary Magdalene had been among the very first to understand the true purpose of his mission, and she knew now that the hours were shortening before he must enter resolutely upon his sorrowful task, that a journey which began in Cana was almost over.

The younger Mary went to the room she shared with Martha and returned with an alabaster jar. Judas stared at it, calculating aloud its worth. While the other women stood in the kitchen doorway and watched, Lazarus' younger sister knelt before Jesus and opened the jar.

The warm evening air was filled with the fragrant essence of nard, the same perfumed cream Mary Magdalene had used to anoint his feet in the home of Simon the Pharisee. Now Mary of Bethany, eyes shining with devotion, sprinkled some of the costly lotion on to the palm of her hand and, using a finger, began gently to rub it first into his feet, then on his face, refreshing and softening skin dried by sun and wind. Tipping more of the pale brown lotion into her palm, she worked it around Jesus' lips and into his beard. Placing her hand on the back of his head she gently pulled it down, close to her, so that she could massage the cream into his scalp.

She was a virtuous and unworldly young woman whose contacts with men were very limited. She had not yet learned the art of disguising her feminine feelings. From their first encounter she had made no secret that she was increasingly attracted by Jesus yet it would never have entered her head that the adoration she so freely displayed towards him would be unkindly misunderstood by others. Martha, on the other hand, was more experienced in the ways of the world; she knew about the potency of sexual attraction, perhaps only too well aware what lay behind the looks she still drew from men in Bethany. She finally stepped forward and tried to attract her sister's attention, to signal with a glance that this kind of behavior was causing unease among the disciples. But Mary was intent upon her task. At last Martha called out to Jesus: "Lord, dost thou not care that my sister hath left me to serve alone. Bid her therefore that she help me." But Jesus, with his eyes closed, and relaxed under the soothing caressing, had failed to see the excitement in Mary's eyes—just as he did not comprehend the anxiety behind Martha's words. Like the kneeling woman, he, too, saw nothing improper in what was happening. He responded: "Martha, Martha, thou art careful and troubled about many things. But one thing is needful: and Mary hath chosen that good part."

When she completed her work, Mary lifted the pot, turning it upside down to show Jesus it was empty. The rapt silence in the courtyard was broken as she deliberately dropped the jar to the ground, smashing it into pieces. Judas leapt to his feet, trembling with sudden anger. Pointing an accusing finger at Mary, he shouted to ask why had she wasted a jar of very expensive ointment—worth at least three hundred shekels. He pointed to his money bag, yelling that it was almost empty; that the money from the sale of the jar could have gone towards feeding and clothing the apostles. Frightened by the unexpected outburst, Mary had started to move backwards, to crawl away from his screaming voice.

Jesus stopped her, placing his hand on her head, soothing her trembling. Then he looked up at Judas, standing beside him, still convulsed with rage. "Let her alone. Against the day of my burying hath she kept this."

Jesus had looked around the circle of seated men. "For the poor always ye have with you; but me ye have not always."

On that prophetic and somber note supper began.

At sunset Jonathan's guards herded the last pilgrims, money changers and vendors of sacrifices out of the Temple. Its outer gates were secured and patrols posted at each one. Teams of Levites raked out the fires in the sacrificial altar and the ovens where the shewbread was baked, and swept up the refuse in the courtyards. Then the Nicanor Gate was shut. Normally the inner court would be deserted, the rabbis and scribes at their evening meal. But hundreds remained under the colonnades, their attention focused on the *Liscat Haggazith*, the chamber where the Great Sanhedrin was in session behind closed doors.

When the Temple crier had returned without news of Jesus' whereabouts, or without any witnesses, Caiaphas had summoned the seventy-one judges to the windowless cavern at short notice. They sat in a wide semicircle on carved seats on either side of him, ranged in order of seniority, their faces lit by oil lamps, wrapped in their heavy woolen blue robes against the chill. The court's walls and domed roof were built from polished stones, cut and positioned when King Jannaesus had ruled; in the suffused light the stones glinted like stars. Normally the court assembled on Tuesday and Thursday afternoons and twenty-three judges were sufficient to provide a *hulikka*, a verdict in a noncapital case. If a capital case extended beyond sunset, no sentence of death could be passed on conviction; the prisoner had to be brought back at dawn, after the trumpeter had sounded the start of a new day, escorted from one of the cells below the Court of the Gentiles. When the accused was standing in the circle of justice, placed immediately before the president's chair, the judges, flanked by beadles and scribes, would file in from the Court of the Priests.

In this case there had not been a pretrial inquiry by the court's two senior secretaries. These experienced lawyers normally had divided responsibilities in preparing a case: one framed the appropriate charges; the other drew up the scrolls containing a broad rebuttal of the accusations. Appended to each set of documents were the appropriate sources from the legal tractates. A quorum, chaired by the president, then met to consider the evidence; the slightest doubt over its admissibility meant the charge being dismissed. Jewish law was deliberately biased in favor of defendants. Evidence could only be given by witnesses of exemplary standing; sinners or suspected sinners were excluded, along with women and children. Agents of the Temple could only give testimony in corroborative support. Any defendant could compel the production of testimony in his favor. The verdict had to be a majority one.

According to some early Christian writing, what happened next in the chamber began with the intervention of a long-standing member of the court. From his seat a few places to Caiaphas' right, Judge Nicodemus, a Pharisee, demanded to know why there had been no preliminary inquiry. He quoted from the tractate *Makkoth* and its insistence that "the spirit of God must shine upon the Beth Din, the home of judgment."

Caiaphas assured him it would; that he, too, would never forget that the basis for Jewish law was appeasing a God angered by wrongdoing. He had convened the court purely in the spirit of that other biblical command, "be holy as I am holy." Because of the circumstances, he had dispensed with a pretrial inquiry in favor of addressing the court on the grave threat facing the Temple—and very likely the nation. He was clearly speaking of insurrection, an uprising which could mobilize the millions within the city and beyond its walls, an unstoppable rebellion the like of which had never struck before. The high priest had paused, knowing he had their full attention, letting his words form their own fearful images in the old and clever minds around him, before he had continued to lead them through excerpts from the sixty-three tractates of the law that dealt with blasphemy, profanation of the sabbath and sorcery and then reminded them they were appointed to represent the common conscience of the people, but they all knew the masses could be fickle; seditious or factious forces could arouse them. That was the danger now at hand.

In building his case the high priest could hardly have overlooked how Jesus had claimed to have raised Lazarus from the dead. That was sorcery, punishable by death. If they had been true to form any one of the Pharisee judges would have objected. Where was the evidence? Who were the witnesses? Had they been interrogated by the high priest and his staff? Had they been put under oath? If so—which one: by God, by heaven, by Jerusalem, by the Temple? Had Lazarus been interrogated to establish he had not been party to a trick? Had testimony been taken from his relatives? Why had the court been convened when even these rudimentary steps had not been taken? Was the case based on this solitary incident? Such questions would have been routine for Pharisees with no liking for the rigid literalism of a Sadducee high priest.

Unperturbed, Caiaphas replied that now was not the time to raise such questions, that he had brought them together simply to vote on whether or not Jesus had a case to answer. With Passover about to begin, the matter was certainly urgent. He could well have set out to demonstrate that the incident involving Lazarus, coupled with all the other claims Jesus had made, must be seen as a trigger factor, one powerful enough, when the news spread, to arouse the ill-informed to action. They must all perform their duty to protect the mob from the consequences.

Nicodemus intervened to ask what evidence was there that the admittedly extraordinary event involving a Bethany man had taken place—let alone been received seriously?

Caiaphas explained that Lazarus and his sisters had fled. In spite of the efforts of the Temple guards they had not been found. When they were they would be interrogated. But the real threat was Jesus. He could proclaim that what he had done gave him divine authority. It would be enough to turn already excited pilgrims into a rampaging mob. That was the threat which must be averted. That after all was why they were here to support his demand for Jesus to be put on trial.

How had Jesus exactly set out to encourage rebellion? Nicodemus challenged. Who were his supporters? How were they equipped to launch such an uprising?

Caiaphas explained: Jesus had given ample proof of his powers of sorcery; that his support had spread as he more openly practiced his magic; that he had predicted wholesale death and destruction unless he had his way. The high priest reminded them of the day Jesus had brought his crusade into the Temple itself at the Feast of Tabernacles—

Nicodemus interrupted once more. Why had Jesus not been arrested then? Surely what he had said on that occasion had been evidence enough?

Caiaphas was reproving. Had the learned judge now changed his mind? Only a moment before he had been among those who had said that the court should not hear a case of such gravity based on a single incident. But in Jesus' case there were any number of such offenses. Together they comprised evidence for a trial.

A judge of Nicodemus' caliber would most certainly have pressed. What was the quality of that evidence? Was it totally independent and sufficiently strong to withstand rigorous professional scrutiny? As a Pharisee, he taught both oral and written law. Would any evidence tendered satisfy the court on both counts?

Another Pharisee, Judge Gamaliel, one of the court's outstanding legal and religious experts, has been popularly assumed to be the one who returned to the critical question of Jesus planning an insurrection. Rebellion was an offense against Rome. The case should therefore be referred to Pilate.

The aged jurist Annas rose to his feet and turned to face his fellow judges. Better than any of them, it has been claimed for him, he knew the inherent risks of involving the Romans. In his long life he had seen how the Romans eventually laid any threat at the door of the Temple. He had not forgotten how many priests had been brutalized when they had marched to Caesarea to protest over Pilate's pagan emblems being erected to overlook the Holy of Holies. Nor had that horrific day faded from his memory when the procurator's troops had actually come into the Court of the Gentiles and slaughtered innocent Jews they suspected to be revolutionaries. Further, he would never forget the blood bath Pilate had unleashed after he sequestered money from the Temple treasury to finance an extra water supply for the city. Hundreds had died or been seriously maimed trying to defend that sacred money. No: to involve the Romans would be the worst possible move. Pilate would seize the opportunity to tighten the imperial hold on their people. That could lead to the very situation they wished to avert—a national uprising. There was, in any event, cause for concern that Pilate would welcome such confrontation as a chance to crush forever the spirit of their people. But to do so he would have to weaken, if not totally destroy, the Temple's paramount influence in Jewish life.

It was perhaps a sign of the rift between the Pharisees and Sadducees in the Great Sanhedrin that Gamaliel is credited in some accounts with conceding that, while all this was undoubtedly true, and that he needed no reminding of Rome's brutality, the nagging central question still remained: what was the precise nature of the revolution Jesus was planning? Was it solely against the Romans? There were hundreds of thousands of Jews who would acclaim such a move. Where was the exact threat to the Temple?

Annas no doubt chose the words attributed to him in the Gospels with care. "He hath spoken blasphemy; what further need have we of witnesses? Behold, now ye have heard his blasphemy."

Nicodemus, cast in the role of popular defender, made a further intervention. Had Jesus actually said he was the Son of God? If he had, then he would support a move for trial; indeed, he was certain every judge present would.

Annas was the focus of silent attention. Finally, the former high priest accepted, he could in all truth do no less, that Jesus may not have used the actual words—but that in all he said was his implicit belief that he was the Son of God, that he had chosen it as a compendious title to enshrine all he claimed to represent: Son of man was designed to conjure up a ready vision of the Messiah for the masses, without risk to himself.

Nicodemus protested. He did not share such a contempt for the people. Like him, he was certain that many knew that the title Jesus had taken was in the book of Daniel; he could argue that he was only carrying on the prophet's work. Where was the proof that Jesus intended the title to be a rallying point, a clarion call to insurrection?

Caiaphas could have insisted that when the time came the evidence would be there: all he wanted was approval to go to trial. Again, the Gospels would recount that the high priest addressed the court and told them that this man was the son of Joseph the carpenter and was born of Mary, but that when he said he was the Son of man, he really meant he was the Son of God. Moreover, that he polluted the sabbath and wished to destroy the law.

Other voices took up the refrain about whether this was still circumstantial evidence or based on eyewitness accounts. The discussion switched among the seated judges, with Caiaphas following the cut-and-thrust of the debate intently. Gamaliel once more had the floor. He reminded them that the Great Sanhedrin was not only a court of law but also a theological forum, that in this very chamber the legendary Rabbi Hillel had debated and formulated some of the regulations that at the time had been considered revolutionary but which were now accepted. Would it therefore not be reasonable and proper that Jesus should be invited here, of his own free will, and allowed to argue his claims? Only then, if they were found to violate the legal code, should he be brought to trial. Such a proposal must only have increased the tension. Caiaphas, outwardly at least, showed that he would consider it most carefully. It would also, of course, mean deferring a vote on bringing Jesus before the court.

The sound of the Temple trumpeter carried to Jesus and the disciples in Bethany. Some of them were still heavy-eyed, having fallen asleep late, kept awake by the troubling episode with Judas. As soon as they had breakfasted and said their farewells to Lazarus and the women, Jesus and the disciples set off for Jerusalem. There was about him the deep courage of someone who had thought long and hard, who saw with chilling clarity what lay ahead. He had calculated the cost in human terms, and had to go on.

Early though it was, the hills were alive with other pilgrims heading for the city, the air filled with singing and with the bleating of animals about to be sacrificed to obtain forgiveness of a sin, to excise an act of ritual impurity, to offer thanks for a birth, to remember the special pact between God and Abraham. Few would have spared a second glance for the group plodding up towards the Mount of Olives. By the time they had reached the base of the hill Jesus had succeeded in getting the Twelve to join him in chanting the ancient hymns; Judas' shrill voice raised loudest of all in praise to the special pact between God and Abraham. Jesus now took the final steps to end that old alliance.

He ordered Matthew to accompany Judas and follow a track around the hill; this would bring them to Bethphage, the first suburb of Jerusalem on the eastern side of the city. If Matthew recognized the irony in being asked to go to where Jerusalem's main customs house was located, he was too busy following the explicit instructions Jesus gave on what to do when they arrived at Bethphage. "Straightaway ye shall find an ass tied, and a colt with her: loose them and bring them unto me. And if any man say ought unto you, ye shall say, 'The Lord hath need of them.'" The sun was still low in the sky when Matthew and Judas returned with the donkey.

Guided by Jesus, the apostles used their cloaks to form a saddle, lashing it in place with their *hazons*. As they worked people began to stop and look: a handful grew to scores, then hundreds. Soon there were thousands of pilgrims standing and staring at the ass with its improvised saddle with Jesus beside it. Old men reminded their younger companions that the Messiah, the liberator of their people, would enter Jerusalem on the back of an ass. Every school child knew that; it was one of the first scriptural lessons they learned. As word spread more people paused on their way into the city, lining either side of the track that led to Jerusalem. The crowd remained silent and watchful, yet united in some mysterious and inexplicable realization that here, at last, was the moment they had all waited for.

As Jesus mounted the donkey, a huge cry went up, surging over the Mount of Olives and down the other side, sweeping on across the Kidron Valley finally to resound against the walls of the city which for so long had not only been the capital of the nation, but the very heart of its belief. The cry faded. There was a moment's silence then it repeated itself, louder than before. It died again. But this time the interval was briefer until the cry once more erupted. Then there was no gap, just a sustained roar.

"Hosanna!"—Save us!

Jesus began to edge the donkey towards Jerusalem, deliberately choosing to ride upon the ass of peace rather than on the horse of war. His ultimate offer of love was contained in the dramatic decision to enter Jerusalem in this way.

"Hosanna! Hosanna!"

The avenue of people extended all the way to the gate King Solomon had built for the day of the Messiah.

"Hosanna! Hosanna!"

Jesus was finally ready to implement the continuous entreaty roaring out around him.

"Hosanna! Hosanna!"

8

PRESSING MATTERS

If they have persecuted me, they will also persecute you.
John 15:20

The Small Sanhedrin was in session. The lower court shared the *Liscat Haggazith* with the Great Sanhedrin, hearing cases every morning except on the sabbath. Caiaphas often presided when they were of a purely religious nature, like the one in which a husband had caught his wife in the act of adultery. There was no possible defense; only one sentence. The high priest pronounced death by stoning and the court *hazzam*, its gaoler, stepped forward to pinion the woman's arms. Then the first tumultuous roar reverberated through the courtroom. "Hosanna!" The continuous sound confirmed that Jesus was coming into Jerusalem under the best possible protection—that of an adoring crowd.

Joseph Caiaphas motioned the *hazzam* forward. After receiving instructions the gaoler escorted the woman from the court.

The incessant wave of noise swept over the battlements of the tetrarch's palace, drowning the screams from the dungeons—and brought a sense of overwhelming relief to Joanna, Herod's servant. She had told Chuza she was ready to die for Jesus. Together, as they had heard him do, husband and wife stood in their room and recited the "Our Father." As the din from the direction of the Mount of Olives drew closer, they gave thanks to God that Jesus was coming to rescue not only her but all others who were suffering.

Pilate stood with Claudia Procula at a window in the eastern tower of the Antonia Fortress watching the hundreds of thousands of pilgrims who formed an avenue. The endless cries rolled back and forth along the ranks. Guards emerged from the Temple, swords unsheathed. Everyone stared towards the Mount of Olives. Over the summit, came a figure mounted on a donkey. Pilate could not identify the rider. But, not bothering to keep the excitement from her voice, Claudia Procula uttered the Greek word—"Christos."

In the palace dungeons Herod Antipas observed the daily round of torture. At the center of this fiendish place was a pit with steep smooth walls, scorched black. Close by was a large trough filled with inflammable liquid, a blend of lamp oil and raw alcohol. Naked prisoners, men and women, were dragged through the mixture and thrown into the hole. When it would hold no more the tetrarch signalled for a gaoler to dip a cresset into the trough, ignite it and toss the flaming torch into the pit, while he remained watching, intent on seeing who would scream the longest and be the last to die in immeasurable agony. Surrounded by his soldiers Herod Antipas rushed to the battlements to observe Jesus descending the Mount of Olives followed by a handful of men. The mighty chorus continued the repetitive chant.

"Hosanna! Blessed is he that cometh in the name of the Lord."

"Hosanna to the Son of David!"

"Hosanna in the highest!"

Then, once more: "Hosanna! Blessed is he that cometh in the name of the Lord."

The tetrarch began to laugh uncontrollably, and it took the men around him a while to recognize that relief lay behind this outburst. Jesus and his group appeared not to have a weapon between them. Nor did anyone in the crowd seem to be armed. What possible threat could they be? Reassured, they watched Jesus coming down the hill, unaware of the significance of the slow and certain tread of a donkey bearing a rider who gave no response to the crowd.

A few yards behind the donkey walked the apostles, their faces dazed and unable to comprehend fully what was happening. Astonishment further deepened when someone ran from the crowd to lay a cloak in the path of the beast. In moments a score more garments were strewn across the avenue, then hundreds, until Jesus and the disciples were advancing over an unbroken layer of cloth; tens of thousands of robes covered the earth in a multicolored quilt which stretched to the Temple gate. Not satisfied with this obeisance, the crowd offered further homage. They cut boughs from the balsam, acacia and tamarisk trees which grew on the lower slopes of the hill. But, above all, they hacked off fronds from palm trees. The branches were placed over the garments, creating a bright green sward. In the meantime hundreds of women and children were fashioning bouquets and nosegays from the profusion of wild spring flowers. These were also placed in the donkey's path. The adulation surpassed even that glorious day when King David had escorted the ark to its final resting place. As Jesus crossed the floor of the Kidron Valley the chanting took on a new resonance.

"Blessed be the kingdom of our father David!"

"Blessed be the king that cometh in the name of the Lord!"

"Peace in heaven and glory in the highest."

Then thundering forth came the now familiar climactic cry.

"Hosanna in the highest!"

The crowd surged forward, blocking the avenue, forcing Jesus to rein in the ass. The singing faded, and men, women and children stared at him in silent awe. They had traveled far, across mountains and seas, by camel and on foot, just to be here for Passover, to commemorate again the night when the Lord, smiting the firstborn of Egypt, had protected the homes of his children. Now, on this day, he was among them again, ready to join in prayers, the offering of the sacrificial lamb and the eating of unleavened bread. Yet, in spite of the rumors down the centuries which had sustained their hopes and deepened their longings, their stunned faces showed only too clearly they simply were unable fully to accept he was here, astride a donkey, finally fulfilling an ancient prediction. They stared at Jesus, not daring to believe, but wanting to so desperately.

Judas, his eyes shining with excitement, was the apostle who traditionally stepped forward and asked the crowd to let them pass. Slowly, and with a reverence the treasurer had certainly never seen before, the people did as he bid. Galvanized, Judas ran from one side of the avenue to the other, urging the onlookers to sing even louder, quoting Scripture to them, reminding those who could hear that God himself had chosen Jerusalem above all other places as where he would be worshipped, and that the city was linked with every happening in their history—as it was on this bright spring day.

Jesus once more edged forward. He traveled only yards before unmistakable Galilean voices cried out.

"Master! Master, we have two blind men here. Give them back their sight."

The pair were brought forward, stumbling over the strewn branches, and Jesus reached down and placed a finger on their eyelids and commanded them to open. Moments later the men were gazing upon the stunned crowd. One of them called out: "I see the Son of David!" His companion cried: "Blessed is the king of Israel."

The procession had assumed a royal importance, reaffirming another hallowed prophecy.

"Rejoice greatly, O daughter of Zion; shout, O daughter of Jerusalem: behold, thy king cometh unto thee . . . lowly and riding on an ass."

The hosannas soared. The apostles saw that the avenue had merged behind them and a great wall of humanity spread towards Bethlehem on one side and Jericho on the other. Beyond it lay the Gate of the Messiah.

If Pilate was not quite transfixed by the approaching procession, there can be no doubting his wish to get a closer look at Jesus. At last the procurator could see his face. He may well have seemed older than Pilate had imagined, thinner, almost gaunt, and the Roman may also have wondered if this was really the man he had been warned about in Jewish literature. Isaiah had predicted the Messiah would assume a certain form. "There is no beauty that we should desire him. He is despised and rejected of men; a man of sorrows and acquainted with grief." Almost certainly Jesus in no way fit that description. He was handsome enough and far from being rejected. Spies had indeed told the procurator that Jesus had increasingly shown symptoms of strange traits such as his frequent disappearance into the desert, almost as if he was driven by wanderlust and a need for isolation; that he was sexually impotent, which would account for the way he rejected the obvious advances of women. Yet, watching Jesus draw closer, there was nothing in his face to show what sort of man he was; all the procurator saw was an inflexibility and certainty he had not seen in any other Jew.

Standing behind Pilate and Claudia Procula was the garrison commander, awaiting instructions. Though untutored in the finer points of Hebrew, he had been stationed long enough in Jerusalem to recognize the ecstatic behavior of the crowd as a clear act of rebellion against Rome. The commander was a man of action and proven valor. Jesus and the disciples should be seized and brought to the fortress while soldiers threw a cordon around the Temple, forbidding all entry, and then began systematically to drive back the mob. A show of such strength and determination would quell the most excitable Jew, dashing hopes as swiftly as they had been raised.

From the balcony of the minaret where the trumpeter sounded the start of a new day, the traditional vantage point of a high priest, Caiaphas stared at an unbelievable scene. From every pilgrim site people were still converging on the city, waving branches and bunches of flowers as they scrambled over the scree. It would be pointless to order the Temple gates closed to keep Jesus from entering and asserting his authority over the very heart of Judaism. No gate was strong enough to keep out such a crowd; it would batter its way in, its fury rising at every charge. The only course was to let him enter; the only hope that somehow he would overreach himself.

In these past three years a great number of Jesus' miracles had been performed before small groups; often no one had been present except the apostles. Even the raising of Lazarus had taken place before a handful of people. Finally, Jesus had given striking proof of what he had often said: that men could close their eyes to his message, but when the time came they would not fail to see.

Judas could well have been convinced that through that miracle of once more restoring sight Jesus had finally launched a bid for supreme sovereignty over the throng around him and the city ahead. He was approaching Jerusalem as a literal rather than a spiritual king of the Jews. With the procession drawing closer to its unbroken curved walls of golden-brown stone, its formidable tower forts and reinforced gates, Judas' conviction could only have deepened that victory had been achieved without a drop of blood being shed; that Jesus would not after all have to die: the crowd would see to that. In the apostle's bedazzled mind that would have been a reasonable explanation of why they were being allowed to advance unopposed. Jesus had flung down his challenge; the enemy had crumbled.

At the Temple gate Jesus turned and faced the crowd. He asked them to be patient; they should return to their encampments and make their preparations for Passover. When they started to disperse, he dismounted and walked into the Temple's immense outer Court of the Gentiles. A silence spread through its length, all two hundred and fifty yards of flagstones, and colonnades, every inch of floor space crowded all the way to the Royal Porch where the doctors of the law debated, and Solomon's Portico, where peddlers went about their business. Only the bleating of animals and the cooing of sacrificial doves broke the sudden tension. People stared expectantly towards the Holy of Holies, waiting for the stone they believed miraculously hovered in the sanctuary to come crashing to the ground. It would be the final proof the Expected One was among them. The silence stretched as Jesus surveyed the scene. Then he turned and walked out of the Temple.

Judas was too stunned to move. While the other apostles slowly followed Jesus, the treasurer remained rooted. If there was a single instant when Judas moved from committed follower to the path of infamy, that was the moment. Around him pilgrims whispered in disappointment that the great stone must still be hovering.

In the *Liscat Haggazith*, Levites lit oil lamps and replenished the jars of water from the Temple's underground well.

Instead of occupying the formal semicircle of seats, the high priest, Annas and the other Sadducee members of the Great Sanhedrin sat on cushions at the rear of the chamber. They had been together since early afternoon, after Jesus had departed and a Roman officer had arrived at the Temple to deliver a warning from the procurator that there must be no repetition of the morning's scenes. Caiaphas had sent back a reassuring message: he would take all necessary steps to reinforce his authority over his people. Caiaphas had told the judges that to avoid the full fury of Rome being unleashed it was vitally important to convince their Pharisee colleagues that they must place the preservation of their own position above all other considerations. The high priest suggested how this could be done.

In recent months Jesus had singled out the Pharisees working in the Temple for special attack: he had accused them of abandoning their roots, of showing hypocrisy, contempt, selfishness and unscrupulous behavior. He had taunted them about their punctilious observance of the sabbath and attacked their teaching. He had accused them of plotting with Herod Antipas to kill him. On one sabbath in Capernaum he had treated "a man with the dropsy" and challenged the Pharisees to show cause why he should not do so on the day of rest. In the synagogue of Bethabara he had devoted his entire commentary on a portion of Scripture to assailing the Temple Pharisees. At Bethsaida Jesus had used a parable further to revile them: "What man shall there be among you, that shall have one sheep, and if it fall into a pit on the sabbath day, will he not lay hold on it and lift it out? How much then is a man better than a sheep? Wherefore it is lawful to do well on the sabbath days. . . ." Around the Sea of Galilee he had regularly condemned Pharisees as vipers, fools and obdurate legalists protecting empty ritualism. In Nain he castigated them as "the children of them which killed the prophets"; in Jericho with "extortion and excess"; in Tyre he referred to their "hypocrisy and iniquity"; and in Sidon accused them of "evil thoughts, murder, adulteries, fornications and thefts." At every opportunity Jesus had heaped maledictions upon their colleagues.

The men around Caiaphas listened attentively, the anger in their faces deepening, as he argued that, in attacking the Pharisees of the Temple, Jesus was destroying their own divine authority to teach and interpret God's will and word. The high priest urged his listeners to stress the danger to their colleagues, bringing an end to the division which had wrecked the last meeting of the Great Sanhedrin. Further discussion ended with the arrival of Jonathan to announce that Herod Antipas was waiting in the Royal Porch.

From the roof of Lazarus' home, Jesus and the apostles continued to watch the increasing groups of men camped out around Bethany. Simon had gone to them and returned with the news they were Zealots and their supporters, there to provide protection. As the night cooled they lit fires and sat talking or occasionally making music, plaintive sounds which carried to Jesus and his companions.

Judas kept his distance, once more his brooding self. Over the meal he finally turned to Jesus and demanded to know why he had not claimed his kingdom. Why had he once more walked away from what had been his for the taking? Why had he not done what the prophets promised and destroyed his enemies? Why was he back here when he could be occupying that throne he had spoken so much about? But before any of the apostles could rebuke Judas, Jesus had quietly reminded him of that evening on the Sea of Galilee when the treasurer, like the others, had been frightened, until he had spoken to them. Soon the faith they had kept since then would be realized. Judas had lapsed once more into sullen silence. After the meal he abruptly excused himself and left the courtyard. Jesus watched him go, saying nothing. The treasurer had not returned before the men on the roof had fallen asleep.

Caiaphas and Annas let Herod Antipas rant on without interruption in the Royal Porch. Jesus, he roared, had come to take away his throne; he had already proclaimed himself king. For that alone he must die. There was no longer a need for covert ambush. Jesus would be cut down in public before his people. If they protested they would also be slaughtered. There was a madness about the tetrarch which might well have reminded the two priests of the last days of Herod the Great: his son displayed the same demented stare and ferocious gesture.

Then, while Levites replenished their wine, they began to reason. Jesus had not actually proclaimed he *was* king of the Jews. Until he did so, however offensive his behavior, it would be hard to get a conviction. But to move openly against Jesus without the support of the law could have dire results. His followers would obey any instruction he gave: they had quietly dispersed when he told them; they could just as easily be mobilized to full-scale fury. Point by point Caiaphas and Annas had carefully cooled Herod Antipas' blood-lust. The safest and surest way, concluded the high priest, was to allow the Great Sanhedrin to find grounds to convict Jesus legally. Herod Antipas reluctantly accepted their arguments and left.

After Annas had retired to his palace, reaching it through an underground passage from the Temple, Caiaphas went to his temporary quarters near the Holy of Holies, it would be a further six days before he could return to his own palace, his wife and children. At some point during the night he was awakened by Jonathan, who had himself been aroused by the officer of the watch with urgent news. The captain of the guard recognized it was of sufficient importance to awaken the high priest. Caiaphas had dressed and, using another of the labyrinth of underground passages, had emerged with Jonathan in the Court of the Gentiles. Standing there, firmly gripped by the officer of the watch, was a man. Jonathan held the burning taper close to the face of Judas.

As noon approached, all male adults, those aged thirteen years and upward, in the Court of the Gentiles, as in all the other courts of the Temple except one—the Court of the Women—prepared to pray. Women, children and slaves were excused the obligation. Each man wrapped himself in a *tallith*, his prayer shawl, and secured with thongs to his forehead or the palm of his right hand a *tefillin*, a small square black box made of the hide of kid or camel and containing identical parchment excerpts from Exodus and Deuteronomy. As the hour approached Caiaphas stood on the podium before the Nicanor Gate. The high priest, along with everyone else, turned towards the Holy of Holies. In the streets of Jerusalem men did the same; in the hillsides still more rose to their feet and faced in the direction of the Temple. At the farthest point of the Diaspora where an adult Jew was located, that Jew would be performing the same precise ritual. It was a compelling example of religious conformity.

Inside the Court of the Gentiles all commerce halted. The most rapacious traders, who had haggled with customers until the last possible moment, hurriedly threw around their shoulders *talliths*, the pure white silk often the most expensive garment they possessed, allowing the ritual fringes to fall around their waists. Caiaphas uttered the first word of the *Shema*—"listen." Voices, piping and deep, wavering and resolute, joined together to recite the phrases of the most famous prayer in their religious life, the one that brought each of them once more into the presence of his Maker.

The consecration over, the trading din resumed, the air a cacophony of sacrificial animals being sold and rates of exchange quoted by the money changers. From his dais Caiaphas looked upon a scene that caused him no offense. Yet the Temple was being desecrated; traders regularly stored their goods in the sacrosanct porches, an offense grave enough to be singled out in the book of Leviticus. Along the length of Solomon's Portico men hawked and spat and trailed their soiled clothes and feet through the sacred area, profaning its purity.

From the far end of the Court of the Gentiles came a sudden and increasing commotion from around the main trading area. The sound of something crashing to the ground reached the high priest, followed by a flock of doves fluttering into the air. Guards ran towards the disturbance. There was another mighty crash as a money changer's stand was hurled out of the portico, its frame splintering and its contents scattering over the courtyard.

Caiaphas saw Jesus, whip raised in one hand, the other holding a cage of birds. One of the men with him opened it and sparrows flew over the

Temple walls. Jesus threw the cage from him and brought his whip lashing down on a money changer's table, toppling it under the sheer force of the blow.

Jonathan appeared at the foot of the podium urging Caiaphas to let him arrest Jesus. The high priest pointed towards the court's gate, through which scores of pilgrims were pouring to cheer on Jesus as he upturned another vendor's table, and very sensibly commanded the captain to hold back his men: the Temple was the last place for a pitched battle. Twenty-three years ago, he could have reminded Jonathan, when the captain was a lowly guard, he had helped to drive out Samaritans who had behaved improperly in the Temple. They had been only a handful, yet it required the entire Temple police force to evict them. While Jonathan ran into the courtyard to order his men back, Caiaphas was faced with the truth that once more Jesus had unerringly calculated the mood of the people.

The commotion interrupted Pilate's reading of a scroll which contained good news from Rome. In the Senate the campaign against Sejanus was mounting. The procurator sensed that the time had come to make discreet contact with Agrippina and her elder son, Nero, once powerful voices in the capital before they had been exiled by Sejanus to small islands off the Italian coast. Their supporters had recently borne Agrippina's standards into the Senate to rousing cheers, a certain indication she and her son would shortly be back in the city. Expressing support for them now could have incalculable benefits later. Nero was the sort of man who could pluck someone from the ends of the empire and install him at its center. The shouting from the Temple courtyard certainly interrupted such pleasurable speculation.

From his window the procurator could have watched Jesus striding through the portico, using his whip to clear the way, pausing only to topple over stalls selling grain, salt, wine, incense and oil. Thousands of birds were being set free; hundreds of sacrificial animals were stampeding around the courtyard. Pilate would not only have heard, but seen the rage in Jesus' face. The calm certainty of yesterday, when he had steadfastly ignored the acclaim for his triumphant entry, had given way to naked fury. The procurator found this reassuring: an angry man could also be a frightened man. And no Roman god had ever shown fear.

Recovering from the sheer speed of the onslaught, the dealers began to vent their own anger, screaming at Jesus, demanding what authority allowed him to behave as he had.

Jesus picked up another table and hurled it at the traders, shouting: "It is written 'my house shall be called the house of prayer,' but ye have made it a den of thieves!"

Escorted by the throng Jesus continued on his path of destruction. The Temple guards kept pace but made no effort to intervene. Jesus was surrounded by the same men who had followed the donkey along the processional avenue. Eleven, Pilate would have seen, were also helping to wreck the merchants' tables, booths and seats. But one, a tiny swarthy-faced man, clutching a *punda* to his chest, was taking no part. Could this be the same man his spies had trailed from Bethany to the Temple during the night and who had only reappeared hours later after spending the time with the high priest?

Jesus reached the northern end of the portico; flushed from his exertion he leaned against a pillar, whip in hand, surrounded by the apostles. They had been as stunned as everyone else by his actions. On previous visits to Jerusalem he had ignored the vendors and their squalid dealings. The traders angrily demanded to know again what authority Jesus had to disrupt their living.

The question held a deeper meaning. The key word was *authority*. Jesus was not a member of the Temple hierarchy, armed with formal authority to interpret the law within its walls: it could therefore be argued that his actions fitted the scriptural definition of "a blasphemous and rebellious elder." That carried its own penalty—stoning. Once more the question was put. "What sign showest thou unto us, seeing thou doest these things?"

Jesus' reply must have silenced all in earshot. "I am able to destroy the Temple of God and to build it in three days."

Without further explanation he led the apostles out of the courtyard. Only when they had left the Temple was the baffled question asked by one trader to another: how could any man possibly destroy and raise a building in three days—especially one which had taken so far forty-six years to erect and was still in the process of construction?

They did not grasp that Jesus had spoken of a very different "temple": his body.

But the face value of the words fit into the choreography Caiaphas was creating.

By the light of the stars Jesus and the others saw movement among the men guarding the track which led from Jerusalem to Bethany. The cordon could only attract rather than lessen trouble: neither the Romans nor Herod Antipas would tolerate it for long. Anxious to avoid exposing Lazarus and his sisters to needless risk Jesus had asked Simon to find a new and secure place where they could sleep, then instructed Peter and John to go to Jerusalem in the morning to make preparations for Passover. On previous occasions they had been guests of relatives and friends. Jesus told the apostles that this time they would dine together as a group with no others present.

He had also explained that his fury with the vendors arose directly from contradiction of the law. Isaiah had defined the Temple as "a house of prayer for all nations." But its priests shamelessly supported the fanatical aims of the Shammai religious cult which had emerged in the wake of Herod the Great's death and was dedicated to promoting a radically pure faith. As part of that creed the sect had also banned the long tradition of non-Jews offering gifts to the Temple at the great festivals. Yet many traders still accepted the tribute and divided it with the priests.

What had enraged Jesus was not only a passion for social justice—the traders *were* swindling scoundrels battening on the pilgrims—but the recognition that they were only a part of a corrupt structure. From the high priest to the lowest Levite, there was a thriving involvement with the sale of sacrifices: they imposed inspection fees to make sure each bird and animal was unblemished; they received bribes from each money changer and every purveyor of goods permitted to operate within Solomon's Portico. In deliberately challenging these arrangements Jesus intended to hasten a confrontation which went far beyond a condemnation that ritual slaughter could never be the substitute for the true love of God. Further, in speaking of "his house," Jesus also made it once more clear that he identified his action as being that of God.

Some of the men guarding the track were in the street below, calling they had brought a visitor from the city. Matthew was the first to recognize the figure in a *chalouk*, a knee-length tunic and a *tallith*, the cloak draped around his shoulders. It was Judge Nicodemus. The apostle's duties as a tax collector had sometimes brought him to the Small Sanhedrin which sat in Sepphoris, one of the country's five main provincial law courts. For a while Nicodemus had presided over the Sepphoris judiciary, and shown himself to be a fair but firm upholder of the law. Matthew introduced their visitor and John asked what "a leader of the Jews" wanted with them.

Nicodemus apologized for the lateness of his visit—strangers rarely called after the supper hour—explaining he had used the cover of darkness so that he would not be recognized. Jesus asked, no doubt more politely than John, why a member of the Great Sanhedrin was here.

"Rabbi, we know that thou art a teacher come from God."

There was no guile about the words. Nicodemus was merely using a judge's right to refer to himself in the plural rather than indicating that a body of support existed for Jesus within the Temple. Indeed, if pressed, Nicodemus would have had to admit that any such support had been eroded among even the most liberal of the Temple Pharisees in the wake of the stinging rebukes Jesus had recently directed at them.

Jesus addressed Nicodemus. "Except a man be born again he cannot see the kingdom of God."

Conditioned by many years of court work never to show surprise, Nicodemus nevertheless could not control his bewilderment. "How can a man be born when he is old? Can he enter the second time into his mother's womb, and be born?"

In a Jerusalem street, the same questions had been put after Jesus had restored sight to yet another blind man. Then they were meant to trap him. Now they were put genuinely to seek enlightenment.

Jesus said that only someone born again "of the spirit" could enter the kingdom.

Nicodemus, as he would have done in the Great Sanhedrin, pressed politely but firmly for a more detailed explanation.

Jesus provided it. "That which is born of the flesh is flesh; and that which is born of the Spirit is spirit. Marvel not that I say unto thee, ye must be born again. The wind bloweth where it listeth, and thou hearest the sound thereof, but canst not tell whence it cometh, and whither it goeth. So is every one that is born of the Spirit."

Nicodemus clearly found the answer still confusing.

Jesus could not hide his irony. "Art thou a master of Israel and knowest not these things?"

Then, once more acknowledging he had come for no other purpose than to learn, the judge asked Jesus to explain where his teachings differed from the existing law. Had Jesus come to offer a new explanation for the written and oral law of the Pentateuch, to tear down the elaborate structures which had stood the test of centuries?

Jesus repeated a now familiar refrain. He had not come to replace or destroy. He had come to fulfill the law. There were many, he accepted, who would remain wedded to their faith. It should be so. What he had come to do was to reveal a new truth, one that not only absorbed all the commandments of existing holy writ, but went beyond them.

Jesus spoke about his meaning of faith; that the time was fast approaching when the sovereignty of God would extend beyond the Promised Land, beyond all other lands, conquered and free, to rule over Rome itself and all the other pagan centers on earth. One age—the one which Jews gave cognizance with their concept of being God's Chosen People—was about to end and a new one begin. It would be one in which the God of the past, present and future would be unified and the kingdom would be within each person, placed there as God's gift to each of those he had created. To receive the gift was both a simple and, at the same time, an extraordinarily demanding process. It required a sense of what was instinctively right and wrong, an ability to forgive, a readiness to offer and accept love. A child found that easy but an adult more often than not difficult. The richer a man, the harder for him to accept God's gift; the greater the stake in worldly life, the more difficult it was to see the larger rewards beyond.

Nicodemus had asked, perhaps with a hint of exasperation, if all those with money, land and authority over others were precluded "from receiving this gift."

Once more Jesus gently chided him. "Verily, verily, I say unto thee: we speak that we do know, and testify that we have seen."

He promised the kingdom of heaven would allow Nicodemus to be in direct communication with God. There was no other way to describe it.

The stars were fading when Jesus invited the judge to join him and the apostles in the Lord's Prayer, so that Nicodemus could repeat words which so perfectly demonstrated what he had been told: that God's purpose would be fulfilled on earth as it was in heaven.

In the east tower of the Antonia Fortress, Claudia Procula prepared to spend another day in her salon. The Jews had the streets to themselves. Her husband had confined all Roman patrols to barracks to reduce possible friction. The centurions sat around the fort, drinking *sheckar*, the local beer, and complaining it was a poor substitute for a Roman brew. The incessant noise from the Temple only aggravated her own mood.

At some point in the morning, from one of the salon windows overlooking the Temple she had seen the throng around the Eastern Gate part to form a corridor through which walked Jesus.

Two chief priests forced their way through the crowd. The first addressed Jesus in the polite and circumlocutory language of the highborn. "Master we know that thou art true, and teachest the way of God in truth, neither carest thou for any man."

The second priest fished in his robe and produced a silver coin, a Roman denarius, and asked: "Is it lawful to give tribute unto Caesar or not?"

To any Jew the Roman tribute was a reminder of their subjugation to a heathen power. If Jesus confirmed the propriety of the levy, the word would most certainly spread swiftly that Jesus supported one of Rome's most hated impositions. His credibility would be destroyed; there was every possibility that the same crowd that had praised him would kill him. The priest asked again if it was lawful to pay.

Jesus put out a hand. "Show me the tribute money."

The rabbi handed over the penny. Jesus held it between thumb and forefinger, inspecting it carefully. On one side was the embossed head of Tiberius and the letters: TI CAESAR AUG D F AUGUSTUS—Tiberius, Caesar Augustus Divi Filius Augustus: Tiberius Caesar son of the divine Augustus. On the other side was an engraving of the empress Julia Livia, with a scepter and flowers and the letters: PONTIF MAXIM—Pontifex Maximus: high priest.

Jesus pointed at the emperor's head and asked whose image and inscription it represented.

The first priest replied impatiently: "Caesar's."

Jesus handed back the coin. "Render therefore unto Caesar the things which are Caesar's, and unto God the things that are God's."

Applause and delighted laughter from the crowd greeted the epigram. The discomfited priests left to report to Caiaphas.

Towards the end of the day the high priest received another visitor. The man followed a prearranged route, a traditional one for informers, entering through a door in the part of Annas' palace which extended into the Lower City. From there he had been brought underground into the Temple, emerging near the *Liscat Haggazith*, from where he was escorted to the high priest's office. Caiaphas had greeted Judas.

What passed between them would leave unanswered tantalizing issues. Was Judas now primarily motivated by mental confusion and disillusionment? Was he obsessed with the belief that he, and he alone, must still bring Jesus into open confrontation with the authorities, not because he wished to see his master die, but because he clung to the belief that Jesus was invincible? Did he *still* think that Jesus primarily intended to topple the authority of Rome—and, when the Temple realized that, its full authority would support him? Had Judas, in spite of being more culturally and politically aware than the other apostles, with the possible exception of Matthew, *still* not realized what the high priest's intentions were after that first nocturnal visit? What had prompted him to return? Had Caiaphas used coercion—threatening to unmask the treasurer unless he continued to cooperate, knowing that exposure would be enough for the crowd to kill Judas? Was that why Caiaphas had reduced Judas' role to one he could more easily understand and manipulate—that of paid informer, offering him money, the thirty pieces of silver? They only raised still further questions. Zechariah had spoken of receiving a similar amount for doing the Lord's work. Had Caiaphas, ever the expert manipulator, persuaded Judas—whose judgment would have almost certainly been further clouded under the tension and danger of what he was about—that he was performing a similar divinely approved function?

After darkness had fallen, Joanna left the tetrarch's palace, wrapped in an *isomuklia*, a heavy outer robe which kept out the chill of the Jerusalem night, and she made her way through the Upper City, along a maze of narrow unnamed streets, many of them stepped, all crowded with pilgrims.

Her destination was a house close to the Antonia Fortress. Despite its modest exterior of roughly hewn stones and a door made of cedar wood, it was the home of the most prosperous businessman in the city, Joseph Haramati, a Galilean who had come south to make his fortune. He was now wealthy enough to have a private burial tomb reserved for himself and his family. It was close to Golgotha.

History would suggest that a year before, on a visit to Galilee, Joseph had encountered Jesus preaching and become a devout follower. He had seen in Jesus many of the virtues of his other religious hero, the Jewish teacher Rabbi Ben Hillel. They both encouraged healing through prayer, did not place undue stress on religious ritual, emphasized the need for giving and receiving spiritual love, and displaying humility, and made no distinction between Jews or Gentiles in God's eyes. To the deeply religious Joseph, Jesus offered still more—the promise of life beyond the grave. Joseph had come to know his mother and friends, and in the past they had sometimes stayed in his home, holding prayer meetings. At one of these Joseph had met Joanna and, on learning of her position in the palace, he realized that she could bring any information to him of moves the tetrarch was contemplating against Jesus. Joseph listened with mounting concern to Joanna's latest news about the tetrarch's attempt to have Jesus murdered.

On the afternoon of what the Jews called the fourteenth of Nisan, but which Pilate preferred to reckon as the fifth day of the first week of the fourth month of the sixteenth year of the reign of Tiberius—and which would become known as Thursday, the sixth day of April in the year of Our Lord 30—the procurator prepared another report for the emperor. It would have to take account of how Jesus had provoked such alarm in the high priest and tetrarch, and how the spies of Herod Antipas were out in force fruitlessly combing the city and hillsides.

The irony of the situation must have appealed to the procurator because it confirmed that the best way to rule the Jews was to keep their leaders divided. If relations between the tetrarch and the Temple had been anything other than icily polite, Herod Antipas would know that Caiaphas had learned from Judas of the new hiding place of Jesus and the apostles within hours of Simon selecting the cavern among the thickly planted groves on the Mount of Olives. It was used to store and squeeze the fruit and accessible only through a small and easily disguised entrance. Locally it was known as *gath shemane*, the olive press—Gethsemane.

The Christian Coptic Church would enshrine such details, and interpret them to allow Pontius Pilate to be included in its calendar of saints on the premise that he was "already a Christian in his innermost heart." It would certainly be one explanation for behavior which would become increasingly baffling to a pagan Roman.

Late in the afternoon Simon bought an unblemished yearling lamb and brought it to one of the priests standing at the Nicanor Gate. Passing inspection, the animal was taken to the sacrificers at the great altar. It was despatched in seconds, one of ten thousand lambs an hour slaughtered in the week before Passover. With the gutted carcass slung over his shoulder and the lamb's hide in one hand, Simon made his way through the throng into the Lower City. Several times he slipped down alleyways, through courtyards, up open flights of stairs and across flat roofs before descending again into streets some distance from where he had begun his evasive action.

The sun was setting when he finally reached Zion, the oldest part of the city, a casbah of souks, sunken courtyards, roof terraces and passages too narrow for a Roman soldier in full armor to negotiate. Simon entered a house which belonged to one of Joseph of Arimathea's servants. Peter had arranged to borrow it for the Passover meal and in return had promised to leave the hide as a traditional form of thanksgiving.

Peter was already waiting in the courtyard, tending the fire he had lit beneath the oven in a corner. Near to it was a well. Checking again that none of the lamb's bones had been broken—an examination required by the Passover tractate—the two men placed it on a grid in the oven. Then they inspected the upper room which John had been preparing. It was a low-roofed chamber supported by heavy beams in the wall and ceiling. On the floor were rattan divans and a low square table. It was set for thirteen, each place denoted by a goblet and platter. Tall candles in clay holders were placed around the table. They would be lit to mark the start of the most important meal in the Jewish liturgical calendar, the *Seder*.

Caiaphas addressed the judges seated around him in the *Liscat Haggazith*. He asked again that the Great Sanhedrin should order the arrest of Jesus. There was a demand from the Pharisees present, perhaps once more led by Judge Nicodemus, to hear the evidence, know the name of the witnesses and their standing in the community, whether they were personally acquainted with Jesus and if their testimony already been formally taken under oath. If so, could the court study it and, if need be, question the witnesses before coming to a decision? That would be the normal procedure.

It would not have needed Nicodemus or Gamaliel to remind the others that, when they had last assembled, Caiaphas had warned that insurrection was imminent. But there had been no sign of any uprising. Indeed, Jesus had actually ordered the crowds to cease their acclaim. Under such circumstances, the senior Pharisee judges clearly saw no cause to rush to judgment.

Not for the first time the supreme court would have broken up in disorder with the high priest walking out of the chamber—the ultimate sign of displeasure at his disposal.

Through the darkness the apostles arrived one by one in the courtyard. Each went to the well, drew water and carefully washed away the dust of the road.

Peter tended the oven, basting the lamb in its own juices. Normally the women in Jesus' entourage would have supervised the cooking, but his insistence on only the Twelve being present meant the oldest apostle was responsible for filling the tiny beakers with drops of salted water which they would all sip before the meal to commemorate the tears of their forefathers, blending the *hazareth*, the red sauce into which the unleavened bread would be dipped, and preparing the bowls of crushed bay leaves, marjoram, basil and horseradish, the "bitter herbs" of the tractate, eaten as a further reminder of their past as slaves in Egypt. While Peter worked John and Simon maintained a vigil at the courtyard entrance. At every knock John peered through a crack before nodding to Simon to open the door. Each arrival was warmly greeted and gave the assurance he had not been followed. Eventually eleven men were in the courtyard. Still to come were Judas and Jesus.

The men in Caiaphas' office would have carefully considered what Judas had said before formulating a plan. At some stage the high priest would have needed to address Jonathan over how many men would be required to capture Jesus. On the captain's part, tactical consideration would have made him hesitate over any attempt to do so in the city, especially in such a volatile quarter as Zion; it was a foregone conclusion that Jesus would have innumerable followers among the predominantly working-class people who lived there. If every one of the five hundred Temple guards were deployed, there could be no guarantee they would be able to extract Jesus without a fierce running battle; an even greater danger was that resistance would not be contained within Zion—the entire city could become embroiled. No doubt Caiaphas and the other priests present had persisted, determined this time not to be thwarted. If the Temple guards were reinforced with sufficient numbers of the tetrarch's soldiers, opposition would be contained and overcome in the casbah; there were enough troops for a cordon to be thrown around the entire area. Such a proposal was still not without risk. The more men involved, the greater the chance of advance warning: the casbah was renowned for its street intelligence: word would travel its length long before any troops were in the area. By the time they would have undoubtedly had to fight to reach the house where Jesus was, he and others would have long gone.

Very possibly still furious over his failure in the Great Sanhedrin, Caiaphas wanted agreement on a viable plan to bring Jesus to the Temple.

That may well have been the moment that Judas chose to ask what would happen then.

Caiaphas, in the mood of the moment, would not have bothered to hide the contempt in his voice. Judas would be paid for his work. When Jesus was captured he would receive thirty pieces of silver.

The amount was equivalent to a laborer's income for four months.

Caiaphas continued questioning Jonathan about his strategy. If he could not take Jesus in Zion, where would he capture him? Before deciding, Jonathan needed to know from Judas where Jesus and the disciples would go after the Passover meal ended. The treasurer, anxious to appease the high priest's anger, replied that the most likely place would be back to the cave on the Mount of Olives. Jonathan would need to be told the exact position of the cavern and what cover there was for his men to approach undetected. Satisfied on those counts, the captain came to a decision. He would capture Jesus in the cavern or its vicinity.

A thought struck Caiaphas. How would Jonathan recognize he had captured the right man, out there in the darkness on the Mount of Olives? Judas said he would identify Jesus by giving him a traditional kiss of peace.

John and Simon greeted Jesus with relief at the courtyard door; not only had he arrived without incident, but also old tensions had surfaced among the disciples. This time the squabbling was over the seating arrangements for the meal; arguments had broken out when John had led the other disciples to the upper room and indicated their places. They returned to the courtyard and immediately began to accuse him of favoritism. James the Less reminded John he had always sat close to his brother: now he was placed farthest away. Thomas objected to where he was seated. Thaddaeus complained at being seated several places below Judas. Philip and Bartholomew both argued they should be closer to Jesus. In vain John had explained that these were places of honor. Peter, because he had organized the occasion, was automatically entitled to preside over the part of the table to Jesus' right. Andrew, because of his seniority, was next to his elder brother. John had placed himself beside Jesus because he had requested it.

The arrival of Jesus put a stop to the acrimony. While Jesus washed, Peter removed the lamb from the oven, placing it on a large plate which he carried upstairs and set in the center of the table, surrounding it with piles of unleavened bread. Peter then went to the well and cleaned himself.

In uncomfortable silence, the Twelve followed Jesus to the table. He lit the candles and invited them to stand at their places. After some hesitation they did so and joined him in prayer. When they were all settled, Jesus reached for his beaker of salt water, blessed it and addressed the table.

"With desire I have desired to eat this Passover with you before I suffer. For I say unto you, I will not any more eat thereof until it be fulfilled in the kingdom of God."

They sipped their salted water. Jesus blessed one of the jars of red wine. Then he rose and filled the first of the four goblets they would drink from during the meal: for *Kiddush*, the sanctification; followed by the wine for *Haggadsh*, the celebration of the lamb; the third glass would be drunk after the prayers of thanks; the fourth to accompany the closing prayers. The goblets symbolized the kingdoms which the book of Daniel identified as having oppressed God's people: the Chaldeans, Medes, Babylonians and the Romans.

Jesus once more spoke. "For I say unto you, I will not drink of the fruit of the vine, until the kingdom of God shall come."

The words were deliberately meant to give the banquet his own unforgettable seal. They were more than a blessing of the good things they were about to eat and drink; within them lay a declaration of gratitude that he had at least been allowed sufficient time to partake in this sacred repast: he wanted them to know he was a condemned man yet one who could sense the closeness of salvation. In those words Jesus had removed the *Seder* from its ancient meaning and bound it forever to his identity. He wanted them to understand that when next they met they would partake of the imperishable nourishment of eternal life. Beneath his allegorical nuances he was saying they would all meet him in the kingdom of heaven. He excluded no one—not even Judas. Instead, he was appealing to all of them to be conscious that, through him, they would ensure the survival of the kingdom. They must see this meal from now on as his own celebration. In time it would become known as the Eucharist or Holy Communion.

John could sense the bickering starting again; a whispered niggardly resentment had resumed over the seating. John looked at Peter, who was visibly upset that, having all heard such words from their master there should still be such unseemly behavior. Only Judas seemed so moved that he sat with head bowed.

Jesus passed the bowl of spicy red sauce to John, who tore off a piece of bread, dipped it into the *hazareth* and then handed the chalice to Andrew. The sauceboat was halfway round the table and the grumbling showed no signs of abating.

Jesus abruptly rose to his feet and went downstairs. In the upper room the argument intensified. Below in the courtyard Jesus stripped to his *nikli*, a short undergarment, and wrapped himself in one of the towels the disciples had used to dry themselves. He drew a pail of water from the well. Carrying the bucket upstairs, he stood for a moment in the open archway listening to the complaining men, then walked over to where Peter reclined and, placing the bucket on the floor, knelt in front of the apostle. He began to wash Peter's feet, saying nothing but making his point as powerfully as any of his words.

Peter, recovering, tried to move his feet away, protesting. "Lord, dost thou wash my feet?"

Without looking up, aware that all eyes were on him, Jesus spoke. "What I do thou knowest not now, but thou shalt know hereafter."

Peter tried again to stop Jesus. "Thou shalt never wash my feet!"

Jesus looked at the disciple. "If I wash thee not, thou hast no part with me."

Peter's voice became eager. "Lord, not my feet only, but also my hands and my head."

Jesus sighed. "He that is washed needeth not save to wash his feet, but is clean every whit; and ye are clean, but not all."

He continued to bathe Peter's feet. Once more, at this late hour, he had to show them what he expected. He deliberately chose Peter because he had not been one of those bickering. Yet Peter, in many ways, had responded no differently from the others. He had initially not accepted what Jesus wanted to do; Peter had shown an obstinacy and stubbornness in insisting he would *not* allow his master to wash his feet. Then, realizing that Jesus was totally intent upon his task, Peter had tried to prolong his personal attention, asking for his hands and head to be bathed. Just as much as the others with their argument over the seating plan, Peter had failed to understand the true purpose of this feast. It was not a Passover, but a farewell meal; yet it was not a time only to remember the past but an occasion to look to the future. By spending time in cleansing Peter's feet Jesus wished to make it clear that there was no time to be wasted on the petty matter of who sat where. When Jesus finished, he walked slowly from the silent room, the sorrow in his face plain.

Dressed, Jesus returned to the table and the meal resumed. He ate little, still preoccupied in driving home that, with the dignity of being his apostles, went the responsibility of working together in harmony: not one of them was greater in his eyes than the other. He wanted to remind them that he, as their host and master, was privileged to serve them—as soon they must serve others.

Around him the Twelve at last began to realize the extraordinary significance of what was taking place. Jesus had brought them to this table not only to express his gratitude for their loyalty—he offered no indication that

Judas was specifically excluded from this benediction—but to give them in trust a task of the utmost importance: the future religious guidance of the people. The meal progressed while he continued to urge that the only worthwhile authority was achieved through humility; that the essence of greatness was found in the depths of modesty; that to be of service was the noblest thing they could do: to each other, to others and, above all, service in God's kingdom. It would require at times hard decisions. But to judge without flinching was the only way to govern over the new kingdom.

Overwhelmed by what he had heard, Peter burst out that he, for one, was ready to follow Jesus unto death. Jesus looked at the apostle. Peter: the very first one he had picked on that hot day on the banks of the Jordan; who had given him a home in Capernaum; who had never wavered in his faith; who had been foremost in recognizing him as the Messiah; who had been given specific instructions about the future of his ministry—the Peter who would one day be the rock on which a new Church would rise.

There was sad acceptance in his voice as Jesus finally spoke. "I tell thee, Peter, the cock shall not crow this day, before that thou shalt thrice deny that thou knowest me."

Peter was too shocked to speak. There was not an apostle who did not sense the troubled mood of Jesus.

Some time during the evening Pilate learned of the plan to arrest Jesus. However, the matter was still purely a Jewish one. The procurator had no grounds upon which to intervene: no evidence to suggest insurrection was at hand; no proof that the high priest intended to do any more than hold Jesus in custody until the end of Passover; no hint that a trial was in the offing. In such cases his orders were clear: the Jews had full autonomy in dealing with religious offenses. To involve himself in the matter could be to put at risk what he and his wife wanted—a speedy and smooth return to Rome.

Claudia Procula would have been unable to offer a countermanding argument to such reasoning. She might well have retired to bed—perhaps indeed burdened with the foreboding her papers of canonization would subsequently insist.

The *Seder* continued along its precise way. The appropriate portion of the Hallel—Psalms 113 and 144—were recited, praising the Lord and recalling when the People of the Book left Egypt. Each apostle then drank. The bowls of bitter herbs were passed around along with the platter of roast lamb, every man taking a handful of meat with his right hand. When they were all served Jesus continued to address them, his face more pensive, his voice as sad as the surviving fragments of the original Gospels were to suggest. As he spoke, John, seeking to be comforting, stopped eating and laid his head against Jesus' chest. Suddenly the apostle sat bolt upright, stunned even more than Peter had been. Around the table equally stupefied men stared at Jesus, unable to believe what he had just said. "One of you shall betray me."

Eyes flashed around the table. These men who thought they knew each other intimately, who had shared danger and joy, stared with sudden suspicion at one another. Simon was half-crouched, ready to deal with any move that might threaten Jesus; following the revelation, he appeared to expect the traitor immediately to take action. Nobody moved: James the Less frozen-faced; Matthew's eyes darting back and forth, looking for a clue in the eyes of others; Andrew turned sideways, transfixed, goblet halfway to his mouth; Thomas repeatedly shaking his head, even more than the others, refusing to believe. Philip, Thaddaeus and his father looking stricken; Judas calmly staring at Jesus. Peter broke the terrible silence. "Master, of whom speakest thou?"

If there was a traitor in their midst he wished to have him named. It was a matter of urgent security. Like Simon, Peter no doubt feared the man would strike without warning.

Jesus ignored Peter's question.

Around the table shattered men were regaining their composure, whispering to one another, turning to those with whom they felt closest: Matthew to Philip, Thaddaeus to his father, Andrew to Peter, Bartholomew to Thomas. John was half-leaning across Jesus, offering his body as a protective shield. Jesus gently pushed him away and broke off a piece of bread. Those who saw the gesture felt relieved. Whoever the traitor was, Jesus clearly did not fear him; rather he was intent on continuing to perform his role. It was a custom that the host at the Seder should offer his guests a piece of bread dipped in a sauce: the gesture went back to the first Passover, when Joshua celebrated the arrival of the Chosen People in Canaan, and he had used it to express gratitude and friendship to all those who survived the exodus with him. Since then the ritual had been observed with full ceremony. Jesus steeped the bread in the sauce.

John repeated Peter's question. "Lord, who is it?"

Concentrating upon what he was doing, Jesus gave no answer. When the bread was sufficiently coated, he held it delicately between thumb and index finger and turned to Judas. His voice almost certainly did not carry beyond the treasurer. "He it is, to whom I shall give a sop."

Judas' response was equally low, meant only for Jesus. It was the reaction of a man who very clearly feared he would never leave the room alive if the truth became known. Leaning into Jesus he murmured: "Master, is it I?"

Jesus placed the morsel of bread on the treasurer's lips. "Thou hast said." His words were so soft that no one, not even the vigilant Simon, seated beside Judas, heard them. The treasurer's treachery remained between him and his master. But that brief exchange signaled the onset of a new phase in the drama. Jesus, in refusing to name Judas publicly, had willingly allowed the betrayal to proceed. After Judas swallowed the bread, Jesus, his voice resigned, the tone of a man who had always accepted he must be the availing victim, spoke once more to the treasurer. "That thou doest, do quickly."

Judas rose to his feet and left the room, clutching his *punda*. John was among those who thought Jesus had sent him to give alms to the poor.

In the tetrarch's palace the celebration had deteriorated into debauchery. Herodias sat on one side of Herod Antipas, Salome on the other. The girl wore a diadem the tetrarch's mother had used at her wedding. Herod Antipas had given it to Salome after spending another afternoon in her company; it was common gossip he had begun to share alternately the beds of mother and daughter. Before them, close to five hundred guests ate and drank in saturnalian revelry. From the rear of the vast hall servants brought more food and wine, while others moved behind the guests, sprinkling them with perfumes. Intent upon draining goblet upon goblet, Herod Antipas did not see Jonathan enter the hall, only aware of his presence when Chuza whispered in his ear. Jonathan stooped and spoke to the tetrarch. Finally comprehending, Herod Antipas nodded. Satisfied, the captain left. He had received permission to include in his force a *centuria* of the tetrarch's troops. It was Caiaphas' idea: if anything went amiss, the high priest could attempt to place the blame upon Herod Antipas' men.

The departure of Judas had the immediate effect of relaxing Jesus. The tension left his voice and face; he was his old tender self, his mood communicated itself to the others. They watched respectfully as he blessed the last of the wine and refilled their goblets. While they sipped, he called them "little children," and said with the poignancy of someone who realized that he would soon be going to where they could not follow, that they must continue to love one another as he had loved them. There was about him—though those present would only see this later—an air of martyrdom: God so loved them, and all those beyond the walls of this room, that he was ready to sacrifice his only begotten Son. Then, in one magnificent sentence, Jesus anticipated his own glorification with the familiar confidence he had always shown when discussing the bond between himself and God. "Now is the Son of man glorified and God is glorified in him. If God be glorified in him, God shall also glorify him in himself, and shall straightway glorify him."

Jesus fell silent for a moment. His look of deep concentration reminded both Matthew and John of that time just before he had raised Lazarus. John sensed a radiation emanating from Jesus' body, as if spiritual energy was coursing through it. They all watched as, once more, he selected a piece of unleavened bread, blessed it and then broke it into eleven pieces. He went from one to another giving each of them a portion before returning to his place. Then he spoke words which would hold a timeless significance. "Take, eat, this is my body." Once they had all swallowed, Jesus lifted his goblet, which had remained untouched throughout the meal, and sanctified it. As Matthew would later record, Jesus passed the cup to John with these words: "Drink ye, all of it. For this is my blood of the new testament, which is shed for many for the remission of sins."

Each drank in turn until the goblet was returned to him, empty.

They looked at Jesus in awe. In a few moments, as if it were the most natural action, Jesus had created a unique new rite which would perpetually remember him. Not since Yahweh had persuaded Abraham to go forth had there been such a comparable moment. From his hands and lips had come a sacrament of the deepest possible meaning. Pieces of the same bread he had given Judas had now become part of his body; an ordinary working man's goblet turned into the chalice of the Lord. With simple commands—"take, eat" and "drink ye"—Jesus had shown them that each time they repeated the ceremony they would be at his table, remembering him, awaiting his return.

He looked around, smiling reassurance, reminding them of other truths: those who believed in God believed in him; that in his father's house there were many rooms, each of which he was as familiar with as the one in which they were seated. He was certain there would be one for each of them. He would never have asked them to have traveled so far with him unless that was an absolute truth. When he had made all the arrangements he would return for them. In the meantime they must always be prepared for that moment; he could give them no advance warning when that would be. But it would happen.

Jesus stood up, allowing them to sense his pure joy at being with his friends. Finally, in a resolute voice he said: "Arise, let us go hence."

The moment had come to take the final steps in delivering himself to the hatred of the world.

Moving in single file, Jonathan led his force out of the Temple. At the Golden Gate, as arranged, the tetrarch's *centuria* waited. Its officer formally placed his men under Jonathan's command. At this late hour the area was deserted, the pilgrims sleeping after the repast. The men moved at a trot into the Kidron Valley, picking their way past the tombstones of the

Jehoshaphat cemetery. Reaching the brook beyond the graves, they found themselves knee-deep in a sluggish flow of blood and animal entrails from the Temple's altar. There were curses and groans as they slithered through the cloying mess and its overpowering stench. The crossing effected, Jonathan led them south, using the tomb of King David's son, Absalom, as a navigating point. There was yet no moon and few stars. Opposite the tomb they paused for Jonathan to divide the force. A sensible strategy would be for the tetrarch's men to continue down the valley a little further and shelter in the rocks there. Once Jesus and the disciples passed over the bridge which formed part of the track between the olive groves and the city, the soldiers were to occupy the crossing, and stop all access. As they left, Jonathan led the Temple guards towards the olive trees. They moved slowly, careful not to awaken the pilgrims in the encampments further up the Mount of Olives. When they reached cover Jonathan motioned them to lie low while he edged forward, pausing from time to time to check his bearings, using the Temple as a reference point. At some point within the trees he waited, hand on sword handle, the chill of the night forgotten. Judas had arrived, turned and led the captain of the guard further into the groves. Finally the treasurer pointed out the entrance to the cavern. Shortly afterwards, Jonathan began to deploy them in a circle around the cave with instructions that no one must move until his command.

Jesus insisted upon being the first to leave the courtyard. When Simon and his brother protested Jesus firmly said there was to be no argument and disappeared into the darkness. Moments later Matthew followed: then one by one the other apostles hurried through the lanes. Simon and Peter left together, quietly closing the courtyard door behind them, Simon scanning the alley for any sign of movement. It was completely deserted.

Moving swiftly Simon led the way to the Golden Gate. It was wide open and there was no sign of the watchman or the Roman patrol which usually stood sentry duty inside the portal. The gate had been left open for Passover, the Romans confined to barracks, and the watchman was at his *Seder*. They followed the trail the others had taken to the olive groves, crossed the bridge and climbed over the scree to the trees.

Jesus waited at the cavern entrance. He greeted the three men and led them inside. He asked Peter to remain with him and beckoned John and his brother to join them. Jesus told the other apostles he was going outside to pray and they must stay in the cave.

Moving through the trees he suddenly turned and confessed to his companions: "My soul is exceeding sorrowful unto death. Tarry ye here and watch."

The disciples sat down against tree trunks and watched Jesus walk on. They whispered among themselves that he seemed once more so deeply troubled as to be on the verge of collapse. Through the murk they heard his anguish. "Abba, Father, all things are possible unto thee; take away this cup from me: nevertheless not what I will, but what thou wilt."

Already tired and emotionally spent from all that they had heard and observed in the past hours, these were words far beyond the comprehension of even men who had come to understand the mystery of the transfiguration. They were unable to grasp that, having been his witnesses on Mount Hebron, Jesus wanted them to see the painful torment which filled him on the lower slopes of the Mount of Olives. By exposing himself so openly at the onset of his passion, he wished them to remember forever the enormity of the suffering he would soon have to bear. He wanted them to realize that he could sense the fearsome pain ahead and he knew he could not escape it: instead, he accepted that through his forthcoming agony lay redemption for all those beyond this landscape of gnarled trees.

As they watched Jesus once more fall to the ground, they heard his plea that "the hour might pass." His was a cry filled with supreme courage and understanding. How long he remained out there, alone, in the first throes of his passion, the apostles would never know. They fell asleep. Jesus awoke them, reproaching Peter in particular. "Couldest not thou watch one hour?" He then moved back into the trees, once more falling to his knees, remaining prostrate before dragging himself to his feet, hanging on to a branch for support, praying all the time. Returning, he had again found them asleep. Jesus admonished them once more and then continued with his agony.

For the third time Jesus found the trio asleep. This time he knelt beside them, shaking them in turn, his voice gentle, without a trace of his previous disappointment. "The hour is come. Behold, the Son of man is betrayed into the hands of sinners. Rise up; let us go; lo, he that betrayeth me is at hand."

They could see Judas standing behind Jesus. From nearby came a shouted command, then racing through the trees were men with drawn swords.

Struggling to their feet the three disciples, sleep banished, prepared to defend Jesus. But before they could move Judas stepped forward and kissed him on the cheek.

Jonathan shouted at the guards to seize him.

A dozen pairs of hands reached to grab Jesus.

HOURS OF TRIAL

O Judgment! thou art fled to brutish hearts,
And men have lost their reason.

Shakespeare, *Julius Caesar*

9

BEYOND ARREST

Jesus answered: My kingdom is not of this world.
John 18:36

Jesus' words halted everyone: Judas, the touch of his lips damp upon his master's cheek, arms around his shoulders, the traditional embrace of a friend, yet who would be judged as plumbing the depths of human depravity; Peter struggling to remove something from under his cloak: John and James the Less beginning to move to his side; the guards reaching forward but not yet touching Jesus. His words, delivered without a trace of surprise, were addressed to those who had swooped out of the night and who, in spite of Jonathan's command, seemed uncertain. "Whom seek ye?"

The tableau dissolved, Judas stepped back among the Temple guards. Peter produced a knife he once used for gutting fish. John and his brother sprang forward and stood fore and aft of their master, warding off the first grabbing hands.

Peter's was the typical response of an impulsive personality. He had been the first to give up his livelihood to become an apostle; the one who, convinced he saw Jesus walking on the water in their first year together, had stepped over the side of the boat and nearly drowned. His companions had also acted in character. John was naturally self-assertive; James the Less, when aroused, had the formidable temper of a physically small person used to defending by force all he held dear.

Jonathan's words cut through the darkness.

"Jeshu Hannosri!"

Jesus responded at once. "I am he."

The guards, confronted by three aroused men, not knowing what reinforcements were close by, perhaps overcome by the authority of his voice, or feeling sudden doubt about arresting someone who faced them so calmly, drew back, stumbling on the scree and protruding roots before falling to the ground.

From behind Jonathan, Judas again shouted. "It is he! Hold him well!"

The words would forever damn the treasurer. Yet was it the cry of a man who again believed that Jesus was about to exercise his extraordinary powers and literally disappear in front of them? Did Judas feel that Jesus was going once more to avoid the confrontation the disciple had always felt was required to prove his master's invincibility, a final prelude to the launch of the kingdom? Had Judas' thinking become so warped that he had failed to understand what Jesus meant by that final command at the *Seder*—"What thou doest, do quickly"—and took it as a positive encouragement actually to produce confrontation?

Jonathan ran forward, roughly ordering his men to their feet, and roared again at Jesus to confirm his identity. Through the trees, led by Simon, came the other apostles, speed carrying them through the Temple ranks towards Jesus. Simon's reaction would have been that of a bodyguard who had been taken unawares. He, above all, should have sensed the presence of danger after years of being hunted by Roman and Herodian forces in the hills of Galilee. Simon would also have quickly realized that the apostles were heavily outnumbered. Those he had led from the cavern had followed him blindly. Seeing Simon's surrender and the bewildering sight of Jesus doing nothing to save himself, they could only have felt helpless and terrified in the presence of such menace.

Jesus motioned all eleven to stand behind him before answering Jonathan. "I have told ye I am he." Jesus pointed to the disciples. "If therefore ye seek me, let these go their way." It was his last act of service to them. Knowing they, like him, were in mortal danger, he had not revealed their identity, so fulfilling a promise made during the first part of his passion: "Of them which thou gavest me, have I lost none." Jesus stepped towards Jonathan, open hands extended, a display of willing surrender, a man going into captivity voluntarily. It would be understandable if Jonathan hesitated. He would have heard so many tales about this man: that he possessed mysterious powers enabling him to control the wind and sea; that once he had fed five thousand people with a few loaves and fish; that he could cure the terminally ill, restore sight and raise the dead. Whether such facts had all been the work of sorcery, as the high priest insisted, or something else, Jonathan almost certainly had no way of telling. But his own experience as a law officer cautioned him that no one gave up so calmly, knowing the outcome must be certain death. The captain ordered Jesus to stand still.

The guards were still scrambling to their feet when Peter made another impulsive move.

Possibly Judas' words provoked it. The treasurer had finally confirmed Peter's suspicions, and he could, in that mercurial mind of his, have intended to murder Judas for his betrayal. Then, realizing that to reach the treasurer he must cut down Jonathan, Peter had lunged at the captain; perhaps intending to drive his blade into Jonathan's neck. With Jonathan dead Peter may have presumed his men would be less inclined to press any action. In the uncertain light, he misjudged his aim. Matthew and John were both in a position to agree that Peter "smote off the ear" of the captain.

Jesus' response was swift as the blow. He sharply ordered Peter to put away the knife, reminding all within earshot that "they that take the sword shall perish with the sword." Then Jesus touched Jonathan's wound, healing it instantly. It would be his last miracle in aid of another—and an act of mercy which would also raise questions. Why did Jonathan not respond to the assault? Was he constrained by Caiaphas' strict order that only Jesus was to be apprehended? Did he fear that if he arrested Peter the others, believing they were also about to be taken, would have launched an attack violent enough to arouse pilgrims sleeping not too far away? Was Jonathan even aware that he had lost an ear and that a moment later Jesus had miraculously replaced it? If he did know what had occurred, had he seen it as striking confirmation of Jesus' powers of sorcery—and had the captain been too frightened to act against Peter in case he evoked even more awesome powers? Jesus' next words certainly left them all in no doubt that he believed ample help was available should he require it. "Thinkest thou that I cannot pray to my Father, and he shall presently give me more than twelve legions of angels?"

The threat to summon over seventy thousand angels might well have seemed to Judas that his master had lost none of his power—that the kingdom was a mere flap of celestial wings away.

Jesus dashed any such hope. "But how then shall the scriptures be fulfilled, that thus it must be?"

The treasurer turned and ran through the trees, his place in historical infamy secured, through misunderstanding to the very end what Jesus had meant.

Jesus' promise of divine help was clearly designed to reassure the apostles, to remind them that, surrounded by enemies, he was giving himself into the care of God. Jesus was telling them that even now, if he wished—just as he had done when threatened in Nazareth, calming the tempest or raising Lazarus—he could once more have called upon God to help him:

he had not done so because that would save him from his chosen path. But, even as he spoke, the apostles were fleeing. It would not matter in which order: whether Thaddaeus went before Thomas, or Philip followed Bartholomew, or James took flight with his own brother, or if Matthew preceded Andrew and if it was finally Simon, John or Peter who was the last one to bolt. But they fled and he understood. The sudden invasion of armed guards, their brutal questions and cursing, followed by the foolhardy gesture of Peter: all this would have panicked the apostles, sending them racing in all directions into the night. It was very human.

Jesus reproached Jonathan and the guards. "Be ye come but as against a thief, with swords and staves? When I was daily with you in the temple, ye stretched forth no hands against me. But this is your hour and the power of darkness." He fell silent, letting them bind him, offering no resistance. They led Jesus down through the trees towards the bridge where Herod Antipas' soldiers waited, dressed and equipped like Roman centurions. That simple coincidence would stir intense controversy.

The fleeing John, his mind filled with a kaleidoscope of impressions identified the tetrarch's men as a "cohort"—normally a force of six hundred Roman centurions led by a tribune. Aside from the fact that guarding the bridge was a *centuria*, only a hundred men, the apostle's subsequent eyewitness account did not attach the crucial word "Roman" to his "cohort." Its absence would not stop apologists from suggesting the arrest was a joint undertaking between the Roman and Jewish authorities and that the Temple hierarchy, in all such matters of common concern, were subservient to imperial control: therefore, the all-important actual *authority* for the arrest should be laid upon the occupying power. The salient weakness of the argument is that it overlooked that the Roman criminal code required a formal indictment before a person could be detained. In fact no warrant had been made out by any competent authority against Jesus. The Great Sanhedrin had been unable to issue one owing to the objections of Nicodemus and Gamaliel. The Romans had not been asked to provide one. Jesus was being frog-marched toward the Golden Gate solely upon the order of Joseph Caiaphas. His decision to act outside all legal parameters was further exemplified by his command not to arrest the apostles. In law, if their master had a case to answer, so did they as accessories directly supporting his teaching; if Jesus proclaimed heresy, then they were his appointed instruments in spreading it. But involving the disciples in such charges would require, under the law, further investigation, proper testimony and independent witnesses. Caiaphas was no longer concerned in working within such a legal framework. The high priest, from whom all hallowed dignity and piety had long gone, for whom only the circumambient ceremonial trappings remained, and even then the most important of those, his robes, the Romans kept in custody, was intent upon subverting the law. The irony would be that John—who hated the existing Temple authorities more than any other apostle—should be the one who would give unwitting credence to the myth that the Romans were ultimately responsible for bringing Jesus through the Golden Gate.

Jonathan very probably was concerned that the flight of the apostles presaged an attempted rescue. He would have deployed his forces to reduce the threat using a standard tactic in which the tetrarch's troops would have been divided, half going ahead, forming a solid wall of shields, the remainder acting as a rearguard, with the Temple guards forming a cordon around Jesus, swords and staves drawn. In their midst would be Jonathan and a guard, holding Jesus by the arms. The force would have properly abandoned silence for speed, and Jesus, bound hand and foot, was half-dragged over the rocky terrain. On the lower slopes they had been hidden by the darkness. But climbing towards the city walls, the moon, which had only been rising when the operation began, was now directly overhead—at the crucial time when the steepness of the ascent slowed their progress. Their presence would have awakened pilgrims in the surrounding encampment: there were shouts; cries of who was there, what was happening. Jonathan no doubt urged the men on. If Jesus stumbled he would have been hauled to his feet. Every breathless step brought the force closer to the sanctuary of the Golden Gate. The advance group of the tetrarch's men may just have passed through the massive portal when a figure raced from the shadow of the city wall, darting among the guards, trying to reach Jesus. Jonathan would have had no more than a glimpse of a boyish face and a body wrapped in a white cloth. One of his men grabbed at the lad, holding fast to the cloth. The youth ducked and twisted, unravelling the sheet, and raced away down the valley, naked. Years later, when he had grown to full manhood and dedicated his life to Jesus, he would include the incident in his account of this night. It would form part of the Gospel of Saint Mark, based also on Peter's experiences.

The moment his force was inside the gate Jonathan ordered it to be closed and left the tetrarch's men on guard. He gave his own men new directions. At a brisk trot they moved through the streets to a gate set in a high wall and with a covered grille. Upon Jonathan's knock the cover drew back, a face peered out, the gate was opened by a waiting manservant and Jesus was bundled into the grounds of the palace of Annas. The gate closed behind prisoner and escort: its grille would come to bear the name of a Judas window. The treasurer had used the gate for those secret visits to the Temple.

The high priest, Annas and a few Sadducee judges were in the palace library when Jonathan arrived with news that Jesus had been brought to an outer courtyard. No doubt they eagerly questioned the captain on everything Jesus had said and done, noting his threat to call upon angels. Caiaphas must have viewed it as a further example of his sorcery. He ordered Jonathan to remove Jesus to an underground chamber and the judges resumed their task of finding ways around the formidable obstacles of the law they were charged with upholding.

No Sanhedrin, Great or Small, could commence criminal proceedings once darkness had fallen; no person could be tried on a criminal charge during a festival. There was also the old problem of the absence of, at the very minimum, a pair of lawfully qualified witnesses who would testify they had, independently of each other, warned Jesus of the criminality of his actions and the penalty they would invoke. The book of Deuteronomy could not be more insistent on those points.

Annas might well, as some accounts were to insist, have pointed out that the case would almost certainly stand or fall on establishing a clear offense in scriptural law, and that he directed each of them to read silently the appropriate paragraph in the book of Leviticus. The scroll was handed from one legate to the next. Only the occasional movement of lips barely visible behind flowing beards and a sudden intake of breath betokened realization that here were the words that could lead to Jesus' death. "He that blasphemeth the name of the Lord he shall surely be put to death, and all the congregation shall certainly stone him: as well the stranger, as he that is born in the land, when he blasphemeth the name of the Lord, shall be put to death."

God's sanctity was an article of faith from the day Yahweh had called forth Abraham, and it had remained the ultimate source of Judaism, the axiom upon which everything else depended. No Jew was permitted to compromise this hallowed principle. Only the high priest in the sanctity of the Holy of Holies could utter God's name. For anyone else to associate himself in any way as equal with God was a capital offense.

For a prosecution to succeed on the grounds that Jesus had committed such a crime it would be essential to have him repeat before a court his claim to messiahship. If Jesus could be forced into doing this in the presence of judges of the Sanhedrin, his conviction would be assured.

The Leviticus passage, being written Scripture, formed part of the old Sadducean legal system and central to its doctrine was that men could be punished solely on their own confessions. The murderer of Saul was executed after confessing to David; Achan had been stoned after his confession to Joshua. These were impressive precedents.

Equally important, there was no legal barrier to a solely Sadducean-based court being convened to apply only Sadducean law—particularly in a time of emergency. Those present in the library would have needed no persuasion of the gravity of the situation. There had been Jesus' triumphal entry, his threat to destroy the Temple. If Jesus had not been apprehended, it would have boiled over into insurrection, and indeed his supporters might yet attack the Temple to rescue him. These were the strongest possible reasons to dispatch him as swiftly as possible by the most convenient means available—in this case the law of the Sadducees. Caiaphas would have needed little persuasion to convince the other judges that Jesus had violated the code. For example, his claim to be able to summon angels at God's will was blasphemy—clearly defined in the eighteenth chapter of the book of Deuteronomy: "There shall not be found among you any one that maketh his son or his daughter to pass through the fire, or that useth divination, or an observer of times, or an enchanter, or a witch, or a charmer, or a consulter with familiar spirits, or a wizard, or a necromancer." The high priest could indeed have argued that Jesus' entire ministry was a prime example of the magical arts: he had interfered with the dead, the elements and the natural laws. Under Sadducean code these were offenses that made it imperative to deal with him urgently—if need be, even without the normal due process of law being applied.

There was a precedent for such action. Some hundred years previously eighty witches in the city of Askalon had posed a sudden and grave threat to the Temple. There had been no time for a trial. Instead the high priest of the day had exercised the executive authority invested in his office and the women were promptly hanged. Caiaphas could have little difficulty in convincing the men around him that the behavior of Jesus fitted into that criterion. Yet almost certainly the high priest had not requested unilateral power—by which he would simply dispatch Jesus to Golgotha without trial. That would be altogether too risky—turning Jesus into a martyr and perhaps even providing his followers with an excuse to attack the Temple. What the high priest wanted was agreement to bring Jesus before a court composed only of Sadducee judges who would examine him, tease out the evidence and obtain the necessary confession.

Caiaphas reiterated that Jesus was a Jew, threatening Jews, and he must be dealt with by the Jews chosen to represent the people, and the finer points of whether it would be possible in every accusation against him to establish a conviction based upon eyewitness testimonies did not apply: there was ample circumstantial evidence. Nor should they concern themselves that there was no precedent for holding an immediate trial at night, or at a time of festivities. The *ultimo ratio* of Jewish law allowed an emergency to override all such considerations. Such an argument could have concluded with a confident Caiaphas predicting that their Pharisee colleagues and the Great Sanhedrin would support their action.

One by one, the men around him agreed on what must be done. First there would be a preliminary examination, with Caiaphas forgoing his right to conduct it, saving his interrogation for later. The initial questioning was assigned to Annas. Attended by his secretary the old priest left the library. Caiaphas summoned Jonathan and ordered him to deliver the prisoner to a nearby room.

Having run from the olive groves, Peter and John sought shelter amongst the tombs of Jehoshaphat where another terror faced them. From the Vale of Hinnom—where Moloch was once offered human sacrifices and which had become the city refuse dump, still a place of evil and smoldering fires—a figure moved towards them. Only the devil or his acolytes roamed Hinnom at night. John and Peter acted in concert, rising to their feet to flee once more. A voice, filled with its own boyish fear, stopped them. They turned and faced the naked Mark.

John gave the boy his *haluk*, an undershift, and Peter ordered Mark to continue through the Kidron to try to find the other apostles.

Then, no doubt in considerable fear, the two men entered the city through the nearby Gate of the Fountain and made their way towards the sounds of activity around the palace of Annas.

Jonathan, still anticipating a rescue attempt, had turned the palace and adjoining Temple into a fortress. His entire force, five hundred heavily armed men, patrolled inside the Temple walls and the palace perimeter. In the palace courtyards and gardens the guards lit fires and ordered servants to fetch food and wine. The entire area was a hubbub of action as figures flitted through the shadows. Realizing it would be a focal point for any impending attack, Jonathan withdrew the tetrarch's soldiers from the Golden Gate and posted them as sentries around the outer walls of the palace. To facilitate easier contact between the troops and his guards, the captain had the palace servants' gate, used for reaching the street, left open. Soon there was a constant milling of domestic staff and soldiery around the portal. No one challenged Peter and John as they edged their way into the palace.

At some point, Claudia Procula awoke in her bedroom adjoining that of her husband. She drifted back to sleep, no doubt hoping her troubling dream would not return. It had been about Jesus.

Another of the unexplained mysteries of this night of unsurpassed drama was how Matthew, whose closest encounter with Claudia Procula may have been no more than glimpsing her on the edge of a Galilean crowd, and who at this very hour was somewhere out in the Kidron Valley, hiding in fear of his life, should come to know about a dream filled with foreboding and ominous reality. More easy to accept is the judgment of Nicodemus in his Gospel that she was by now a "a pious woman of Jewish tendencies." Less convincing would be the claim that in her premonitory dream Socrates appeared to Pilate's wife and urged her to intercede on behalf of Jesus.

Dressed in the regalia of a judge of the Great Sanhedrin, Annas sat on a high-backed wooden chair, a symbol of his further authority as a doctor of the law. His secretary squatted on a stool, tablet and *stilus* on his lap, beside a lamp on a metal stand, its flame bright, a sign that its oil was refined, not like the rancid-smelling liquid burnt by the poor. On the edge of the pool of light stood Jonathan, gripping Jesus by the arm. His feet had been cut in several places during the journey into the city; the hobbling rope around the ankles chafed the skin; his wrists were similarly bruised.

Annas ordered Jonathan to remove the bonds before the questioning began.

He asked Jesus his name.

Jesus gave it. The secretary's *stilus* marked the wax.

Annas went straight to the point. He asked Jesus what work he did.

Just as the Temple vendors had hoped to trap Jesus by questioning his *authority*, so did Annas. Establishing Jesus' lack of Temple approved *authority* was an essential step towards a conviction. Behind the word lay a range of accepted public manifestations of Jewish religious life: the *authority* of the rituals, the ceremonies, the consecration of every working moment. *Authority* was accepting the sabbath as a day of rest as God had himself rested on the seventh day of creation. *Authority* was recognizing that any violation of this or any other divine commandment would be punishable by death. *Authority* meant never to challenge the will of the men who sat in God's Temple.

But Jesus had consistently implied that, like John the Baptist, his authority came directly from heaven; that he was the appointed link between God and man. Once that claim was established in this room his fate would be sealed. Annas put the question: on whose authority did Jesus work?

Jesus made no answer.

Annas would have known the value of keeping silent—and the psychological advantage he held. With his followers scattered, and himself rushed through the night like a dangerous criminal and confined in darkness before being brought here, Jesus must have been unsettled. He continued to wait, studying Jesus, no doubt estimating his strength and weaknesses. Jesus remained silent and impassive. The deadlock stretched.

Inside the palace grounds Peter and John separated, each apostle tagging behind servants carrying food and wine to the guards. Emboldened at being able to move without challenge, Peter drifted from one group of guards to another. Their talk could only have given him sudden hope: they feared that if rescue was attempted it would be impossible for them to hold off the throngs Jesus had shown he was capable of arousing. Peter set off to find John.

John had been hovering around the servants' gate, trying to get some idea of the number of soldiers patrolling the outside walls, critical intelligence for any rescue. Peter's arrival provoked questions. Should they both go in search of Simon—the Canaanite would certainly know where to find the men and how best to organize a rescue mission—or should one of them remain and try to locate exactly where the master was being held in the palace? Any further discussion was interrupted by the gate portress—John would remember her as young—who broke off her badinage with the soldiers to point at Peter. "Art not thou also one of this man's disciples?"

Peter vehemently shook his head and said emphatically he was not, glad no doubt that his face was in shadow.

The girl continued to stare at Peter trying to make up her mind. The light was poor; she could have made a mistake. They had both come from within the palace; they might even be Temple agents.

While she hesitated, John calmly steered Peter back into the palace grounds.

Annas had sent for several judges from the library. They stood along one wall, black-robed figures, staring fixedly at Jesus. Jonathan stood immediately behind him. Annas was intent upon creating a threatening atmosphere—to break the iron will of the man who had so far avoided every pitfall in his path. Jesus had said little apart from confirming the number of his disciples, where they traveled and the synagogues he had preached in—

Annas interrupted. He asked Jesus what he had taught there.

Jesus patiently explained that all the essential themes of Judaism were incorporated into his teaching.

Glaring at Jesus, Annas could not contain his frustration. What else had he taught?

Jesus could have included in any explanation the fact that, like any rabbi, he placed the highest value on moral purity; that, for instance, he believed that adultery was a cause for a man to put aside his wife, but that did not give him the right to take another. To do so was also an act of adultery.

This teaching proclaimed his strong support for the sanctity of wedlock and condemnation of sexual licentiousness. Jesus concluded: "I spake openly to the world! In secret have I said nothing."

The men along the wall murmured angrily. No prisoner had ever dared address a judge, let alone a former high priest, in such a way.

Annas continued to probe, perhaps believing that the man before him—for all the absence of diffidence, humility, submissiveness and fear—could be irked to the point where he would bear witness against himself. What did he mean?

In that first year when he had selected the Twelve Jesus had told them: "What I tell you in darkness, that speak ye in light; and what you hear in the ear, that preach ye upon the housetops."

He delivered a sharp rebuke to Annas. "Why askest thou me? Ask them which heard me, what I have said unto them. Behold they know what I said."

The words were followed by Jonathan's savage slap on Jesus' face. The captain shouted in his ear: "Answerest thou the high priest so?"

The judges could not contain themselves. They spat at Jesus. He looked at them stoically then turned to Jonathan, the mark of the blow clear on his skin. "If l have spoken evil, bear witness of the evil. But if well, why smitest thou me?"

For the best part of a Roman watch—the accepted way to measure time at night—Annas had tried every maneuver: alternately threatening and placating, being coldly dismissive and feigning politeness. He had asked a series of simple questions before smoothly inserting a deadly one. He had tried to establish that Jesus was the founder of a school of teaching that really was no more than a secret society, open only to the initiated. He had attempted to make the kingdom sound like a form of *Sheol*. Yet, every time he had scented victory, Jesus had calmly removed himself from danger. He had turned the claim of secrecy against his interrogator: there had been none on his part; it was the Temple which had behaved in an underhanded manner, sending agents to listen surreptitiously when he would have been happy to come and explain openly. The more Annas had tried to defeat Jesus, the greater must have been the priest's sense of personal failure. Even Jonathan's slap had drawn forth a majestic rebuke. But it had also ended any pretense this was a legally convened preliminary inquiry. Annas ordered Jonathan once more to bind Jesus and take him to the lord high priest. But first Jesus must be taught a lesson.

Thomas and Philip had fled the length of the Kidron Valley, stumbling through one pilgrim encampment after another before scrambling down the slopes which led to the aqueduct Pilate had built to improve Jerusalem's water supply. It had taken two full years to lay, and the hewn stones used to form the pipe were all double-flanged to make the joints watertight. The exhausted apostles rested, their backs against the pipe, staring towards Bethlehem where his story, they believed, had properly begun and which, they could not yet grasp, was almost at its earthly end. Disoriented, convinced they faced certain death if they entered the city, they struggled to find common solace in what Jesus had said towards the end of the meal: he would return. But, in any event, they knew the way to where he had gone.

On that bleak hillside they continued to recall the certainty of his words: that he was the revelation of God and that as long as they accepted that they could face the future without his bodily presence.

John and Peter had separated, trying to establish where Jesus was being held. Peter passed beyond another arched portico into an open courtyard when he hesitated. Ahead of him a soldier was peering through a window opening. From inside came angry voices. Then, above all the shouting, clear and authoritative as always, Peter heard Jesus. The room where he was being held was deep inside the palace. There was no guarantee that rescue could be effected before he would either be moved or killed.

Peter set off to find John, walking as nonchalantly as possible through another courtyard, taking care to stay clear of the men warming themselves around a fire. Peter could not have forgotten that only a few hours ago Jesus had spoken of the unique bond which existed between himself and the disciples. Judas had already departed from the *Seder*—and how Peter now hated him—when Jesus finally pushed aside his plate. Then, leaning across John and Andrew, he addressed Peter about the mission the apostle must fulfill. In the warmth and friendship of the room that had seemed easy to accept. But here, alone in the darkness, surrounded by enemies, Peter knew he had already failed: that moment at the gate when he had made his denial still must have hurt deeply. Yet alongside the pain Peter could have drawn strength from how Jesus had described not only the immense task ahead but the victory which would be all the sweeter for overcoming the obstacles. As he entered another portico, staying close to the wall, a shadow to the guards moving restlessly around the adjoining courtyard, Peter could have begun to be certain that Jesus after all would have forgiven his denial.

Jewish legal procedure did not have an official prosecutor. Witnesses performed that function. Throughout the night a number of Temple vendors, as well as some of the guards in the arresting party had been brought to the palace to fulfill that role. Assured that they would face no penalty for bearing false testimony, all had cooperated. Caiaphas' only problem could have been the lack of time. Given a day he could without doubt make them word perfect. But, in their eagerness to please, the men continued to stumble over the details of the perjury the high priest had added to the other illegalities.

John had concentrated his search upon the lower end of the palace grounds, an area of servants' quarters, chicken pens, ornamental and vegetable gardens. He also began to sift impressions of this fearful night. What Judas had done was too despicable to dwell upon. John would never describe the treasurer's kiss; he would leave that to Matthew. Nor would he reveal his own feelings at having to run into the night as the guards seized and bound Jesus.

John suddenly heard Peter's voice shouting in protest, momentarily drowning that of a woman. He ran towards the altercation. Peter stood in a courtyard, surrounded by several men and women servants. A maid wagged a finger at her companions to emphasize her claim. She had been in the crowd when Jesus had ridden on the donkey. She pointed at Peter. He *had* been walking behind the animal.

Peter uttered an even louder denial. "I do not know the man!" He started to shove past the woman. The others blocked his path.

A manservant prodded Peter in the chest. "Thy speech betrayeth thee."

Peter roundly cursed him as a liar and troublemaker, roaring that he did not know *the man*—once more putting a verbal distance between Jesus and himself: he was a stranger, someone Peter wanted them to believe he had never set eyes upon—*"the man."* So vehement was his protest that the servants cowered. Peter undoubtedly had a country accent, but so did many of the spies of Herod Antipas—and he was infamous for punishing anyone who upset his men. *"I know not the man!"*

Peter stormed past the servants. John called from the shadows. As they hurried back into the Lower City a cockerel crowed.

The room was close to the palace library yet far removed from its scroll-filled elegance and had been chosen for one of the most shameful incidents in the passion of Jesus, one almost certainly engineered by Annas and approved by Caiaphas.

Trussed hand and foot, Jesus stood while a guard slapped his face; next a judge spat in his face. The intention of his tormentors was to show Jesus the hopelessness of his situation and make him realize they could do as they wished with him; that here in one of the foremost palaces of his people he was regarded as scum, abandoned by everyone: once that penetrated his stubborn pride, he would confess. Another judge sent spittle dribbling down Jesus' face. A third Sadducee member of the Great Sanhedrin contemptuously delivered a further punch. Jesus stared calmly at the persecutors. A guard delivered another resounding clout. A trickle of blood ran from Jesus' mouth. Jonathan spoke to one of the guards, who hurried from the room. Yet another judge spat into Jesus' eyes and said he was a blasphemer. The guard returned with an empty grain sack. Jonathan thrust it over Jesus' head and down around his shoulders. The captain motioned for two of the guards to begin spinning Jesus around. As the grotesque pantomime began, judge after judge stepped forward and struck blows at his hooded head.

One of the guards shouted: "Prophesy unto us, thou Christ, who is he that smote thee?"

Raucous laughter greeted the sally. The blows continued, each strike accompanied by further abuse. Jesus bore it all without flinching.

Mark found four apostles: Andrew, Thaddaeus, Bartholomew and James the Less. They huddled in the cold darkness of early morning near the tombs of Jehoshaphat. Jesus' mother and Mary Magdalene joined them. The women could have contributed little as they sat staring helplessly toward the silent city, listening to the men's accounts of Jesus' last hours with them—and how he had prayed for all who believed in him, not only now but in the future. But the women would have had no trouble in imagining how Jesus had felt: deeply loved yet so little understood, and in the end deserted by all those who had been so close to him. Yet they would also have accepted that what had happened showed the true greatness of his soul. Through the intensity of prayer Jesus had crushed his human self but left his spirit intact. They had every reason to believe that nothing or nobody could destroy that.

Simon and Matthew chose the same escape route—southwards intending to reach the Wilderness; and after a few *strades*, realizing they were not being pursued, Simon suggested heading for Bethany to break the news to Lazarus and his sisters. Mary was distraught, Martha practical. It would be perfectly in keeping if she had broached the possibility of rescue.

Protest by Matthew would have been meant for Simon. Jesus had specifically ordered, after Peter's intervention in the Garden of Gethsemane, that there was to be no more violence. He had told them that the kingdom could never come through armed force, that they must love their enemies. If Simon mobilized his contacts to march in their tens of thousands upon Jerusalem, then the whole purpose of the past three years would be destroyed.

While Martha and her sister prepared breakfast, the men sat on the ground, accepting the truth.

10

RUSH TO JUDGMENT

He said unto them: if I tell you, ye will not believe.
Luke 22:67

The sound of the priest-trumpeter heralding a new day carried clearly to Annas and the twenty-one judges assembled in the largest of the many magnificent halls in his palace. Its lofty ceiling was supported by two rows of Corinthian pillars. Between them were window openings, their lintels decorated with molded profiles of griffins and capricorns, figures from Greek mythology. The consoles flanking the wide entrance arch were in the shape of palm trees. Above the arch, in relief, were a pair of lions. The judges sat in a semicircle of throne-like chairs in the center of the hall. Each was either a chief priest or elder of the Temple. All were practicing Sadducees. They included the judges who had spat upon and assaulted Jesus. Behind them were members of the permanent staff of the Great Sanhedrin: beadles, ushers and Levites who would fetch scrolls, summon witnesses and maintain order in the spectator area, an enclosure to one side of the seated judiciary.

Every effort had been made by Caiaphas to give the setting the aura of the supreme court. He knew from long experience how intimidating that could be: accused sometimes fainted when faced with the row of silent robed judges, and witnesses had quaked even before being bound by oath. The high priest recognized it was doubly important to create an overwhelming legal presence: Jesus was more than just another prisoner; under Jewish and Roman law the forthcoming trial would be a travesty. No witnesses had been sought to testify on his behalf. The Temple crier had not been sent forth on the previous day, the minimum notice required under the law, to announce all those who wished could attend and, if need be, give evidence providing their depositions had been properly sworn to beforehand. No formal evidence had been taken by the court in advance of the trial. No public notice had been posted in the Temple, an obligation under the Sanhedrin rules of procedure. No prior written notification had been sent to the Antonia Fortress—which would have allowed the procurator the right to send an *assessore* to the Jewish court and decide whether there was a need to intervene. When this intervention was exercised a new trial was mandatory before a Roman court, where scriptural law was inadmissible. The ancient "right of the sword" was sometimes not always easy to discern. If a religious crime had elements which impinged upon Roman law—sedition, and any challenge to the emperor's divinity were high on the list—then, while a Jewish court could pronounce a death sentence, it had to ratify the verdict with the procurator before it could be executed. It was another reminder that imperial authority overrode all else.

The studied scene-setting to suggest this would be a serious investigation had the trappings of a carefully managed show-trial. Almost certainly there was not one genuine member of the public present in the enclosure; it was filled instead with priests, Levites and Temple vendors, virtually a handpicked audience. Caiaphas entered the hall in the wake of a procession of priests who sat among the spectators, while the high priest took his place in the midst of the semicircle of robed men. The two clerks of the court who would keep the official record perched on stools at his feet.

Attention focused on the arrival of Jonathan escorting Jesus. The captain led him to a point directly in front of where Caiaphas sat; it was marked by a freshly made daub on the marble floor. Jonathan stepped back, coming to attention. He had taken no chance that a rescue might yet be attempted. Guards stood shoulder to shoulder around the courthouse, swords drawn ready. More armed men were in the archway. The tetrarch's soldiers had been withdrawn from outside the palace walls to surround the hall. It all strengthened the impression that even in custody Jesus was dangerous.

This was the moment when the *Balil Rib*, a court-appointed defense advocate, would have been asked to step forward and offer his services. None did so. Caiaphas should then have formally inquired whether Jesus intended to defend himself or send for an attorney. The question was not put.

In the strengthening light all eyes in the hall continued to stare at Jesus. Here at last was the man who had stirred the imagination of thousands, who had offered himself as the crystallization of their hopes, the symbol of their burning nationalism. Spontaneously they had elevated him to the level of the Expected One. But now he had to answer for himself. The air seethed with suppressed excitement.

Jesus' bonds had been removed but the marks of violence were visible: bruised cheeks, swollen nose and lips, puffed eyes, dried blood on his beard and a welt around his neck from the halter. Yet his gaze was calm and quietly determined as he continued to meet the cold and hostile stare of Joseph Caiaphas.

At this point the high priest should have formally reminded the court that the case would be tried under the tractate that specified "Capital charges open with a verdict of 'not guilty' and not with a verdict of 'guilty.'"

Rather, what seems to have happened is that Caiaphas rose to his feet, took a shuffling couple of paces towards Jesus, then turned and faced the judges. He said the accused, "Yeshu Hannosri," was brought before them on a capital charge grounded in the following clauses: not having the proper fear and respect of the Name in his heart but, having been moved and seduced at the instigation of Beelzebub, falsely and repeatedly claimed in this city and elsewhere to be endowed with authority and powers he did not possess; blasphemed against the Name and profaned the Temple; altered, subverted and overturned its appointed constitution; attempted to raise insurrection by various statements and actions against the Temple and the lord tetrarch, the sovereign temporal ruler.

Amid all his other activity, Caiaphas had supervised the formulation of the indictment. It was pregnant with implication, a combination of theological necessity and political convenience. It would allow for exploration of the purely Judaic offenses that Jesus had presented himself as being in kinship with God and that the superhuman powers he claimed came from demons and accounted for why he was a charismatic exorcist. Conviction on either of these counts carried a death sentence. At the same time Jesus was charged with having sought to bring the Jewish state into conflict with the rule of Rome by disputing the authority of its appointed representative, Herod Antipas. This was an offense against the imperial code, punishable by crucifixion. The underlying implication of the indictment was that, in attacking the priestly authority of the Temple, Jesus had challenged the mandate of Rome which had also appointed the high priest and upon whose power the untroubled functioning of the Temple depended. Caiaphas would have total freedom in his indictment to raise any action which had been initiated by Jesus and supported by his disciples and all those who had shown only too clearly that they believed him to be the Messiah, the divinely designated king of the Jews. While the high priest had based his strategy for the trial around that factor, and everything else would build to it, and lead from it, he knew that ultimately a conviction very much depended upon Jesus confirming he regarded himself as the Messiah.

The reading of the indictment marked the formal start of the trial. It was preceded by further breaches of procedure. There had been no roll call of the judges. This was more than a legalistic formality. It was an integral part of the law that "the spirit of God" must always favor the defendant: anything which fell short of that ideal was not permitted. At the calling of his name any judge would stand down if the prisoner was personally known to him or if there was any other reason why he could not fairly try the case. Each, for instance, should have been asked if he had any prior knowledge of the charges. The judges had been at the meetings of the Great Sanhedrin and had supported Caiaphas in his attempts to obtain an arrest warrant; having participated in those proceedings, they were precluded from trying the case. A challenge from either Jesus or somebody on his behalf at this stage could have wrecked Caiaphas' carefully crafted plan. None came. The second procedural breach was that the *Shema* had not been recited before the indictment was read. This profession of faith held an even deeper meaning in a criminal case. It was an implicit oath that those who would give evidence and try the proceedings were bound by several sacred commands of truth and fairness; they would always speak, listen and judge by the strict rules of their religion.

Caiaphas addressed his fellow judges. In trying the case they must constantly have before them the national interest—"our place and our nation." The words no doubt were chosen and spoken with care. Behind them was the specter of Roman intervention which could have deprived everyone in the hall, excepting Jesus, of their position and seen the end of Jewish autonomy. The phrase was an emotionally charged reminder that the court should remember all those who had struggled and died to achieve a measure of independence; that no one must forget the still desperate hopes and aspirations of the people behind any threat to "our place and our nation." In those words Caiaphas had conveyed an impression of Jesus cynically exploiting the masses with a new and dangerous teaching which masked a plot to destabilize the nation—and perhaps even destroy it. The high priest had reinforced fear and anger.

Jesus made no protest. He remained perfectly still, an unprepossessing figure in his soiled robes.

Caiaphas returned to his seat and ordered a court usher to summon the first witness, so further straining the legal credibility of the proceedings. The Sanhedrin tractate stipulated that immediately after the charge was put the prisoner was entitled to have the court hear argument for an acquittal on the grounds that the charges were unsupportable. There was an impressive number of precedents for such dismissals. Jesus was not invited to challenge. The law also required that adequate time be allowed after the indictment was read for a prisoner to reflect whether he or she would prefer to let the case continue in the expectation that the prosecution witnesses would be unable to establish guilt and might themselves be punished for bearing false testimony. The prospect of exacting revenge was often a decisive factor. The *lex talionis* of the biblical command—"an eye for an eye, a tooth for a tooth, a hand for a hand, a foot for a foot, burning for burning, wound for wound, bruise for bruise, life for life"—still had a strong appeal, part of the general principle of vengeance being authorized by God. But until the accused indicated his or her intention, hearing of evidence for the prosecution could not begin. No one questioned a further lapse from normal procedure. Jesus continued to gaze impassively at the judges.

The various and flagrant breaches of the Jewish legal system would have serious and far-reaching consequences. Ultimately they would make it all the more difficult to establish what did occur in the pale light of a new day in that hall. Unraveling the facts, deciphering the many ramifications of the proceedings, requires a clear understanding of a number of separate yet interrelated factors.

The first, and the root cause of all subsequent difficulties, were to arise from early Christian doctrinal interests. Struggling to survive, then to expand, the faith of the Fathers of the early Church needed a focal point. Unable in the beginning, from a sheer lack of numerical strength, to apportion any blame upon the Roman imperial system whose evils had spawned a renewed yearning for the Messiah, and subsequently unwilling to do so—Rome, through the emperor Constantine, eventually became the way for the Church to expand—it became an act of Christian faith that *the Jews* arrested him, brutalized him and staged undoubtedly the most celebrated show-trial in history. A web of vile circumstances, woven by a few, became the mesh from which an entire people would not be allowed to escape.

The stigma of collective guilt upon the entire Jewish people would form the source of the harassments, the humiliations and the pogroms which culminated in the Holocaust. Jews would be expelled, uprooted, looted, pillaged and vilified for what was done in their name in that palace in Jerusalem on a spring morning when anti-Semitism was already rife. The events in that courtroom would foster the great collision between one of the oldest religions and a lusty upstart of a faith which, in the spirit of the time, would have no compunction in distorting truth to give semblance to *the Jews* having collectively provided the true climax to a night of genuine horror for Jesus: all that followed would flow from that monumental misrepresentation.

The truth of what happened in that hall—between perjured witnesses and a handful of morally bankrupt priest-lawyers—would be further removed from reality by an understandable, yet seriously flawed, attempt to rebut the monstrous allegations against *the Jews.* The claim would be made that what Caiaphas and his cohorts intended to appear as a legally constituted full trial was in reality an *inquiry*. Such dangerous dissembling would be a crude attempt to rewrite history that in a way is as historically improper as shifting the responsibility upon the entire Jewish people. But Jewish apologists would make much of there being no Christians in the courtroom, or that there was no likely way Christians could have had access to an objective account of the trial proceedings; that, in any event, followers of Jesus were primarily peasants with no grasp of the subtleties of legal procedures and would be unable to distinguish one kind from another. Such a multi-accusation has been disputed on the grounds there is no evidence that some of those in the courtroom did *not* subsequently become converts to Christianity; indeed the annals of the early Church are filled with accounts of Jews and Romans who embraced his teaching. On the matter of the trial record, again what may have happened is that as well as the official court clerks there were also certainly present the secretaries of the judges, keeping records for their masters; it would perhaps not be entirely fanciful if one of them had made available his account, to form subsequently the basis for the Gospel versions. More sustainable would be the argument that Matthew was far from being an uneducated peasant. As a tax collector he had been grounded in law and would certainly have known the difference between a *trial* and an *inquiry*. But what at least can only be a rough approximation of what happened could be lost in the welter of anti-Semitic polemics.

Early Christian calumny that not a handful of Jews but *the Jews* were implicated in the trial of Jesus would produce an intense and degrading hostility between two religions bound by an umbilical cord which cannot be severed: the Old Testament. The Gospels, Acts, the Epistles of Paul, right to the last verse of the book of Revelation would grow from that earlier testament. All Christian claims for Jesus would be based in Scripture from that source; a belief in the primacy of its faith would be based upon the texts of the Pentateuch. Without the books of Israel there could be no meaningful testament of Christianity. Yet, because of what Jesus suffered on that night—shock, outrage and travail—the understandable and righteous wrath of his followers, perhaps even their claims to vengeance, would be extended to far beyond those directly involved and solely responsible—a few Jewish notables who, out of ignorance and fear, set out to destroy a man who had done his best to help the afflicted and those with sin. The behavior of the priests in that hall, acting secretly and illegally, could never, by any accounting, be taken as representing the legitimate will of the Jewish people, yet it would be presented as such.

A great deal of energy would be expended to try to establish discrepancies within the testimony of those not actually present: Matthew, Mark,

Luke and John. Matthew and Mark would, incorrectly, set the trial as taking place during the night. Luke would indicate, correctly, that there were no proceedings during the hours of darkness. From this simple and relatively unimportant mistake would grow the Jewish argument that if the apostles could be wrong on timing they could be in error in other areas. John's Gospel, the most anti-Semitic of the evangelical accounts, would, for that reason, be called in defense of Jewish claims. Much would be made by apologists of John's omission of any mention of the trial in the hall. Why should he, of all the apostles, would run the argument, miss this opportunity further to blacken the name of *the Jews*? It is an unattractive question which takes no account of how much else John excluded. His Gospel is the most selective; that does not give it any more, or less, historical authority. Equally the other accounts should not be treated with suspicion when measured against John's. His silence apart, they based them on what they discovered actually happened in that hall.

The first prosecution witness stood a few feet to the right of Jesus, facing the semicircle. Defense witnesses would have given evidence from his left. Each witness in a capital charge had to be solemnly put on oath, have its significance explained and be given a firm reminder of the punishment for false testimony. Caiaphas ignored the requirement.

At this stage Annas rose to his feet to begin establishing that Jesus was guilty of blasphemy, had threatened the Temple and planned an insurrection; it fits into what is known about Sadducee legal procedure, which allowed the most senior judge, next to the high priest, to cross-examine. It was a task for which the old priest was well suited. In spite of his years Annas had retained a rhetorical delicacy, a mental capacity to juggle, to ridicule, and to make the most innocent action appear the product of an evil and calculating mind. His working life had after all been spent in continual meditation upon the *corpus divini* of the Jewish penal code.

Assuming he was no different from any advocate, the examination would have quickly developed its own pace, a litany of standard questions and answers. Where had the witness first seen the accused? On that day Jesus had arrived at the Eastern Gate on a donkey. Did he know the significance of that gate? It had been built by Solomon for the Expected One. What had people said when they saw him on the back of a donkey? That he had come to free them. Why? Because they said he fulfilled the prediction of Scripture. Had he resisted that claim? No.

An interrogation along such lines would have been important to establish the expectations of Jesus being the Messiah and a liberation leader. Annas would then have had to confirm the popular concept of the Messiah: that his appearance would be preceded by a precursor—Elijah. The interrogation and responses continued. Had the witness seen any evidence that the prophet was once more among the people? No. But Jesus had been acclaimed? Yes. How could the witness explain that? Jesus had deceived the crowd. How? By his silence. An answer along such lines would have helped to imply that Jesus not only had a special relationship with God—but was determined not to deny it. The offense to Jewish religious susceptibilities had been rooted. The questioning continued. Before he had seen the prisoner had he heard of him? Yes: his preaching was widely known to be about a kingdom over which he would rule and which only those who obeyed him could enter; all others would perish. Did he believe that? No. Why not? It was talk that would arouse the Romans.

Annas would have needed to set about establishing a direct link between that dire prospect and Jesus' entry into Jerusalem.

What had the witness felt in the presence of such a throng? Coached by Caiaphas, the witness remembered. Fear. He had felt fear. Why had he felt fear? What had made him fearful? "Fear." "Fearful"? The words echoed around the hall. The man expressed what some undoubtedly may have felt: an unease that Jesus *could* have such power. What had the mob shouted? Hosannas. That he was king. Words like that. Swiftly and smoothly, "fear" had been followed by "mob," "shouted" and finally a claim to "kingship." The whiff of insurrection drifted in the air from the judges' semicircle to the spectators and back to Annas. It is by such advocacy—if not the precise detail, then the substance—that men like Annas are remembered.

Jesus had been established as the harbinger of the long-awaited apocalyptic revolution. He had presented himself as ready to overthrow the existing political and social order, end Roman domination and restore the Chosen People to their rightful place. Whatever the merits of such a vision, Annas had managed to imply such a role was reserved solely for the Expected One.

So it could have continued. When had the witness next seen the accused? In the Temple. Where in the Temple? Near his stall. What was the defendant doing? Destroying other stalls. It would only have been natural for Annas to let the impact of the scene once more settle over the courtroom. *Destroying stalls in the Temple.* No further repetition would have been needed: Annas' silence had its own telling eloquence; it seemed to say he did not have to remind them where matters would have ended if Jesus had not been brought to justice.

By this stage Annas had established what he had set out to do: not only had Jesus offered himself as the Messiah but he had begun to fulfill the mob's expectations through violence; that beneath the teaching claims he made for his ministry—the nation would only be delivered from bondage if they followed him—lay an altogether more dangerous intention.

To discover what that was required Annas to show that Jesus was familiar with Temple procedures and customs. His own mother had purchased a bird for sacrifice after his birth and he knew there were no legitimate grounds to attack the traders and overturn "the tables of the money changers and the seats of them that sold doves." What, then, had driven him to do so a few days ago? Annas would have left the court in no doubt. Jesus' action was not against a handful of tradesmen, earning a legitimate living, but was directed at the Temple administration. It was a deliberate and premeditated attempt to gain control of the Temple and dispose of all those lawfully appointed to run its affairs. The first rumble of anger had come from the spectators as Annas wove a damning portrait which went far beyond any temporary interference with petty business transactions. Jesus had made the first probing move to launching wholesale insurrection.

The ensuing questions and answers were designed to confirm the extent of this sinister design: Jesus on the rampage; the posse of men protecting him; the mob cheering him on; the vendors, honest God-fearing men, helpless in the face of such evil violence.

Annas would have failed in his task if he had not turned and faced the semicircle of judges and asked what clearer evidence did they need that an act of blasphemy had been established? Jesus had come in the guise of a pilgrim but was plotter-in-chief of a monstrous plan. Nor was there any question that he had behaved impulsively. What he had done had been a carefully prepared attack. The court should look upon his action as that of someone not only filled with evil intent towards the chief priests but falsely proclaiming his own messianic mission. Who would deny that in the guise of religion he had not sought to take absolute power? How easy it is to hear the deadly trip of the questions and to accept the premise of the judges staring at Jesus, waiting to see if he would offer any challenge.

Jesus remained silent.

The next witness was sworn; the same corroborative evidence. Had he been terrified at the destruction the accused had unleashed? He had. Had he been too terrified to oppose the violence? He had. Even when the defendant had destroyed his own stall? Yes. Had others been equally terrified? They had.

(All the Gospels—not just the four evangelical accounts but the other books discreetly discarded by the early Fathers of the Church at their councils at Nicea and Chalcedon—suggest that events in the great hall unfolded broadly along these lines.)

Annas set about nailing down another plank. Had Jesus been alone? No: he was accompanied by his usual followers and some of the mob who had called him the Messiah on the previous day. What had they done? Supported his actions. Once more Annas had cleverly exposed the threat of insurrection. He would have needed to return to Jesus' behavior so as to leave no room for doubt. Did the witness remember what Jesus had said during this destruction? After being tutored by Caiaphas, the witness did: that the Temple was a place of thieves. Was there any basis for that reaction? No. Had he ever heard anybody else refer to the Temple activities in that way? No. Like any astute lawyer, Annas would not have overlooked a chance to bolster favorable testimony with the law; in this instance it provided for the Temple to offer a number of ancillary commercial services in conjunction with its religious role: the Temple was a bank and a treasury and it derived valuable income from such facilities. Any challenge to that could be construed as an attack on the sacerdotal authorities and seem as yet another step to the rebellion Jesus had plotted.

Again it is not hard to envisage Annas turning back to the witness. What else had Jesus said? He would destroy the Temple. What had he taken this to mean? That Jesus would use magic to accomplish the feat; it was impossible by any other means.

Annas would not really have needed to remind the court that such a clear and carefully articulated prophecy could indeed only be construed as being aimed at the religious heart of the nation. The threat to Jewish survival had been buttressed. The spectator area seethed at this proof that Jesus had intended to commit the ultimate act of violence which gave further substance to the charge of insurrection.

Witnesses came and went, stitching together a portrait of a man who traveled the land working his spells by the power of Beelzebub. Inevitably there was one who testified to his shock at being told the accused had brought Lazarus back to life, and that it was either fraud or induced through sorcery; another said he had seen Jesus restore sight and was convinced it had been done through the power of darkness; a third insisted the look on Jesus' face when he had destroyed the money changers' booths was of someone possessed by the Evil Eye. A guard who had been in the Gethsemane arresting party said he personally heard Jesus threaten to call upon a host of angels to help him. What kind of angels? The messengers of the Evil Eye. Caiaphas would hardly have needed to remind the court about these fallen angels who made their lairs in trees and went about their wicked work under cover of darkness. The inference was only too clear: what better place for Jesus to plot than among the olive groves of Gethsemane, with the evil hosts ready to do his bidding? Why, with their help, if he had not been seized, he would now be on the way to Galilee to gather the Zealots for an all-out attack on the Temple. In gilding the prosecution case, none had been more eloquent than Annas as he continued to enhance the image of Jesus as a dangerous revolutionary.

Jesus said not a word.

Yet another witness took the stand. It may have been a momentary relaxation on the part of the old priest, it may have been overeagerness on the part of the witness: the reason would be lost—but not the effect. The man said he was sure Jesus had made the threat against the Temple on the *same* day he rode through the mob. Annas moved to head off disaster. He urged the witness to remember. Surely it had happened on the *following* day? The man looked doubtful. Perhaps. But he was certain of one thing: it had occurred *after* morning prayers. Think again, rasped Annas. Had it not been *before* morning prayers? The hapless man pleaded that the fear he had felt at the time had confused him. Perhaps it had been *early* in the morning.

A furiously disappointed murmur came from the spectators. This time the judges dared not publicly ignore the tractate that specified the slightest contradiction by witnesses for the prosecution rendered all previous testimony invalid.

Annas waved away the man and abandoned calling further evidence.

In spite of this spectacular failure the parade of witnesses must, inevitably, have made an impact—the more so because their perjury had passed without challenge. Ironically, Jesus, who had offered as the basis for his teaching the ideal "Blessed are they which are persecuted for righteousness' sake for theirs is the kingdom of heaven," by that same silence which brought him closer to his preordained fate also ensured that countless millions of other Jews would suffer torment, degradation and persecution in centuries to come; they would find small consolation in those words he had spoken on Mount Hattin. "Blessed are ye, when men shall revile you, and persecute you, and shall say all manner of evil against you falsely, for my sake. Rejoice and be exceeding glad: for great is your reward in heaven." Through accident or by intent the Christian monopoly of truth would ensure that the matter of responsibility for what was happening in that hall would be obfuscated, and all Jews forever blamed for a trial whose ultimate and sole responsibility rested upon an old man and his son-in-law.

The Court of the Gentiles was once more filled with pilgrims come to make their offerings. Mingling with them were the usual *goyim*, men and women nonbelievers, come to meet a landlord, settle a debt or enter into a contract. Pagans and believers were united in discussing a number of puzzling features: Solomon's Portico was virtually deserted of traders; there was not a Temple guard in view; only a solitary priest stood vigil at the Nicanor Gate.

Those first through the Eastern Gate had noticed Caiaphas hurry from the podium and that he had not been seen since. Nicodemus and Gamaliel had arrived and gathered the twenty-three other Pharisee judges of the

Great Sanhedrin into one of the courts of the Temple that led from the Royal Porch. Its door had been closed behind them. The more knowledgeable wondered if it marked the start of some new doctrinal dispute with the Sadducees. The absence of the sect's judge-priests caused further speculation; something had happened, or was about to; but no one could say what, or when it would occur.

Pilgrims who had camped on either side of the Golden Gate recounted the disturbance of the night and the glimpse of soldiers hustling along a prisoner. In the past few days there had been several arrests in the hills. The most notable had been that of the capture of a Zealot leader, an elderly warrior who could no longer outrun his captors. He was known as Barabbas of Galilee. He had been handed over to the Romans and languished in the Antonia Fortress; it was a foregone conclusion he would be crucified.

Travelers from the Bethany area reported there was still no sign of the man upon whom they had begun to attach so many hopes, the one they increasingly called the Expected One. Jesus had not been seen in public for the past twenty-four hours. The more cynical speculated whether he would turn out to be another of those self-styled messiahs. Old men in the courtyard would still have remembered those heady days when the Master of Justice of the Essenes had briefly claimed himself to be divine; there were those who recalled praying that either Judas of Gamala or Sadduck the Pharisee was the Messiah. Those who had experienced previous disappointments wondered if they were about to do so again; that, while Jesus had been more dramatic and direct in his impact, he could still turn out to be no more than a symptom of the national desperation.

Very likely no one paid any special attention to a trio of women, one old and frail, the other in her middle years, their companion younger: the courtyard was always filled with such anxious-faced pilgrims. Mary, the mother of Jesus, Mary the mother of two of his apostles and grandmother to a third, and Mary Magdalene, who loved him with devotion and unconsummated passion, were filled with growing fear as they tried to discover his whereabouts. At Annas' palace, the portress at the servants' gate, hearing their broad Galilean accents, had very likely eyed them suspiciously. They had hurried to the Temple, the natural source for all news. But no one had answers for their diffident inquiries. No one probably noticed—why should they?—the man who walked through the crowd. Judas' presence would only be verified by what he was about to do.

Back in the hall, undoubtedly concerned to regain the initiative, Caiaphas needed to establish that Jesus had deliberately thrust himself forward as the symbol of Jewish nationalism. To do so he asked a series of questions designed to lay out the historical situation of Jesus: how he had grown up in a milieu of alternating violence and tension; how his formative years had been influenced by the apocalyptic plans of terrorists like Judas of Gamala and later by visits to the Sepphoris theater. Who could doubt that there, among the painted faces, he had learned how to make a continued attack upon established authority? Who could doubt that there he had developed his contacts with the criminal *kanna-im* movement, the Zealots? When Judas of Gamala had been executed, his followers had fled to the desert. Was that the real reason he had gone to the Wilderness? To make contact with the surviving criminals? Was it there he had first planned the assault on the Temple? Was it there he had prepared his attack on the existing legal system? Was it there that he had planned a social structure that would leave the legally appointed authority of the land helpless? Was it there that he had perfected his sorcery? Who could doubt there was a menace about the question that even Annas had not equalled?

There was no response from Jesus.

Caiaphas needed to introduce the arrest of Barabbas, to portray the Zealot who had been captured close to Gethsemane as a pitiless killer. Where had he and Jesus met? Where had they plotted? With Barabbas arrested, had Jesus been about to take over his followers? Were his own disciples no different to the Zealots?

Circling Jesus, careful to keep a distance as if he might have feared contamination by coming too close, Caiaphas continued asking questions about the disciples and their sobriquets. Was it not true that *Shi'mon* was a professed Zealot? That Peter was known in Capernaum as *Banjora*—Terrorist? That the brothers, *Ya'kob* and *Johanan*, James and John, were called *Boanerges*, Thunderers, because of their threatening behavior? That the *son of Tolmai*, Bartholomew, had been a renowned fighter round the taverns of Galilee? That not one of the apostles was a placid man, content to follow his faith like all good Jews? Were they not similar to the one called *lover of horses*, Philip, given to violence, even threatening the lawful agents of the Temple? Were they not like the one born with a Greek name, *Didymus*, who now called himself Thomas, but for whom no change of name could disguise a revolutionary nature? Had not even *Matthai* been seduced from his lawful work, however unpleasant those in the court would find such an occupation, to help launch a movement that from the beginning had been concerned with rebellion? The impact of the high priest's examination was made that much more impressive by Jesus continuing to remain silent, staring fixedly ahead.

Caiaphas explored other matters. Had Jesus not reviled the lord tetrarch? Had he not claimed total authority over those who listened to him? Then, once more, had Jesus not done everything to undermine the very citadel of the nation's authority, namely the Temple? The questions still failed to produce a solitary response or reaction.

The high priest had to dispose of another matter. Jesus was *not* to be grouped with other itinerant preachers: for all their doctrinal fallibility, they were men of essential passivity. But they did not have a contempt for the Temple's authority, which was clearly stated in the book of Deuteronomy: "The man that will do presumptuously, and will not hearken unto the priest that standeth to minister before the Lord thy God, or unto the judge, even that man shall die." Jesus, imbued with his own authority as eschatological prophet, had refused to submit his teaching or himself to the authority of the Temple. Moreover, from the outset of his ministry, Jesus had been preoccupied with action, at every turn determined to prey on the ignorance of people. Whatever else he could *not* lay title to, there could be no denying he *was* a political leader; that the purpose of his ministry was not primarily religious but to excite the crowd into accepting him as their deliverer. Even his teaching reinforced that. Caiaphas could have quoted passages his agents had noted which all amounted to one thing: Jesus was *not* a man concerned with doctrinal issues. He was preoccupied with action—action and violence were opposite sides of the same coin.

The interrogation conveyed only too clearly the obsessive fear that Jesus was imbued with demonic powers, whose most dramatic manifestation had been seen in the triumphal entry. That everything he had done had been in preparation for arousing the people on the eve of the *Pesah*. The consummate skill of the high priest reminded them of the sound and tumult of that climactic moment, presenting it as a supreme example of his defiance of Scripture, a belief he had the right to reinterpret Holy Law. Yet, absolutely to ensure a conviction, Caiaphas constantly kept to the fore that, behind Jesus' visions and predictions, was a man who had inherited the sheathed dagger of Judas of Gamala, and was even more dangerous because he knew how to stir people with his claim to heal the sick and raise the dead. Performing such tricks to heighten public passions, and deluding people to the point of hysteria into allowing him to enter the city on the back of an animal to fulfill a promise of the Name: what else was all that but a clear attempt to raise a rebellion? What had the mob called him? "The king!" They had heard the witnesses. All had agreed upon that. "The king!" That had been followed by physical assault upon the very Temple. How else could that be regarded other than as a prelude to insurrection? Were not he and his men *biastai*, the violent ones? Whatever of this kingdom he spoke of—did he not intend to seize it by force? And in proclaiming a kingdom he had set himself up in direct opposition to the lord tetrarch, the Temple and, of course, the Romans. That was rebellion. Nothing would soften the hammer-blows. No one could deny what followed.

Caiaphas turned and confronted Jesus with yet another question. Dared he challenge one word?

There would be those who were not there who would claim Jesus looked at the high priest "calmly and with authority," "without a trace of fear," "knowing what he must say." Perhaps.

But his words would become a matter of acceptable record. "If I tell you, ye will not believe."

Caiaphas stood closer to Jesus, an arm-length separating them, no doubt staring into his eyes, no doubt waiting.

There would be those who would recount that Jesus had "stared back with certainty," had "never wavered in his gaze."

The certainty is that, when Jesus spoke again, the words were framed as a question, but offered as a statement. "And if I also ask you ye will not answer me, nor let me go."

Everyone in the hall must only too clearly have realized a critical moment had been reached. Somehow Caiaphas had forced Jesus to remain silent no longer. His decision to speak, to reveal himself, was all the more unexpected because Jesus had hitherto seemed untroubled by the relentless pressure of the examination.

Caiaphas weighed his words. "Art thou the Christ?"

Jesus repeated what he had said. "If I tell you, ye will not believe."

Caiaphas must have sensed how close he was. His last question had been delivered with the ring of metal striking metal. Jesus had hesitated for a moment. Now, without any prompting, he moved a sentence closer to the victory the high priest sought. "Hereafter, shall the Son of man sit on the right hand of the power of God."

Caiaphas held his breath.

Suddenly, Jesus was close to destroying himself. Casually, and not at all declamatory, as if he was raising a question in a Temple debate, knowing he was master of the situation, the high priest asked:

"Art thou then the Son of God?"

Jesus did not hesitate. "Ye say that I am."

A collective gasp came from the court. Jesus had done what no one in Judea had ever done, what Abraham, Jacob, Moses, and all the other great prophets had never considered doing: he had made himself the equal of God. He had made himself God. There could be no greater blasphemy.

Caiaphas turned away, suddenly weary. Slowly he raised a hand and then ripped his tunic. The gesture was not a histrionic response to victory; it was the ritual prescribed for any priest who had heard a blasphemy uttered. Around him other priests were tearing their garments, not along a seam, but in the middle of the cloth so that the damage was beyond repair and the skin exposed over the heart, a sign of grief.

Caiaphas addressed the judges. "He hath spoken blasphemy. What further need have we of witnesses? . . . What think ye?"

Once more procedure was ignored. In capital trials voting was designed to avoid the senior members of the bench influencing their juniors. The youngest member voted first, then a verdict was given by each judge in ascending order of seniority. The high priest would normally have been the last to cast his vote. But Caiaphas had made clear his own feelings on what the verdict should be. One by one, they gave the same answer. "He is guilty of death."

The high priest had a final matter to settle. He told the court that not only had Jesus been found guilty of blasphemy but he had also committed crimes punishable under Roman law. To claim divinity was a direct affront to the emperor and a capital offense. Imperial law also prescribed the death penalty for anyone convicted of threatening a sacred building, and that protection had been extended to include the Temple. Further, the court had seen how Jesus had refused to offer any defense to the many questions put to establish political crimes which were further offenses under Roman law. Therefore Jesus must be sent forthwith to the Antonia Fortress to be dealt with by the procurator. The judges agreed.

Caiaphas left the hall, the bells of his regalia the only sound to break the silence. By sending Jesus to Pilate the possibility of a defeat within the Great Sanhedrin had been avoided.

11

ROMAN RESPONSES

And Pilate asked him again; saying: Answerest thou nothing?

Luke 15:4

Since sunrise on the day that would become known as Good Friday, Pontius Pilate had been at work in his salon. The large room resembled a counting house as the collectors responsible for tax gathering arrived with bulging *pundas* of coins.

The procurator derived considerable satisfaction from this most important task. There was the spur of showing Rome that once more he had increased the amount of tax gathered, something his predecessors had never managed, and the challenge, one which required his total concentration, of dealing with the collectors: they were sharp and devious and always ready to seize an opportunity to cheat. But not even the most rapacious would dare to go about his business during the forthcoming week. Judea, in an administrative, legal and commercial sense, would cease to exist during Passover. Even Golgotha would be cleared of its crucified by this nightfall. The two convicted thieves being held in the fortress before carrying their crosses to the mound would find their agony that much shorter when they reached there. If they had not succumbed before sunset they would be killed by a centurion's spear.

Because of its importance—this salon was where her husband made all his administrative decisions and received visitors while in the Jewish capital—Claudia Procula had given extra thought and care to its decoration and furnishings. The stone walls had been chiseled to a smooth tawny-colored finish and adorned with paintings and tapestries depicting scenes from

Roman mythology. The furniture was the finest Rome could offer, including several pieces she had inherited from her grandfather's palace. A bust of the emperor Augustus stood on a marble plinth behind the handsomely carved table which served as Pilate's desk. The sculpture was a reminder of her hope that one day he would also be sufficiently important to be immortalized in marble. Placed around the salon were divans and the statues of imperial gods and the floor was covered with rugs from Persia, India and China. At one end were wide stone steps that led down from the procuratorial sleeping quarters; a heavy curtain drawn across the upper stairway protected the bedrooms from prying eyes. The salon was ordinarily a magnificent example of Roman taste surpassed only by that of his wife one floor below. Now it was the focal point of a sordid business. At the outset of his administration Pilate had recognized how effective it was to gather taxes when the Jews were concentrated in one place and during the ten days the procurator had been in Jerusalem the collectors had combed the city and hills. Each man had his own team to reinforce demands; a few cudgel blows and the threat of more severe punishment were usually sufficient to quell resistance from any who hesitated to pay his dues. On the previous day a collector and his men had been working their way through an encampment on the road to Jericho when a force of Zealots led by Barabbas attacked them. One of the tetrarch's cohorts patrolling the area came to the rescue. There had been a skirmish in which several of the tax collectors had been killed before the Zealots fled. In the pursuit Barabbas had been captured and brought to the fortress. Pilate had not yet sentenced him to death.

That incident apart, the collectors had gathered their usual levies for income tax, poll tax, road tax, toll-bridge tax, house tax, boundary tax, market tax, meat tax and salt tax. There was even a tax payable by all pilgrims for the right to enter or reside in Jerusalem during the Passover period. It was a thorough system and one impossible to evade. After Passover the collectors would pursue any outstanding debt to the remotest corner of the country. They were encouraged to do so because an imperial edict allowed them to garner for themselves any additional money they could obtain; from this source they paid their own men and built often substantial fortunes. Impositions were so financially crippling that victims were frequently driven to flight or suicide. Their families were then invariably shipped to the slave markets of the empire by the collectors, who divided the purchase price with their Roman masters.

Before a collector left the salon he deposited a sum in Pilate's personal coffer. The amount was calculated against the official tax collected—the assumption being that the larger a collector's return the greater his own personal profit. This form of cynical exploitation was common throughout the procurator's staff. Each Roman official received payment from those who called at the fortress seeking imperial seals and signatures on documents granting permission to work in a garrison, to become a supplier to the occupying forces, to be exempt from an order to provide free grain and meat to a local fort or free transport for the army. There was a bribe payable for every service. The largest was for an exemption from having to deal with the Roman businessmen who roamed the countryside and cornered the harvest at often half its true value and then sold off the crop for substantial profits in other parts of the empire. A Jewish landowner could pay the equivalent of a worker's salary for a year to have one of Pilate's men provide a scroll which said his crop was reserved for the Judean market.

If Pilate needed a pause from his scrutiny of the counting and apportioning of money, the windows of the salon provided views of the Temple courtyards, the Lower City, Herod Antipas' palace and the hills around Jerusalem and immediately below the huge fortress courtyard with its iron scourging post. The thickness of a mature cypress tree trunk and three feet tall, it stood in the center of the courtyard. A prisoner would be stripped naked and fastened to shackles at the top and bottom so that his body was tautly arched against the post. He was then lashed with a scourge, strips of leather, each with a slug of metal or animal bone at the end; under Roman law the face and genitalia could also be beaten. There was also scourging to death, in which a man was cut to the bone, his skin left hanging in shreds and his innards spilt on to the ground. Julius Caesar had decreed that the scourging was too severe for Italian soldiers to administer; Pilate's entourage included two Syrian conscripts who shared the task. The Jews had a modified form of the punishment, using a rod for blows to the shoulders and buttocks, limiting them to the scriptural "forty stripes save one."

At this hour Pilate saw no sign of unusual activity beyond the fortress walls. Sentries patrolled on the tetrarch's battlements. Annas' palace seemed as deserted as it always did. Now that the vendors had appeared in the Temple courtyards, there was the usual bustle to buy last-minute sacrifices; by late afternoon the last of the unsold sheep and birds would be removed for Passover. In the hills pilgrims were on the move once more, and no doubt informers would have begun to report that priests were moving through the city and encampments spreading the word that, far from being the Expected One, Jesus had planned to attack the Temple with the help of Barabbas. Pilate would not have been surprised to learn that a groundswell of feeling against Jesus was developing: he had always said that Jews were even more fickle than those Romans who patronized the arena in Rome.

Nevertheless, it would be prudent for him not to ignore warnings that Barabbas' compatriots could launch a reprisal attack on the procurator's column when it headed north to Caesarea in a week's time. While Pilate could have had little doubt that his vastly superior force—a full-strength legion, six thousand men—would be able to drive off even the most fanatical assault, there would undoubtedly be Roman casualties which would have to be reported. Administrators had been punished before for what Sejanus decided was an unnecessary loss of men. Rather than provoke confrontation Pilate would want to avoid it.

Very possibly, as the hagiography of the Christian Coptic Church claims, the procurator was once more interrupted by the return of the fortress commander asking for a decision on Barabbas.

The commander felt that Barabbas should be executed with the thieves. Probably not for the first time Pilate took the long view: if Barabbas remained alive for the moment there was a better chance the Zealots would hold off retaliatory action, perhaps even doing so in the hope that Barabbas might at least be spared the ignominy of the cross to die in the *zystus*, the Hippodrome built by Herod the Great, and one of the dominant features of the Lower City, with its outer walls rimmed with gold, silver and precious stones. Every week, except during Jewish festivities, gladiatorial shows were staged for the benefit of the Romans and the tetrarch's soldiers in which men fought to the death against each other and lions and leopards. Criminals were regularly sent to the arena rather than to Golgotha.

Any decision on Barabbas was overshadowed by the news that Jesus was about to be delivered to the fortress. Pilate's reaction was understandable, if only because already during his time in Jerusalem he had been confronted with what must have seemed arrogant demands. Pilgrims from Egypt had delivered a petition to the fortress reminding him that the Jewish community in Alexandria possessed total autonomous jurisdiction in *all* cases. Could not the same freedom be enjoyed by Judean courts? A group of Jewish lawyers from Sardes had written that an edict of Julius Caesar gave them civil jurisdiction over Roman citizens. Would the procurator support their proposed appeal to Rome to grant a similar privilege for the Jerusalem courts? Pilate had no doubt fumed that such arrogance only confirmed the more freedom Rome gave Jews the more they wanted. The impending arrival of Jesus furthered his anger with the Temple for daring to have proceeded without advance notice with a capital-charge trial and then arrogantly to refer Jesus for sentencing under Roman law.

Caiaphas, Annas and other Sadducee priests had prepared the scroll listing the tractates under which Jesus had been convicted. The parchment also indicated the infractions of Roman law. The paperwork would accompany him to the Antonia Fortress. They were interrupted by the arrival of Judas Iscariot, whose attitude must only have confirmed Caiaphas' view that he had been right not to call the treasurer to give evidence. Judas was agitated. Caiaphas gave him a purse containing the thirty pieces of silver.

Judas put the bag on the table upon which Caiaphas had been preparing the scroll and lamented: "I have sinned . . . I have betrayed the innocent blood!"

It may have been Annas who picked up the *punda*, threw the purse at Judas and ordered him to leave.

Judas ran from the office, very probably still shouting in remorse and despair. As he passed the altar in the Court of the Priests he opened his bag and hurled the coins at the startled sacrificers and, still screaming, continued through the Nicanor Gate and out of the Temple by the Mourner's Gate, and on through the Lower City to the Golden Gate. He finally halted his headlong progress at an outcrop of rock high over the boundary-strewn Hinnom valley and its smoldering refuse fires. There were several trees growing on the outcrop. The treasurer chose one and climbed its trunk. Standing on a branch he removed the girdle from around his robe and, with some difficulty fashioned one end into a noose and tied the other to a bough above his head. He then placed the noose around his neck and stepped into space. He may still have been alive when the girdle broke, sending his body plunging on to the rocks below. The Acts of the Apostles would recount how he "burst asunder in the midst and all his bowels gushed out."

While the treasurer was plunging to his death, the sacrificers had recovered the money and taken it to Caiaphas' office. Once more the high priest was forced to interrupt his work, this time to deal with a minor point of law. The silver could not be placed in the Temple treasury because it was contaminated. Equally, it would be unthinkable not to make use of it. After a brief discussion, it was decided that the coins could be used to purchase a plot of land near the Golden Gate as a burial place for pilgrims who died on a visit to the city. Caiaphas then summoned Jonathan and ordered him to prepare to take Jesus before Pilate.

Pilate was hampered in deciding how to prepare for the arrival of Jesus through a lack of information. He did not yet know what Jesus had been charged with or convicted upon. It would have been perfectly sensible for Pilate to have ordered a halt in the procession of collectors while he sent for the two *assessores*, the advocates who could advise him on any point of law in a Roman trial.

The lawyers were young and cautious. Jerusalem was a junior posting in the imperial legal service; their hope would be to complete their tour of duty without making serious mistakes and either return to Rome or be sent to a more congenial and important part of the empire. They would have tempered advice with caution, but no matter how hesitant they were in recommending any specific action they would know there was no precedent for the Jews to transfer a prisoner to Roman jurisdiction on the eve of the most important religious festival of the Jewish year.

Within their enclosure in the Temple, Nicodemus, Gamaliel and the other Pharisee judges heard nothing to reassure them there had not been a grave miscarriage of justice. The broad sweep of their discussion must have taken into account that the conflict between Jesus and the Temple on doctrinal and politico-religious grounds required a full and proper examination. Caiaphas had been all too clearly wrong, in both a legal and a moral sense, to stop at the one question, "Art thou the Son of God?" He should have pressed the matter after Jesus', at best, ambiguous answer. It had not even begun to be established that Jesus had arrogated to himself an exalted relationship with God which would satisfy any Pharisee judge. Further, the law contained the proviso that a *unanimous* verdict of guilt presupposed bias on the part of the court. In Jesus' case that should have meant his automatic acquittal. These were serious issues. The prelude to Passover was clearly not the time to probe them, and it would be far more sensible if the whole matter could be postponed for a later date, when both the pilgrims and Pilate would have left Jerusalem and the Temple judges and scholars could deliberate in their usual careful manner.

Such a laudable sentiment became irrelevant, as did the role of the Pharisees, with the report that Jesus was about to pass out of the jurisdiction of the Jews and into that of Rome.

Among the apocalyptic literary forms used to couch early Christian faith—writings, it must be added, that often reflect a naive positivism—are accounts of Claudia Procula receiving her husband early on in the morning in her salon, no doubt an oasis of silk and perfumes in the midst of militaria. She immediately launched herself upon a further account of her dream. Her obvious distress would survive in her words; there was also a revealing passion about them. "Have thou nothing to do with that just man: for I have suffered many things this day in a dream because of him."

Her plea was grave and urgent and that much more important and significant because the dream must have lost some of its initial terror. She had had time to think and had become a woman deeply troubled and concerned to stop her husband becoming embroiled in a situation she recognized as highly dangerous. Was this ambitious, willful and highly strung woman purely concerned with *their* future—and only wanted to avoid any precipitate action that could affect it, especially at such an emotionally charged time as Passover? Her well-developed understanding of Jewish attitudes would have left her in no doubt that for the Romans to become involved with the fate of Jesus could have an effect on her husband's career; if civil unrest ensued, it was bound to bring criticism—or worse—from Rome. Was that the sole reason she had taken the highly unusual step of interrupting her husband at work and sending for him? Clearly, Claudia Procula was a woman desperate to get across the point that her husband must not, under any circumstances, involve himself with the case of Jesus. No longer did she bother to keep secret her own attitude. For her Jesus was a "just man." Then she had added a poignant and wifely appeal: she had suffered, perhaps greatly, from what she had learned in the dream; only her husband could ensure she would endure no more. They were the words of a woman in torment; a virtual confession: she had come under the impress of his spiritual message and it finally had wrenched from her the admission that he *was* a powerful influence on her life—a "just man." In accepting and admitting that, she had rejected all she had been taught to revere: paganism, emperor- and idol-worship, the indisputable authority of Rome. Hers were the words of someone suffering all the agony of withdrawing from the past into an uncertain future. A sentence of such brevity had conveyed so perfectly her position. The words were a determined effort to influence the fate of someone she had come, if only from afar, to know. In that one sentence she had mingled her aspirations for her husband's future with her love for Jesus.

Mary, his mother, and her companions only had a brief glimpse of Jesus as he was marched, bound like any common criminal, across the Court of the Gentiles. The three women could hardly have recognized him: his face was a blotch of bruises, his beard and hair matted with sweat, spittle and dried blood, and his robe ripped. After his conviction the priest-judges and guards had once more punched him and spat and torn at his clothing, releasing their pent-up fury against the man who, throughout his ministry, had branded them as hypocrites and leaders of the blind.

This, then, was the son Mary glimpsed. Even he had most definitely not warned her of this: the hatred on the faces of Caiaphas, Annas and the other Sadducee priests who led the way across the courtyard under the protection of Jonathan's men, swords unsheathed, shields touching to form a solid wall around Jesus. More guards stood at the Eastern Gate, parting only for prisoner and escort to pass before closing ranks again. Unable to continue, the three stricken women watched helplessly as Jesus disappeared from view.

Herod Antipas continued to follow the pattern of his normal day in Jerusalem, alternately plunging from the icy coldness of one tub into the steaming waters of another in the colonnaded splendor of his bathroom and its cathedral-like tepidarium. Naked and dripping, his skin flowing with renewed vigour, all signs of his hangover gone, the tetrarch had walked to the massage block to have his body pummeled and kneaded. He then went to his private apartment and breakfasted with Herodias and Salome.

The women represented a curious psychological parallelogram of forces. They undoubtedly sensed how delicately balanced was their position. That their master needed them both meant neither alone could satisfy him: one wrong move and they could both be forever banished. That prospect very possibly influenced their attitude to the arrest of Jesus. In the past they had encouraged Herod Antipas' wish to kill him. They would almost certainly have seen the danger for them all if he now pursued such a plan. In the volatile atmosphere of Passover, his followers would retaliate; once more Jew would kill Jew. Rather than risk such a possibility, a wiser and safer course for them would be to urge Herod Antipas to allow the Romans to deal with Jesus. Even the most inflamed of his followers would hesitate over confronting the occupying power.

Advancing in wedge formation, shields and swords creating a menacing wall of metal which forced all before it, the Temple guards led Jesus through the narrow streets, heading eastwards, climbing as they went over the cobbles. Behind the wedge came rows of chief priests. They formed a further protective cocoon around Caiaphas. Behind him marched Annas and the other trial judges. Flanking them was a double line of guards which narrowed to form a further wedge at the rear of the force. In the midst of the formation was Jesus, held on one side by Jonathan and on the other by a guard. Behind the main group trotted several further ranks of guards, ready to stop any attempt to follow or get close to the prisoner. In all there were over five hundred people hurrying him through the streets.

The size of this force would subsequently reinforce the fiction that "the Jews" were collectively responsible for handing Jesus to the Romans: it would be represented as the *vox populi*—the voice of *the people*. That accusation would form a further basis for the early Christian Church successfully to inveigh against the Jewish nation. Its people would be forever damned by the action of the closely bunched men taking Jesus to Pilate.

It was midmorning and the sun beat down on their heads. The air was pungent with the stench of the hot grease of cooking and the sickening smell of rubbish rotting in the smaller alleys. Long before they reached its walls, the presence of the Antonia loomed over them. Built upon fortifications dating from Solomon's time, the citadel was only surpassed in height by the actual Temple. Its towers rose a full hundred feet above the main walls, themselves soaring fifty feet above street level. Rectangular in shape, the fortress was almost four hundred feet long by two hundred feet wide. They could see centurions in full battle dress assembling on the battlements, and beyond the walls came shouted commands and the distinctive sound of Roman soldiers running at the double in their armor.

When Jonathan's men swept round the corner of the south flank of the fortress to approach its main entrance they found themselves confronted by several rows of centurions blocking any approach to the portico. In the vast courtyard—three thousand square meters and paved with immense slabs of stone—the remainder of the garrison was mobilizing. Almost seven thousand men and their officers stood poised for action.

The front wedge of the Temple force halted a few feet from the Romans. Jonathan went forward to consult Caiaphas. The fortress was a pagan place which no Jew, let alone the high priest, could enter during the Passover period without resulting in legal impurity. But normally the Roman tribunal sat near to the whipping post in the center of the courtyard; in that way its members could see a sentence of scourging performed without having to leave their seats. Caiaphas proposed that the tribunal should assemble in the vaulted gateway, the procurator and his *assessores* sitting inside the arch, while Jesus and his accusers remained out in the street. The high priest gave the scroll to Jonathan, who marched to the portal, saluted and addressed the officer and suggested where the trial could be held.

The officer took the parchment from the captain of the guard and disappeared into the fortress. The silence stretched behind him.

One by one the apostles had made their way back into the city and had taken up positions near the fortress. They were tense and nervous, whispering among themselves, not knowing what to do. With them were Mary and Martha of Bethany and Joseph of Arimathea. Whatever else they felt, they must have shared a common feeling of dejection. Barely five days ago, Jesus had made his triumphal entry, been acknowledged as the Messiah. Now he was trussed and battered and covered with the spittle of contempt, waiting for his fate to be decided by the all-conquering Romans. It was an image they could only have found agonizing to witness. As they stared helplessly there was sudden activity in the gateway. Soldiers were positioning three handsomely carved wooden thrones.

Wearing his procurator's cloak over his toga Pilate emerged from the east tower accompanied by the garrison commander and the *assessores*. Maniple after maniple came to attention as they passed. In his hand Pilate held Caiaphas' scroll. Crossing the courtyard they reached the west portal. The commander ordered the centurions to break rank and form an avenue on either side of the throne that extended to where the Temple party stood. The *assessores* took their seats. They would have no part in the proceedings unless Pilate sought their advice on a point of law. He would act as prosecutor and judge; upon him alone would rest the final judgment. While the commander took his place behind the procurator's seat Pilate continued to stare at the throng of priests and guards.

Caiaphas turned and spoke to Jonathan. The priests and guards divided so that Jesus stood alone. Jonathan nudged him and he stumbled forward between the silent ranks of centurions. When he was a few feet short of the thrones Pilate motioned for him to stop. Ignoring Jesus, the procurator addressed Caiaphas. "What accusation bring ye against this man?"

The second trial of Jesus had begun.

The question was put in Greek, the language commonly used within the imperial legal system, and had a special significance. Pilate now knew the charges under which Jesus had been convicted in Jewish law: they were in the scroll. It also contained a broad outline of the offense under Roman law of threatening the Temple and a summary of the questions Jesus had refused to answer. Pilate could have confirmed the judgment of the Jewish court and formally ratified the sentence. That would have been the end of the matter: a few words, a nod of assent could have concluded his involvement. Instead, by putting that question he had ignored the Jewish proceedings and verdict and indicated he wished to exercise his right to hold a completely new trial under Roman law.

Was it curiosity to know more about the prisoner which prompted him to take this course? Was he showing himself as the supreme arbitrator anxious to weigh the truth to the last gram? Did he recognize that the high priest and his companions had behaved with the cunning dexterity of conjurors in that, having convicted Jesus, they wanted to use the cover of Roman law to have him killed—so reducing the risk of any action against the Temple? How much had his discussions with his wife affected him? Did he anticipate that any accusation brought by the Jews would not be sustained in Roman law—and, having established that, he would leave Caiaphas with a difficult decision of whether to risk carrying out the Jewish penalty on the eve of Passover? Whatever its grounding, the question Pilate had put produced an immediate response from the high priest. "If he were not a malefactor, we would not have delivered him up unto thee."

Pilate considered the words. There was a wheedling certainty about them. But Caiaphas had not answered his question. The procurator came to a decision. Pointing at Jesus, he addressed the high priest. "Take ye him and judge him according to your law."

Caiaphas flinched as if he had been slapped. When he spoke, his next words had certainly lost their arrogance. He pleaded that the political offenses Jesus had committed were outside the jurisdiction of the Jewish legal system and their seriousness transcended the purely religious crime of blasphemy upon which he had been convicted. Therefore, because Roman law superseded all other, "it is not lawful for us to put any man to death."

Pilate considered the point.

Already emotionally drained and physically exhausted by the events of the night, several of the apostles found it intolerable to continue observing what was happening at the gate. They began to slip away into the crowd that had begun to assemble. In the end only Matthew, John and Peter remained with Mary and Martha and Joseph of Arimathea. They all clearly heard Pilate repeat his question as to what were the specific accusations.

Caiaphas strove to keep his anger under control when he realized Pilate had cleverly outmaneuvered them. In bringing Jesus before the procurator the high priest had conceded the Temple's *jus gladii*, forgoing any further right to implement the sentence they had passed. But Pilate showed a clear reluctance to carry it out for them. Instead, he had given all the signs of being determined not merely to act as their executioner.

The high priest broke into a furious torrent. "We found this fellow perverting the nation and forbidding to give tribute to Caesar, saying that he himself is Christ a king."

Those words ensured Pilate could not, after all, escape. Caiaphas' accusations placed Jesus totally within Roman competence. The charges could not be more damning. "Perverting the nation" spoke of insurrection. "Forbidding to give tribute to Caesar" was a direct affront to the imperial mandate for taxation. Most serious of all was the accusation of kingship. If proven, that was high treason. The accusations did indeed supersede the charge of blasphemy under Jewish law and invested Jesus with the grave political offense of having set himself up as a direct threat to the emperor. Whatever Pilate's original motives for prolonging the matter, he now had no alternative but to continue. The charges must be examined and, if proven, he must pass the only sentence possible—death.

Pilate rose to his feet and spoke to the garrison commander. Then, followed by the *assessores*, and ignoring the onlookers, the procurator walked back into the fortress.

The commander took Jesus by the arm and led him through the gate. Behind them the centurions re-formed to block the view of the mystified onlookers.

The window in Claudia Procula's salon provided a view of the courtyard. She would not have been the woman she was if she had not watched her husband and his prisoner passing through the ranks of centurions to enter the east tower. She had urged Pilate to have nothing to do with "that just man." Yet he was bringing Jesus into the heart of the citadel. Could there be any doubt that her mind was filled with desperate hope?

Pilate himself settled behind the table in the salon. There would have been no time to remove the tax lists or the chests of coins. The *assessores* sat to one side of the procurator. The commander remained on guard at the top of the stairs. Jesus stood in the center of the room. Pilate came at once to the core of the matter. He realized that the final part of Caiaphas' accusatory words—the reference to kingship—implicitly included the other charges of subverting the gathering of taxes and plotting rebellion. His question to Jesus was without equivocation. "Art thou the king of the Jews?"

Pilate had tried to establish grounds for a simple confession or denial, a straightforward plea of guilty or not guilty. Jesus answered in almost the same terms he had responded to Caiaphas. "Thou sayest." Yet the answer was steeped in philosophical distinctions. Where Jesus had showed no difficulty in affirming his status to Caiaphas as that of "the Son of God," to say he was "the king of the Jews" was a different matter. Jesus did not want Pilate to think he was invested with royalty in any practical, earthly sense—any more than the kingdom he would rule over was of this world. Instead, Jesus wanted the procurator to realize he had never intended there to be the misunderstandings which had filled his fellow Jews with unrealistic expectations and the Romans with unnecessary fears.

Jesus now began an exchange which would prove to be of supreme importance. He amplified his response with a question of his own. "Sayest thou this thing of thyself, or did others tell it thee of me?"

He wished to establish a basic fact before going any further: was he going to be judged on hearsay, or receive an impartial hearing? It was an extraordinary display of confidence. In spite of all the punishments and insults, Jesus had effortlessly taken command of the situation. There was a natural dignity about his words that could not fail to have moved his listeners: here was a man of noble stature, who knew how to conduct himself in the face of death. They could well have thought of no higher tribute than to say he was behaving like a Roman. Nevertheless, realizing he was being disadvantaged, Pilate displayed impatience. "Am I a Jew?"

The procurator wished to make clear he would not be drawn into discussing Judaic doctrine—let alone his own view on the accusations. His next words were a sharp reminder. "Thine own nation and the chief priests have delivered thee unto me: what hast thou done?"

Pilate wanted to bring Jesus back to earthly reality to defend himself. But Jesus was determined to establish another reality; he returned to the main reason for his arraignment. "My kingdom is not of this world; if my kingdom were of this world, then would my servants fight, that I should not be delivered to the Jews."

Pilate must have sensed that once more he was being dragged into a doctrinal debate beyond his competence to judge. He made a further attempt to regain control of the situation. "Art thou a king then?"

Jesus might well have paused, perhaps even sighed and wondered how he could make his position clear. "Thou sayest that I am a king. To this end was I born, and for this cause came I into the world, that I should bear witness unto the truth. Every one that is of the truth heareth my voice."

Even in confessing to kingship, Jesus had manifestly tried to make Pilate understand the one salient reason they were having this dialogue; that he had been born solely to bear witness to a great new religious truth; that his kingdom was in the minds of all those who sought it; that his royalty was spiritual; and his empire no smaller, or greater, than the willingness of each person to hear his teaching, become his disciple, a citizen of his kingdom. He had given "truth" a new grandeur, one that was totally divine in its concept. Finally, he had issued a personal invitation to Pilate and the others in the room: they were part of his "every one"; if they wished, they, too, for all their pagan Roman ways, could enter his kingdom. It only required that they should embrace the new "truth."

Did Pilate ponder, even for a moment, the idea of accepting the invitation? Or was he already so blunted by the limitations of his life that there was no room for such a revolutionary vision? Or did his skepticism once more surface and take control? Was that why he put the question "What is truth?"

Pilate rose and ordered the commander to take Jesus back to the gate. Accompanied by the *assessores*, the procurator led the way.

Matthew and John, the sisters from Bethany and Joseph of Arimathea must have been alarmed by what was happening around the gate. More priests had come from the Temple to occupy the entire frontage of the fortress. There were many hundreds of them, black-robed and silent, eyes fixed on the portal. When Pilate and the advocates appeared, the throng began to chorus the accusations Annas had made. Ignoring them, Pilate turned and beckoned into the courtyard. The commander lead Jesus before the men seated on the thrones. The tumult increased so that the apostles had difficulty in hearing the procurator's words.

Pilate leaned forward and raised his voice to make himself heard above the crowd. "Hearest thou not how many things they witness against thee?"

Jesus made no response; his silence was filled with an innate sense of propriety; he did not wish to quarrel with his countrymen before the Roman tribunal.

Pilate, undoubtedly vexed by what was happening, recognizing that he was being used, addressed Caiaphas. “I find in him no fault at all.” The high priest raged that Jesus had incited the people; that he had intended to raise rebellion through the country from that first day he had appeared in public in Galilee—Pilate interrupted. The mention of Galilee provided a solution that would absolve him from any further involvement. Jesus was a subject of Herod Antipas. He should be sent to the tetrarch for judgment. It was a satisfying Roman response.

12

TO HEROD AND BACK

> And Herod with his men of war set him at nought, and mocked him and arrayed him in a gorgeous robe, and sent him again to Pilate.
>
> Luke 23:11

It is not difficult to imagine the foreboding of Chuza as he went to convey the news to Herod Antipas that Jesus was on the way. At this hour of the morning the steward would have known where to find the tetrarch and Chuza's sense of fear could only have increased as he descended a flight of stone steps to the palace dungeons. No sane person would willingly come to this place. The steward edged past the near-dead suspended from hooks, and the half-mad held in chains. Among them moved gaolers with whips and other instruments of torture. They catcalled and shouted coarse witticisms and abuse. There was an air of boisterous vulgarity that made it all that more frightening; the men in charge enjoyed their work. They went to and from a forge to heat branding irons used for burning into a forehead the dreaded *stigma*, marking forever a man as a thief. Sometimes a gaoler thrust too hard and the white-hot metal burnt through a skull and cauterized a victim's brain. Men were being destroyed by the *furca* each bore, a heavy wooden yoke across back and shoulders. Unable to move because their arms were chained above their head, the sheer weight of the *furca* would eventually wrench limbs from torsos, leaving prisoners to bleed to death. There were treadmills and racks from which death was almost a merciful release. One of the most feared punishments was the crusher in which a man's body was placed between two thick planks. These were then inexorably tightened by other prisoners turning ratchets until first the shoulders and hips were crushed by the pressure then the ribcage and finally the head pulped. It could take hours. The stench was overpowering: excrement, vomit and the pungent body odor of men and women in mortal terror. The women were kept in a separate cage. They were regularly raped—though none would live long enough to give birth. The life expectancy of all those consigned to the dungeons was weeks rather than months.

Herod Antipas must have appeared an incongruous figure as he strode back and forth through the dungeons in his regal garb that included a splendid purple silk cloak which had once belonged to his father. He could spend hours discussing with his turnkeys the merits of a specific torture before ordering it to be carried out. He would stand at the edge of one of the pits filled with slurry and watch a man being lowered into the cesspool and drowned; he would wait patiently for a tallow-coated stake to be impaled in someone's upper and lower jaws and then lit, so that the wood burnt away the lower part of the face. He would sometimes inspect the hand of a woman caught stealing before it was severed. He could stare, his eyes bulging in excitement, watching the desperate struggle of a man being garrotted by a rope held by two warders pulling on either side. Even then his craving for witnessing punishment was not satisfied. He would watch the specialists at work who pulled off fingernails one at a time, who gouged out eyes with a hook, who disemboweled a living man with a few cuts of a knife. At the end of a spell in the dungeons the tetrarch would emerge sated and cheerful and at his most unpredictable. On this day after sunset there would begin a week's pause in the torture, for Passover. However, in the past he had come down here on holy days and personally killed a prisoner to appease his bloodlust.

Upon receiving his steward's news the tetrarch left the dungeons to prepare to receive Jesus.

Pilate resumed his business with the tax collectors. They could well have looked at him with sudden curiosity. His behavior was by any reckoning beyond anything they would have known: men in power, whether Romans or Jews, did not behave as the procurator had done. First he had hesitated over Jesus; now he continued to prevaricate over the fate of Barabbas.

Jonathan had re-formed the wedge-like formation around Jesus, Caiaphas, Annas and the chief priests. But there was no way his guards could encompass the other priests who insisted on accompanying them across the city. There may have been three thousand members of the Temple marching upon the tetrarch's palace.

In trying to understand why the high priest and his cohorts were probably angry and close to panic a number of factors must be taken into account. They had confidently gone to Pilate expecting swift confirmation that Jesus should be executed. Instead the procurator had created a precedent in having a Roman court hand back a Jew to the Jewish authorities. Further, because there had been no time to consult the appropriate texts, they would be almost certainly in some doubt whether Herod Antipas had any legal right to hold a trial after the Temple had done so. There was, in fact, no precedent for such a hearing. More alarming still would be the thought of the tetrarch hearing the case and then acquitting Jesus. That would leave the high priest and his cohorts in a dangerously exposed position. They would then either have to bring the case before a full plenary session of the Great Sanhedrin—or else release Jesus. Both prospects were fraught with risk. The supreme court might not come to a verdict before sunset, when it would have to rise to observe the Passover. If that happened it would not be able to meet for another week. In the intervening period there would be no knowing what could happen.

In this increasingly uncertain and anxious mood they reached the palace entrance. Caiaphas ordered the chief priests and guards to accompany him into the palace with Jesus while the others were to maintain a silent vigil at the gate—a brooding presence which held its own menace.

Inside the palace hundreds of court officials had hurriedly assembled, probably in the banqueting hall from where, on the previous night, the tetrarch had been carried out senseless with drink. They stood on either side of the hall forming a corridor which led from the closed double entrance doors to the empty throne of Herod the Great brought from the tetrarch's own salon. A measure of the importance of the occasion would have been the presence of Herodias and Salome, seated on adjacent thrones, the women formally caped and robed, possibly even with diadems in their hair. Chuza waited before a curtained alcove. A hush, part curiosity, part anticipation, fell upon the massed courtiers.

The Temple procession and its escort of palace soldiers were greeted by the tetrarch's high chamberlain, secretary and other senior officials in an antechamber near the hall. The high chamberlain formally asked why they were here. Caiaphas explained. Perhaps it had been left to the tetrarch's secretary to demand that Jesus should be untied, and any protest would have been met with the explanation that Herod Antipas never received anyone who was not a free person: it was a way of demonstrating that in this palace he alone decided when a person's freedom should be restricted. Caiaphas reluctantly told Jonathan to remove Jesus' bonds. Only when the work was completed did the high chamberlain order the hall doors to be opened.

Beyond, over a hundred paces away, was the still empty throne from which Herod the Great had dispensed judgment on so many of his subjects.

Pilate's anger was understandable. The counting had already been seriously interrupted and it was almost certain this could not now be completed before sunset, which in turn would mean carrying over the process beyond Passover, an unwelcome prospect. The departure for Caesarea would have to be rescheduled and the port authorities would have to delay the galley carrying the money chests to Rome. That must provoke questions from the imperial treasury and perhaps even from Sejanus. Under these circumstances the last thing the procurator would want would be any further distraction.

Jesus walked through the densely packed assembly. Ahead strode the high chamberlain, immediately behind came the tetrarch's secretary. These were the positions they normally occupied when escorting an important dignitary into the presence of Herod Antipas. They were followed by Caiaphas who was flanked by Jonathan and Annas.

The chamberlain halted before the empty throne then stepped back to stand on one side of Jesus while the secretary moved forward to stand on the other. Chuza drew the curtain and Herod Antipas emerged wearing his father's cloak and crown and smiling that dangerous and demented half-smile which made him look so uncannily like his father as he sat on the throne.

Earthly ruler and subject stared at one another; a king with a kingdom beyond this world faced the most powerful Jewish ruler on earth. The tetrarch's half-smile was followed by a courteous greeting. It drew suppressed laughter from the courtiers. Herod Antipas stared about him, eyes darting, the smile more lopsided than before. There would be those who would say that the smile was the clue to what followed.

The meeting between Jesus and Herod Antipas would become one of the most hotly debated, and contested, events of his passion. Disagreement would start over whether it was an impulsive whim which made the tetrarch receive Jesus in this extraordinary manner, or whether he was driven by some deeper compulsion to humiliate the high priest and his cohorts. Had the tetrarch, caught in the grip of one of his fantasies, decided to show that, in spite of being a vassal of Rome, he was Pilate's equal in judicial power—at least when it came to dealing with a Jew? Or had he, in that devious and disabled mind of his, prepared this charade to show contempt for the way the Temple had mismanaged matters?

Yet, where Caiaphas had at least attempted to create an impression of legality, there was no question of Herod Antipas doing so. What he was embarked upon was neither an informal inquiry nor a trial. There had been no time for the tetrarch to prepare for either. What followed—though it would be called the third trial of Jesus—was beyond all known jurisprudence.

Sifting possible fact from pure legend, what happened in the hall unfolded something like this.

Having received no response from Jesus to his words of welcome, Herod Antipas addressed the audience. They had all heard a great deal about this man, and those miraculous happenings. He came before them with impressive claims and they should all be properly impressed. But who among them had actually *seen* him perform a single feat?

The courtiers would have been less than their groveling selves if they had not dutifully laughed at the tetrarch's baiting.

He asked a further question. Who would like to see Jesus perform just a single miracle which would show that he was, after all, the Messiah?

The mockery was now a full-throated roar which had its echo in that sabbath when Jesus had stood in the synagogue in Nazareth. Once more he was assailed by the same demand to prove himself.

Herod Antipas, signaling for silence, addressed Jesus. Would he tell them first how he performed his sorcery? Would he then show them? Perhaps he would once more turn water into wine? Maybe he would wish to have a broken body to heal?

Who could doubt that once more raucous laughter erupted.

Jesus maintained complete silence.

Herod Antipas rose to his feet, the smile on his lips, if anything, more alarming and dangerous. He unclasped his cloak and walked up to Jesus. He asked him a further question. "Thou art the king of the Jews?"

Jesus gave no flicker of response.

The tetrarch draped the cloak over Jesus' shoulders and stood back to admire the effect. He addressed the hall. Surely now, with a king's robe around his shoulders, they could expect him to behave like a king? The tetrarch bowed mockingly before Jesus. The courtiers did the same. The low chanting began.

The tetrarch's mocking banter gave way to a sudden surge of anger. He began to attack Jesus, reminding him of the defamatory words he had used. *A fox!* He had called his lord tetrarch that! *A fox!* Why had he done so? What gave him such a right to do so? The questions tumbled forth, a furious spittle-laced torrent of words. There was madness in the air.

Then, as abruptly as it had begun, the abuse ended. Perhaps exhausted by his tirade, Herod Antipas returned to his throne, slumped in thought.

Finally, indicating Jesus, he once more addressed the gathering. Did they think that even in a king's robe he looked like a king?

They chorused they did not.

The tetrarch at last spoke to Caiaphas. He reviled Jesus and ordered the high priest to return him to Pilate.

As the high priest began to rage Herod Antipas walked from the hall. Herodias and Salome followed him.

Emerging from the palace—Jesus once more bound and wearing the ridiculous and demeaning cloak and surrounded by furious priests and Temple guards—Caiaphas and Annas only too well recognized they had reached a supremely critical moment. Twice they had failed to have others put Jesus to death. For themselves to order carrying out the sentence of the Sadducean court was still fraught with risk. The Pharisee members of the Great Sanhedrin could intervene and force a postponement; that would be perilously divisive and seriously damaging to the authority of the Temple. But, more serious still, the longer Jesus lived the greater was the threat he posed of public opinion being aroused against the priesthood. All he represented would be seen by the masses to be *right* and the Temple shown to be *wrong*; if his teaching prevailed, then the Temple and all its functions would be regarded as totally irrelevant and would be cast aside. That would see the end of the priestly life of privileges and perquisites that included the second bird used in the ritual purification of a woman after childbirth; the portions of each animal presented to the sacrificers at the great altar; the *terumah*, the choicest gathering of all fruit and vegetables; the *challah*, the giving of one twenty-fourth part of the dough used in any baking; the *tithes*, one tenth of every other item which could be used for food. These gifts ensured that, from the high priest down, the Temple employees were a highly privileged and pampered group in a nation where poverty was rampant. It was human for men like Caiaphas and Annas not to wish to surrender their rewards willingly.

Most serious of all, Jesus was a direct threat to their position which placed them between believers and God. The law insisted that sacrifices must only be offered at the Temple and only through its priests, and that they alone had the authority to decide the penalty to be exacted to restore a supplicant to good standing with God. Jesus threatened this supremacy. Caiaphas and Annas realized they faced a simple and clear choice: either they destroyed Jesus—or he ruined them. If Jesus lived, he would remain a constant threat to their life of power and luxury and their position as the ultimate arbitrators in all spiritual matters. He must die.

Standing outside the tetrarch's palace, the sun high in the sky—a reminder of how little time they had left to act—the high priest gave instructions to Jonathan.

Some time before the change of the morning watch, Pilate came to a decision over Barabbas. He would send him to Golgotha, with the two thieves. He had barely made up his mind when he received word that the Temple hierarchy was back at the west portal with Jesus and demanding to see the procurator.

Pilate's full fury burst upon Caiaphas when he reached the gateway. "Ye have brought this man unto me, as one that perverteth the people: and, behold, I, having examined him before you, have found no fault in this man touching those things whereof ye accuse him. No, nor yet Herod, for I sent you to him; and, lo, nothing worthy of death is done unto him."

It was an exemplary summary of events to date. In the procurator's view nothing had changed; his angry words contained the explicit reminder that under the Roman *Lex Julia*—the Roman law originally enacted by Julius Caesar—Jesus had not caused any injury to the majesty of the emperor. The definition of an offense under *Lex Julia* was so far-reaching that it included virtually anything the emperor or, in this case Pilate, would regard as diminishing the authority of Rome.

Standing before the massed ranks of the Temple, the procurator had so far kept his nerve—perhaps it had been bolstered by the restraining influence of his wife. Nevertheless he must also have sensed that the seething priests would *not* relent—any more than they had done so that time when they had marched to Caesarea to protest about the Roman insignias fluttering next to the Temple. There was certainly about the men before him the same grinding and growing opposition he had witnessed before—and all that more dangerous with Passover almost upon them; they were torn between a need to prepare for the *Pesah* and their self-evident determination to obtain some imperial action. Notwithstanding the presence of his numerically superior troops, Pilate made a decision which would forever implicate him in the fate of Jesus. "I will therefore chastise him and release him!"

He ordered centurions to take Jesus into the courtyard. Under Roman law "chastising" meant scourging—and that form of punishment generally formed part of a Roman death sentence. There was no precedent for releasing a prisoner after such a whipping. Caiaphas and Annas must have been filled with sudden hope.

Mary, Jesus' mother, Mary Magdalene and the elder Mary had found their way to Joseph of Arimathea's house. There they found Mary and Martha,

Joanna, John and Peter. They sat quietly, weeping, occasionally asking questions. The legend would take root that it was here that his mother said she would make every effort to be with her son as the end approached.

Pilate was making his way across the courtyard to go back into the fortress when he was stopped by a momentous and growing new chant. "Crucify him! Crucify him!" He returned to the west portal. The crowd of priests had grown and their demand bounced off the fortress walls. "Crucify him! Crucify him!"

The cry rose and fell, an echo of that very different tumult six mornings earlier when Jesus had made his triumphal entry into the city. Now, instead of Judas leading the hosannas, Caiaphas and Annas were at the forefront of a very different roar. "Crucify him! Crucify him!"

Once more events overtook Pilate. Standing there, uncertain and perhaps even a little afraid, the procurator was interrupted by the arrival of one of his wife's servants. She handed over a scroll written by Claudia Procula, again urging her husband not to become involved: that even now he must not be swayed by the vociferous urging of the crowd. "Crucify him! Crucify him!"

Pilate strode out into the street, centurions flanking him, swords drawn and shields extended, ready to do battle at his command. It was a dangerous and ugly situation. The procurator halted a few feet from the high priest. Pilate turned and indicated Jesus, standing between two centurions inside the fortress gateway. "What evil hath he done? I have found no cause of death in him. I will therefore chastise him and let him go!"

They were the words of a man who had fallen prey to some inner force. As a sop to the howling mob, he was going to subject Jesus to the cruelest punishment possible, short of crucifixion, and then release him. It was unprecedented.

In the courtyard the priests could see the two thieves and Barabbas being prepared for the journey to Golgotha. Once more Caiaphas and Annas motivated those around them. Hundreds of hands pointed at Jesus and an even more thunderous roar assailed Pilate. "Away with this man and release unto us Barabbas!"

Pilate stood transfixed by words which would spark one of the bitterest controversies to divide the two faiths represented before him: Judaism and Christianity.

The argument would stand or fall on two questions. Was there *privilegium paschale*—a Passover pardon? Did Pilate have the authority to implement it?

Both in Roman and Jewish law there existed specific and clear grounds for granting an amnesty on the occasion of the onset of great festivals. The Romans had inherited the custom from the Greeks and had refined it to two kinds of pardon. There was the *indulgentia*. Only an emperor could grant this and it was normally only extended to a conquered enemy leader who had shown exceptional courage in the face of defeat. There was also the *abolitio*, which was an integral part of the Roman legal code; this pardon could be granted at any point *before a Roman sentence was passed*. An *abolitio* ended proceedings and freed a prisoner before his guilt or innocence had been formally established. The prerogative was in the hands of the chief imperial administrator in a province. Under Roman law both Barabbas and Jesus would qualify for an *abolitio*: the Zealot leader had not been tried; Jesus had been adjudged not guilty of any offense.

The Jewish tractate, *Pesahim*, allowed at Passover for the release of a prisoner from either Jewish or Roman custody—providing he or she was *not guilty* of a religious crime; those charged or condemned for secular offenses—including *any political crime*—could be freed. The custom of granting a prisoner freedom at Passover and other great Jewish festivals dated from these turbulent times when the Hasmonean dynasty ruled over Jerusalem, civil war engulfed the nation and the number of purely *political* prisoners dramatically increased; anyone who opposed the Hasmonean king was deemed to be politically motivated. Hundreds, perhaps thousands of such prisoners had filled the city gaols. To ensure a measure of peace during the Passover, the Hasmonean king regularly pardoned and released an inmate. The gesture was underpinned by a strong commercial consideration. The dynasty included a large number of princes who were Temple priests whose income virtually depended on the number of pilgrims who came to Jerusalem. Granting freedom to one man was a small price to pay to encourage pilgrims from the Diaspora to accept they would not be embroiled in the civil war if they came to the city. The custom became a recognized ritual. When the Roman occupation began, the imperial power consented to it continuing—seeing it as a shrewd way to reduce the extra emotional tension always present at times like Passover. In an equally calculated move Caiaphas had used it to try to force Pilate to heed the will of the Temple.

Barabbas still clearly qualified for release under the tractate. Jesus, who had also been convicted of blasphemy, did not.

The tumult engulfed the procurator. He had been repeatedly confronted on his doorstep, an unpleasant and draining experience. Added to this was the realization he would now be definitely forced to remain after Passover in a city and among a people he hated. His personality was most probably ill-equipped to deal with such vagaries; the essential and reassuring links which governed his life were being strained over the fate of one man. The relentless cry bore in on him. "Release unto us Barabbas! Crucify him!"

It was too much for Pilate to cope with: the unconscious forces previously held back finally burst into his consciousness. The shouting was coming dangerously close to violence. In a moment he would be engulfed in an uprising—trampled to his own death by the crazed mob of aroused religious fanatics. The procurator's self-preservation overcame all else. Once more he walked over to Caiaphas. They stood feet apart, divided by religion and social mores, but linked by a loathing which was mutual and vibrant. A gradual silence settled over the crowd. Pilate's question cut through the hush. "Whether of the twain will ye that I release unto you?"

The response was immediate.

"Barabbas!"

Pilate's next question showed the increasing strain he was under.

"What shall I do then with Jesus which is called Christ?"

That question marked the formal abdication of his prerogative as impartial judge. It saw the end of what skills he had in handling a complex and perplexing situation, of showing that Roman justice, for all its severity, could not be misused and exploited. Now, in the face of a mob of aroused priests he had capitulated, sunk to the point where he had asked them for advice. He had accepted the rule of the mob. It roared at him. *"Let him be crucified."*

The procurator turned and walked to the gateway. Beside it was a drinking fountain for the sentries. Pilate washed his hands in water. Then, standing near Jesus, he addressed the Temple cadre. *"I am innocent of the blood of this just person. See ye to it."*

The words were lost in a renewed chant, no longer furious but triumphant. *"Crucify him!"*

Pilate ordered Barabbas to be released and Jesus to be taken to the scourging post. Then he returned to his salon. In one sense the trials of Jesus were over. In another they were about to begin.

BEYOND THE CROSS

Vicisti, Galilae—Thou hast conquered, O Galilean.
Julian (alleged dying words)

13

THE PLACE OF THE SKULL

To give light to them that sit in darkness and in the shadow of death.

Luke 1:79

Led unprotesting into the courtyard and through the ranks of centurions, hardened men largely indifferent to what was to happen, Jesus knew his brief mission was almost over. He would face an excruciatingly painful ritual death knowing he had done all that had been asked of him, that it had always been intended he would go to his earthly end without any idea of the efficacy of his teaching, miracles and cures. The one certainty had always been that after he had planted the Word all that was required of him was to die.

The more he sowed, the closer it came, and these last three years had been an accelerating race towards death. He had lived all his public life in readiness for this and had announced his fate to those closest to him as an inevitability. If they could see him approaching the scourging post he would have urged them, as he had done so often in the past, not to regard what was about to happen as either a disgrace, a failure or the inevitable consequence of his actions. The destruction of his body—though not his soul—had always been intended as the climax to his mission on earth.

Crossing the courtyard under the scrutiny of men wedded to other gods; watching Barabbas, freed and making his way to the west portal, where the Temple cadre continued their triumphant chanting; passing the two thieves who had just been scourged and were bowed under the crosses they must drag to Golgotha: Jesus saw and accepted it all.

The two Syrian conscripts waited at the post. The ground around it was slippery with the blood of the thieves. Each held a *flagellum*, made of strips of leather soaked in brine, and a *flagrum*, whose thongs were studded with pieces of bone and small metal spheres with spiked surfaces. The choice of whip rested on the garrison commander standing beside the post. The thieves had been brutalized by the *flagellum*. He ordered the *flagrum* for Jesus.

One of the conscripts stepped forward and ripped Herod the Great's cloak from Jesus' shoulders and handed the garment to the commander. The two Syrians then shoved him, face forward, against the post, shackling his hands and feet. Using a knife, one of them slashed his robe from the neckline to the hem and yanked it free. Another stroke cut away his undergarment. Jesus was as naked and defenseless as the day he was born. The Syrians stepped back, each measuring his distance, expertly flicking his whip so that for the moment the thongs only caressed his skin. From beyond the west gate came another roar. "Crucify him! Crucify him!"

The commander ordered the punishment to commence.

The first Syrian stepped forward and delivered a lash, the *flagrum* opening the skin, the first slivers of flesh torn from his body and his blood starting to spurt on to the flagstones, mingling with that of the thieves. A further roar came from the priests as the second blow landed.

Each *flagrum* made a whistling sound as it snaked through the air, then a dull thwacking as the strips of reinforced leather struck home. Jesus was being steadily cut open from the back of his head to his heels. After every few lashes the commander stepped forward to estimate how much more he could bear. Each time he motioned for the shameful torture to resume.

Matthew, Mark and John would all limit themselves merely to recording the punishment. The apostles, like every other Jew, had grown up with scourging: they well understood the shame of its nudity, the unbearable physical pain and, above all, the infamy of Jesus being condemned to a punishment normally reserved for slaves and criminals. Their understandable discretion would be used by the early Church to argue that the punishment was too horrific to be recorded; further, that in not protesting at it, *the Jews* tacitly accepted a barbarism far crueler than any kind of ritual slaughter.

The claim would be made that Pilate had inflicted this revolting suffering upon a man in whom he had found no fault at all as a last resort to appease the bloodthirsty clamoring of *the Jews* and it was they, not he, who wished Jesus to be punished in this vile manner. The story would flourish that the whips made by Romans, wielded by Roman conscripts, on the authority of a Roman commander and procurator, which curled and coiled across the body of Jesus, did so at the behest of *the Jews.*

The scourging would produce its own grim literature: eventually a library of several hundred books devoted to the subject would occupy a gallery in the secret archives of the Vatican detailing the history of the torture and the precise method of manufacturing its weapons—"the pieces of bone came from previous victims"—and how scourging came to be part of the Jewish penal code. In these books can be found claims that the flogging lasted between three and five minutes; that it produced widespread subcutaneous hemorrhages on his body and that throughout the ordeal his lips seemed to be moving in prayer, as if Jesus "forgave the Jews who had instigated all this." There were numerous descriptions of how Jesus must have been a pitiful sight when the Syrians—much would be made of their Semitic background—finally set aside their whips and wiped the perspiration from their brows. His chest, neck, shoulders, back, hips and legs were slashed as if with knives and streaked with blue welts and swollen bruises. Even his face was cut and disfigured by the lashes that had rained down upon him. Having recovered their breath, the Semitic Syrians, with no more feelings of compassion than the priest had for the lamb with its head through the rung, unshackled Jesus. He was in such a state that he could scarcely have been recognized even by those who knew him best. The scourging had exposed the mechanism of his flesh, even to the very veins and arteries.

What had happened was indisputably appalling—but so was the subsequent shocking accusation that *the Jews* had brought it upon him: that they were somehow collectively responsible for the gruesome sight of Jesus lying at the foot of the scourging post, unconscious.

From the west gate came the ceaseless chanting of the high priest and the Temple cadre continuing to demand his crucifixion. One of the conscripts picked up a pail of water mixed with salt and sloshed it over Jesus: the stinging brine was a routine way to revive a victim and help to stem the flow of blood. Jesus was hauled to his feet and held upright until he could feel some return of strength. His body ached with pain, which grew in intensity as full consciousness returned. The blood matting his body hair, he stood shivering in shock. These were standard responses to a scourging. What followed added cruel insult to torture. The soldiers—no doubt bored and certainly without pity—began to taunt Jesus. Any fear they may have felt in his presence had gone; with it went the respect normally accorded to a man who had survived the *flagrum.* He now became the plaything of the centurions. While Jesus struggled to reclothe himself as best he could, they addressed him with mocking gallantry, finally draping the purple cape of Herod the Great over his body. One of them fetched a fagot of dead thorns used as firelighters from a pile stacked in the courtyard. The soldier shaped it into a *pileus*, the oval-shaped hat Romans often wore when attending festive occasions. He placed the plaited ring on Jesus' head. Another stripped a branch of its spikes and shoved it in his hand.

The centurions knelt before Jesus, each on one knee, and bowed their heads, their chants matching the cries from the west gate. "Hail, king of the Jews!" The mockery which Herod Antipas had begun was complete.

Obtaining no reaction from Jesus, the soldiers became more unpleasant. They rose to their feet and approached him, one at a time, as if to bestow a kiss of peace. Instead, they spat in his face. One grabbed the stick and used it to beat him. He handed it to a companion who repeated the process. The cane was passed from one hand to another to strike Jesus. He gave no response. A centurion drove the crown of thorns into his lacerated scalp. Jesus stoically bore this further pain. The soldiers grew increasingly furious, kicking and punching as they chanted: "Hail, king of the Jews!"

Beyond the gate the priests screamed that Jesus must be crucified *now*: the sun was already directly overhead. Time was running out if he was to experience the full agony of the cross. In the courtyard the soldiers, tired of their savagery, began to shove Jesus towards the east tower. Propped against its wall was the cross intended for Barabbas.

John, unable to bear the strain of not knowing what was happening, had risked his life to return and stand among the priests. Suddenly they fell silent. Through the fortress gate came Pilate followed by a small detachment of soldiers with Jesus in their midst, bedraggled and bloody, the crown of thorns rammed into his skull, the robe hiding his terrible injuries; prisoner and escort remained inside the gate. The procurator addressed Caiaphas. "Behold I bring him forth to you, that ye may know that I find no fault in him!"

Pilate motioned for the soldiers to bring Jesus out of the shadow of the archway and expose him to the bright sunlight. John and those around him saw the brutality Jesus had suffered. Pilate spoke again. "Behold the man!"

Caiaphas' response was immediate. "Crucify him!"

Thousands of other voices took up the refrain around the anguished apostles.

That brief exchange, recorded by John without comment, would foment further tension between Jews and Christians. The tableau at high noon outside the fortress would be explored and exploited. Pilate, who *had* ordered the scourging, but almost certainly not the subsequent mockery and brutality of his soldiers, would be presented as determined to make a last desperate plea to *the Jews* to recant and let Jesus go; that the words "behold the man" were a straightforward appeal to the compassion of the priestly cadre: the procurator was saying that Jesus had already suffered enough, and that he stood before them, bloodied and physically broken, an object of derision, no longer a threat to the Temple. What more did they want? There would be others who would see in the words an even more profound meaning by capitalizing the word "Man." It would become a sentence used to portray the procurator in a still more appealing light—in spite of the fearful whipping he had ordered. "Behold the man" would be seen as meaning: "Behold him; here was a Man unique among men; one filled with mystery; humbled he retained an indefinable grandeur." It could have been a description of the Messiah.

Pilate would be presented, in that moment, as having regained his integrity and become once more the dispenser of imperial justice, a proud ruler who could hardly restrain himself from saying to *the Jews* that their behavior disgusted him; that he would no longer involve himself with their injustice. Instead, the Jews had continued with their raucous demand. "Crucify! Crucify!"

All that is certain is that in doing so the high priest and his staff brought further odium upon their people.

Pilate finally did not bother to hide his displeasure. "Take ye him, and crucify him: for I find no fault in him!"

John would record that *the Jews*—though almost certainly it was Caiaphas—answered: "We have a law, which by our law he ought to die, because he made himself the Son of God."

Originally Jesus had been brought to the bar of Roman justice on a charge of treason. Now Caiaphas was attempting to reintroduce the religious charge which had no counterpart in the imperial code; he was clearly casting about for anything that would persuade Pilate to have Jesus crucified.

The procurator put a question to Jesus far beyond any geographical significance. "Whence art thou?"

Jesus caught the uncertainty in Pilate's voice. He was asking Jesus to explain what he stood for, to amplify those values Jesus had hinted at earlier, when they had spoken in Pilate's salon and Jesus had said his kingdom was not of this world.

Jesus did not reply. But his silence was not purely that of suffering; he wanted to see if Pilate could grasp for himself the answer to his question.

"Speakest thou not unto me? Knowest thou not that I have power to crucify thee and have power to release thee?"

Pilate was saying, perhaps even pleading, that even now, after all that had happened, he would still free Jesus—and no doubt arrange for his safe conduct through the hostile mob of priests. All the procurator wanted were explanations he could understand.

Jesus put aside any thought of freedom. "Thou couldest have no power at all against me, except it were given thee from above; therefore he that delivereth me unto thee hath greater sin."

Jesus wanted Pilate to understand that not only did he sympathize with the procurator's position of having a very limited earthly authority, but that Jesus was speaking of a far more exalted power—God's and his own. Both were interchangeable and equal. Then almost as an afterthought he had firmly apportioned blame for those who had brought them *both* to this situation: Caiaphas and his priests.

Their renewed shouts interrupted further discussion. The high priest shouted into the gateway: "If thou let this man go, thou art not Caesar's friend: whosoever maketh himself a king speaketh against Caesar!"

In final desperation the high priest had been driven to invoke the emperor; to proclaim that the high priest of the Jews was more loyal to a system he hated than was the procurator he equally loathed. Pilate, whatever action he may have been contemplating, now had no alternative. He must show that he, too, had no loyalty other than to Caesar Tiberius. The procurator ordered the cross to be brought to the gateway. He summoned a secretary. When the man arrived Pilate dictated a sentence to him in Latin, Greek and Aramaic. "Jesus of Nazareth. The king of the Jews."

Pilate ordered the inscription to be nailed above the crosspiece of the cross. Then, his voice filled with all the bitterness the Gospels would imply, he spoke to Caiaphas. "Behold your king!"

The high priest, as he had done at the end of the trial in Annas's hall, sensed victory. It would have been natural for him to stare at Pilate, waiting. In keeping with his entire behavior the procurator uttered a last despairing question. "Shall I crucify your king?"

His victory complete, Caiaphas replied: "We have no king but Caesar."

Pontius Pilate nodded to Jesus' escort and walked into the fortress.

Claudia Procula's "just man" must, after all, die on Golgotha, the place of the skull.

Pilate's question was the last recorded words he spoke, leaving unresolved a tantalizing issue. The procurator was certainly a more complex person than the Gospels would accord: their failure would be to offer any plausible explanation why Pilate—who had previously shown insensitivity to those he governed—should have gone to such exceptional lengths to save Jesus before being finally driven to deliver him—and then only in the face of that threat to report him to the emperor.

The threat was hardly enforceable. Caiaphas had no avenue to report anything directly to Rome; his channel to imperial authority was through the tetrarch. After the latest behavior of Herod Antipas there was no way the high priest could have been certain that any complaint he made would be forwarded. And, if it did reach Rome, there was no guarantee it would be treated seriously. Caiaphas could have been under no illusion about the contempt in which he was held in Roman circles. Finally, before daring to protest about the procurator to the emperor, he would need the full backing of the Great Sanhedrin: high priests simply did not act unilaterally in such grave matters. That would almost certainly have led to further fierce debate. Pilate, then, should not have been unduly troubled by the threat.

But had he acquiesced to it for a very different reason? In his conversations with his wife he would not have failed to grasp something of her feelings that Jesus was in every sense an exceptional person; his own conversations with him could only have reinforced that view. Could it, then, be that Pilate finally realized that Jesus not only *had* to die—but that he was actually prepared to? Could the procurator have come to believe that the last service he could perform for Jesus was to hand him over to be crucified as king of the Jews? Could it be that Pilate had, after all, at least an inkling that nothing could stop the coming of his kingdom?

Once Pilate agreed to the crucifixion and disappeared into the courtyard, the scene at the gate took on a military precision. The commander detailed one of the officers to act as *exactor mortis*, responsible for taking Jesus to Golgotha.

It was a coveted duty: the *exactor mortis* had first choice of the clothes and any other personal effects of the condemned. Three soldiers were ordered to complete the deathwatch that would remain at the execution site until Jesus was dead. The commander took the unusual step of sending a *centuria*, a further hundred troops in full battle dress, to accompany them: undoubtedly it was a precaution against any attempt to intervene in the proceedings.

The officer ordered the men to dismantle the cross, made from two balks of roughly hewn timber, the vertical span a standard ten cubits tall, fifteen feet. Assembled it weighed around three hundred pounds, beyond the strength of even a physically fit man to carry to Golgotha, and an impossible feat for someone who had been severely weakened by a scourging. The *patibulum*, the crossbeam, weighed over fifty pounds.

With the officer pulling forward Jesus' head, the beam was lowered on to his neck and shoulders. Then Jesus' arms were extended and tied to the span. Fresh blood seeped from the wounds on his body. The *exactor mortis* unfastened the Herodian robe: he had made his first acquisition. He ordered the crown of thorns to be removed; it had been part of private sport and had no place in the ritual of the Roman crucifixion.

The soldiers hoisted the upright onto their shoulders while the officer fastened a rope around the waist of Jesus which he then tied to the back of his own belt; sometimes a condemned man had to be dragged to his execution. Attached to the belt was a hammer, an awl, a pouch of nails and a flagon. In one hand he carried two stout poles, forked at the top; in the other a pair of wooden shovels.

It was early afternoon when the procession formed up. First came five ranks of centurions, ten abreast, followed by the execution party, then a further five rows of soldiers. Caiaphas and the priests along with Jonathan and his guards walked behind them. The public followed; in all there may have been already close to four thousand persons going to see Jesus die. Among them was John. But he would write nothing about that journey; like the kiss of Judas it was almost certainly too awful for him to record. Around him were those who would provide details for Matthew, Luke and Mark; like the best of reporters they would confine themselves to simply relating what they learned happened.

The distance to Golgotha was short, no more than five hundred yards to the northwest of the Antonia Fortress. To reach the mound required passing through the business quarter, a warren of shops which largely depended on the Temple for their livelihood. As the procession wended its way the priests ordered the shopkeepers to follow; scores did so, swelling the monotonous chanting. "Crucify. Crucify."

Climbing towards the gate which led from the city towards the execution hillock, Jesus finally began to falter. The officer ordered a halt, almost certainly not from pity but of necessity; if Jesus died before being crucified there would be disciplinary proceedings. Coming through the gate was a peasant, Luke's Simon, "coming out of the country." He was ordered to take over the burden of the *patibulum*, and made to walk behind the soldiers carrying the upright.

The procession restarted but only went a few more yards before there was a second and equally dramatic intervention. During the changeover of the spar a number of women had managed to infiltrate the escort; seeing his pitiful state they began to weep and wail. There would be subsequent speculation that they included Jesus' mother and the other women from Joseph of Arimathea's house. More likely they were members of an organization of pious women who devoted themselves to helping the condemned along this final stage.

Freed from his crippling yoke, Jesus spoke to them. "Daughters of Jerusalem, weep not for me, but weep for yourselves and for your children.

For, behold, the days are coming in which they shall say, blessed are the barren, and the wombs that never bare, and the paps which never gave suck. Then shall they begin to say to the mountains; fall on us; and to the hills; cover us. For if they do these things in a green tree, what shall be done in the dry?"

He had spoken in the timeless manner of the great prophets. His phrases may well have been broken by gasps of pain; almost certainly he had not strength left to deliver a sustained discourse. Every word must have cost him dearly, draining further his steadily diminishing strength. Yet they contained all the sobering eloquence of a visionary: Jesus was once more peering into the future and what he saw was apocalyptic: a world where it was better not to bear children, a time of great catastrophe. These were crushing predictions, a series of paralyzing images through which he wanted everyone who could hear clearly to understand that ahead lay great misery if they had the courage still to follow him. It was unflinching and without a shred of compromise: the way of the cross was essential to enter his kingdom.

The *exactor mortis* ordered the women away and the procession continued through the city gate. To the left rose the ramparts of the tetrarch's palace; the screams of his prisoners must have carried clearly. A mere hundred feet ahead and slightly to the right rose the skull-shaped mound of Golgotha. The two thieves were already suspended from their *cruxi*. The *centuria* were instructed to form an outward-facing circle around the hillock and let no one pass. The officer led Jesus forward. Behind came Simon and the trio carrying the upright. They moved among the centurions who had accompanied the robbers, and who, their work completed, sat on the ground, sharing out their possessions.

The three men dropped the balk and began to prod the ground around the erected crosses. Finally they selected a spot between and slightly forward of where the naked and very likely semiconscious thieves were suspended. Two of the soldiers used the shovels to dig a hole; when they judged it deep enough they positioned the upright, wedging the post firmly in place with rocks, forming a cairn of stones around its base so that it would not sway and fall under the load it must bear. While they worked the *exactor mortis* untied the rope which bound Jesus to him and stripped Jesus of all his clothes; the officer chose what he wanted and left the rest to be divided among the squad.

The early Christian Church, understandably anxious not to remind its members that Jesus was going to his death as a circumcised Jew, would go to considerable lengths to suggest that he wore a loincloth; volumes would be written arguing that "naked" could mean "relative as well as total nudity"; that the Romans made an exception of Jesus and allowed him to retain an undergarment. But Roman practice considered that part of the penalty of crucifixion should include total degradation of the victim: the only permitted concession was that women were crucified facing the cross—though they, too, were completely nude.

Once the upright was firmly positioned and Jesus was naked the squad began the task of attaching him to the crossbeam. After Simon laid the *patibulum* on the ground near the upright he was dismissed from the mound, his chance encounter with history over, his place in Christian lore forever assured. Jesus was ordered to lie on his back so that his shoulders were resting in the center of the beam. A soldier grasped each of his arms and stretched them out on the wood. The *exactor mortis* then used the point of his spear to make a scratch mark near each wrist. Jesus' arms were momentarily raised above his head while the officer used the hammer and awl to make a hole in the timber so that it would receive a nail more easily. Jesus' arms were then repositioned, the soldiers holding them taut. A nail was hammered through his wrist into the wood. The other hand was similarly pinioned. This was standard Roman procedure; what followed had been absorbed from Judaism.

The *exactor mortis* uncorked the flagon and offered Jesus a drink to ease the pain: the apostle Mark was sure it was the usual mixture of wine and myrrh, a potion which produced a quick-acting narcotic effect, dulling senses and pain. The Romans had, almost certainly reluctantly, been persuaded to offer this relief to Jews: the book of Proverbs and the Talmud both contained instructions to ease the suffering of the condemned. Jesus allowed the drink to moisten his lips but he would not swallow a drop. In the Garden of Gethsemane he had accepted that his passion must be borne without any relief: that he must sacrifice himself in full possession of his faculties, including those which stimulated his terrible physical pain.

The ground around Golgotha was crammed with onlookers, now silent; even the Temple cadre at last showed a sense of respect for what was being done at their behest.

The four Romans bent over his body, working efficiently. Ignoring the involuntary twitching of his body and the fresh blood oozing around the nail wounds, they began the most difficult part of any crucifixion—raising and attaching the *patibulum* to the upright. Jesus was now a dead weight and unable to assist them—and so perhaps make it easier for himself. Two of the men grasped either end of the beam, the third held him around the waist while the officer supported the back of his head. At his command they lifted Jesus on to his feet and positioned his back against the upright. The officer handed the two men supporting the beam each a pole. They placed the forked ends under the beam close to his body. The third soldier grasped Jesus, this time around the knees. At a further command from the *exactor mortis* the soldiers with the poles raised the beam while their companion supported Jesus' body as it inched up the main spar. When they had lifted him several feet, the crossbeam slipped into a notch already cut into the upright. The officer took a stout peg with a metal spike at one end and hammered it into the wood between Jesus' legs. The weight of his suspended body was now divided between his arms and crotch. His feet were then nailed to the wood, two nails driven through each tibia.

The squad's work was over. They sat on the ground a few feet from the cross dividing up his clothing and, in Luke's sparse yet chilling graphic account, "cast lots" for the raiment as they kept watch.

The priests reminded the onlookers that the book of Deuteronomy said there was a curse upon any man hung from wood—such a person "was not the elect of God." They should therefore not feel any sympathy let alone have any lingering thought that Jesus could be the Messiah. After a while the crowd began to disperse, no doubt influenced by crucifixion being a drawn-out affair in which little appeared to be happening.

Looking down from his cross, dying, Jesus must have experienced the very depths of rejection. He had been betrayed, denied and forsaken. His flesh had been torn and pierced and his blood had flowed copiously. He had been hoisted up from the earth in a final barbaric operation, placed between two common thieves, the parchment proclamation above his head a derisive reminder of his failure. As he looked down he would have noticed the crowd thinning—though it would be uncertain whether he would have still been able to see his mother, Mary Magdalene, Mary the mother of two of the apostles, and Joanna. With them were Mary and Martha, Nicodemus and John.

They could only wait.

Below the *cruxi* the soldiers played with dice made from knuckle bones, drank *posca*, a vinegary wine, and haggled over the meager spoils of the three men suspended above them. From time to time a centurion rose and walked around the crosses, trying to judge how close death was by the swarm of flies settling on the bodies and the number of carrion birds circling in the blue sky. In this manner an hour, perhaps longer, passed. It may have been the effect of the *posca*, boredom, or the innate cruelty of any deathwatch. Whatever the cause they began to mock and insult Jesus.

Caiaphas heard the jeers from the mound and began to shout: "He saved others! Himself he cannot save!"

Annas and the other priests took up the refrain. "Let Christ, the king of Israel, descend now from the cross, that we may see and believe."

After the outrages they had perpetrated what came from them now was a miserable evil.

At some point during the torrent of abuse, Jesus found the strength to turn his head to the men on either side of him and encourage them to bear their suffering. Then, with what could only be a superhuman effort, he raised his voice so that his words reached the chanting Temple cadre. "Father, forgive them; for they know not what they do."

They were genuinely heroic words—an unforgettable contrast between the behavior of the availing victim and his executioners. Jesus was actually praying for all those who had brutalized him; he wanted to bestow upon them his limitless pity, charity and forgiveness; he wished them to know that whatever they had done, or must do, would not ultimately matter if they came to understand who he was. It was a haunting and thrilling reminder of what he had said on Mount Hattin. "Love your enemies, bless them that curse you, do good to them that hate you and pray for them which despitefully use you, and persecute you."

His forgiveness of those who had treated him so grievously would forever ennoble the somber horror of Golgotha.

While the priests continued to behave shamefully John had started delicate negotiations with the officer commanding the *centuria*. The apostle explained that Jesus' mother and his closest friends wanted to go to the foot of the cross to be near him when the end came. What passed between the two men would forever be uncertain: there would be suggestions of bribery, of John handing over money; others would say that the stricken beauty of Mary Magdalene stirred something in the officer; or that it was his mother's dignity which finally influenced the Roman. Whatever the reason, he allowed to pass through the cordon Jesus' mother, the elderly Mary, Mary Magdalene and Joanna. John was allowed to accompany them. The four women and the apostle picked their way up the mound.

When they reached the foot of the cross they knelt and averted their eyes: they had been raised with a proper sense of modesty; to be exposed completely naked in public was a humiliation almost beyond equal. John was beside Mary, Jesus' mother; he could sense her resolve, knowing she only wished to encourage him in his sacrifice, to let her son understand she supported this total submission to the will of God. In centuries to come that would be the moment that the Church would say she became blessed among all women.

Jesus called down to her. "Woman." The word was filled with formal respect, the way he had always addressed her in public since that evening in Cana when she had asked him to perform that first miracle and he had said, "Woman," and that his time had not yet come, but they had both known and accepted even then it would come to this. "Behold thy son." Jesus wanted her to know he would not turn away from the sacrifice; that while he would shortly no longer exist in this world they would next meet in a better one. In the meantime, she must be protected. Jesus turned his gaze to John. "Behold thy mother." He was asking John not only to take care of her—but to remember always that through Mary his presence would always be there: she had been chosen to give birth to him; she still possessed the sacred authority to make him live in her.

Peter, to whom Jesus had chosen to give the keys to the kingdom, may well, as the Catholic Church still insists, have made a deliberate decision not to come to Golgotha, and sent John to bear witness for him. It would be a suggestion that neither enhanced Peter's position nor diminished the role of John. Of the Twelve he alone continued to show himself as worthy of that original invitation—"Come, follow me."

The mocking voices were now joined by another. One of the thieves began to curse and revile Jesus for not using his power to save them. It was the understandable and desperate reaction of someone embittered by his fate, and who, sensing his own end was very close, wished somehow to distract himself from its torment and terror. His companion delivered a rebuke. "Dost not thou fear God, seeing thou art in the same condemnation?"

The robber wanted to urge the other thief that, while they were both irretrievably doomed, he should not behave like those who had condemned them. Then, with another glance and a movement of his head, all he could manage, he continued to remind his companion of reality. "We receive the due reward of our deeds. But this man hath done nothing amiss."

The honesty of the words was the more moving under the horror they were all enduring; through them, that petty criminal, uncouth, roughened and hardened by a life of sin, had found grace. Having shamed and silenced his companion, he now called out to Jesus. "Lord, remember me when thou comest into thy kingdom."

In confessing his own sins and proclaiming a firm belief in the innocence of Jesus, the thief, with the simplicity of the untutored, had found the way to look beyond his own immediate fate. He wanted Jesus to know he believed in him—and that he accepted his kingdom was only a few further tortured moments on earth away. This man, whose name and appearance would be lost for ever, asked for nothing except to remain in the memory of Jesus.

An endless and futile debate would ensue as to whether the thief could have known Jesus before they became brothers-in-misery. Rationalists could ponder whether his conversion was the climax of lengthy exposure to his teachings and that was why he had felt able to speak with such familiarity: "Remember me." The most likely possibility was that the thief would have heard the discussions in the Antonia Fortress that had led to the release of Barabbas; he would have seen the parchment nailed to Jesus' cross; if he could not read, the robber would have learned of its meaning from the mocking taunts of the priests. Above all, he would have been a witness to his dignity, patience and overwhelming goodness and had heard Jesus ask God to forgive and pardon all those who had brought him here. This had all helped the thief to receive the grace of God which alone could explain his immediate and total conversion. His profession of faith would have remained one of the most unforgettable events in history even if Jesus had not responded. But his reply would be incontrovertible proof that as earthly death drew closer for them both so did the threshold of eternity. "Verily, I say unto thee: today shalt thou be with me in paradise."

There was an urgency to the promise. Soldiers were prodding the other thief with their spears to confirm he was dead. Jesus knew that the man on his other side, who would simply become known as the Good Thief, like himself, could not last much longer.

Until a short while ago the sky had been cloudless; now it grew steadily gloomier, almost obscuring Jesus and the men on either side.

The darkness over the land finally silenced the abuse. Caiaphas and Annas led the Temple cadre back into the city; the few remaining spectators followed. Jonathan and a handful of his guards remained on watch outside the ring of Roman troops.

The soldiers on Golgotha huddled together, shields over their faces. Of all the meteorological phenomena of Judea, the one the Romans disliked most was the *khamsin*, the black sirocco which scooped up tons of sand in its swirling progress out of the Wilderness. In minutes it once more obscured the sun and filled the air with a dark choking. It was widely believed by Romans that it was sent by the gods as a mark of grave displeasure. The centurions peeped around their shields at Jesus' cross, understandably suddenly fearful.

Mary, his mother, and her companions saw that Jesus was sinking rapidly. Blood dripped steadily from the wounds in his hands and feet. From time to time he had tried to redistribute his weight, attempting to ease himself upward to relieve the agonizing pressure in his chest; this only increased the pain in his legs. Jesus' movements were now more sporadic and weaker, little more than twitches. He was still alive, but barely. The sand of the *khamsin* coated his body giving it a strange grayish appearance as if he had already been turned to ash and dust. Then the wind passed, leaving a gloomy stillness.

Suddenly, Jesus pulled himself once more against the upright, forcing up his body, gulping air into his lungs. He stared out over Golgotha and beyond, to the towers of the palace of Herod Antipas and further, to the Antonia Fortress, and finally to the Temple. Then he cried out: "My God, my God, why hast thou forsaken me?"

The mystery of those words would remain forever inexplicable unless they were seen as the final proof that Jesus wished to spare himself nothing; that right to the end he would remain his own master and, with the help of his Father, become the immolated victim through which all those who accepted him would be saved. Not for a moment was he complaining of rejection, though he well understood that everyone was quite alone at death; rather he was reminding himself of why he had to suffer. He knew, and accepted, that in dying he had to sink to the depths before he would ascend to the peak of liberty. His words were not spoken in despair, or reproach, let alone anger; they were a reminder that he was about to be rescued from his present misery—just as a short while before he had saved the Good Thief.

The sky began to brighten, though the sun was still obscured. The centurions returned to their posts, staring at him, openly incredulous that Jesus was still alive. From his lips came two words which showed how far his agony had gone. "I thirst." No longer had he the strength left to speak loudly; almost certainly it was the barely audible moan of man in the burning fever of death.

The words aroused something in the *exactor mortis*; he alone had the authority to intervene. He took the sponge used as a stopper for the flagon of *posca* and poured some of the wine into it. He placed the sponge on the tip of a spear and raised it to Jesus' lips. He sucked upon the sponge. When the officer lowered the spear, Jesus bowed his head. All those around the cross heard the next words. "It is finished."

It was the beginning of the ninth hour, his third on the cross: the moment the sun once more appeared; the end of his suffering. Even in dying Jesus had acted on his own volition. His head had not dropped on his chest *after* death. Instead he had bowed in acceptance that his physical life was finally over—and he acknowledged this before his spirit returned from whence it came.

But the *exactor mortis* had to be certain. He removed the sponge and drove his spear into Jesus' side, working its broad blade around the ribs and into his heart. He withdrew the weapon leaving a large hole. John and the others watched as from the opening came a mixed flow of blood and water. The lancing of the heart, itself almost a banal act, the pointless desecration of a victim already beyond further earthly destruction, would be given a special significance by the evangelist: he would see in the flow the image of Christianity itself emerging; the mixture would symbolize for John the two great sacraments, baptism and communion.

The spear thrust signaled the end of the Roman presence on and around Golgotha. The usual imperial custom was to leave the crucified exposed for a few days as a salutary warning: in that time they became the prey of wild animals and carrion birds. When the stench became unbearable the remains, still on their crosses, were dumped in the Hinnom Valley.

The centurions came down from the hillock leaving Jesus and the two thieves hanging. The *centuria* re-formed and marched back to the barracks. The way was clear for others to join John and the women at the foot of his cross: Joseph of Arimathea, Nicodemus, Mary and Martha. There was both uncertainty and a sense of urgency mingling with their grief. In two hours' time the Passover sabbath would begin. From then on it would be forbidden to remove his body under Jewish law—as this would violate the edict of not working on the sabbath. But before Jesus could be buried they must find a sepulchre.

Joseph said he would go to Pilate and seek authority to have Jesus removed and buried in Joseph's own tomb. The sepulchre was close to where they stood and Jesus could still be properly laid to rest before the onset of Passover. With the accord of the others, Joseph hurried into the city. He was back on the mound as the sun began to dip beyond the Temple. With him was Mark. The boy carried what would be described in his Gospel as "fine linen," which Joseph had purchased in the city to provide a burial shroud. The only hint of what had transpired between Pilate and Joseph would be Mark's revelation that the procurator had expressed surprise that Jesus was already dead; he had sent for the *exactor mortis*, and only when the officer had confirmed the fact did Pilate agree to release the body.

In the face of the advancing afternoon there was grisly work to do. While Nicodemus went to the Street of the Perfume Makers to purchase embalming materials, John and Mark undertook the task of taking Jesus from the cross.

They began by pulling out the nails from his feet, most likely using the hook-like tool Joseph, like any other businessman, carried on him to remove stones trapped in the hoofs of his donkey. Then, with the women supporting the body, the men stood on the cairn and nudged the crossbar from its socket and lowered Jesus to the ground. The nails from his wrists were pried loose. Owing to rigor mortis there was undoubtedly a problem in placing Jesus' hands to his side; equally likely, it was resolved by forcing them into position and securing them with perhaps the cincture of a robe. Still completely naked, Jesus was carried by the three men, the women following, to the tomb.

Befitting a man of Joseph's position, it occupied a prime position among the burial sites in the vicinity of Golgotha. Barely a hundred paces from the execution mount, it was sheltered from its sights by being placed in the lee of another hummock and further protected by a low stone wall inside which had been planted trees and shrubs and the ground cleared of stones and seeded. The tomb had been carved from the hummock and was reached by rolling a boulder, shaped like an outsize millstone, in its groove: this provided effective protection against animals yet made it easy to gain access. Because the sepulchre was unoccupied the stone had been left moved back, exposing the entrance.

Jesus was laid on the ground before the opening.

The women in the burial party took over. Led by Mary, his mother—custom dictated no less as she was his closest relative—water was fetched from a nearby well and the body bathed. John and Mark were too overcome to report the undoubted horror they must all have felt as the full extent of his injuries became clearly visible when the thick coating of dust and caked blood was removed.

Nicodemus returned laden with sacks of myrrh, resin and dried aloes; they were standard burial preparations. John was astonished at the sheer weight the elderly judge had managed to carry—"about an hundred pound weight." The load was not only heavy, but expensive: it required a very wealthy man to afford such homage.

The sticky myrrh was worked into the skin, coating the wounds with a thick light-brown covering. Afterwards the sweet-smelling powder of aloes was sprinkled on the body. The men then wrapped it in the shroud, starting with the feet and winding the linen tightly. When they had covered up to his shoulders they paused so that all those present could view him for the last time. Then the head was covered.

The sun was barely visible above the city wall. When it sank below the horizon it would be the great Sabbath of Passover. Already, in the windows of the tetrarch's palace the first lamps were lit and over Jerusalem itself a hush was settling. The men carried Jesus into the burial chamber, stooping to pass through the low entrance. A ledge had been cut in the rock on one side of the vault. Jesus was placed in the niche. Then they left the tomb, pushing the great round stone in its groove to close the sepulchre.

The news that Jesus' body had been buried and not consigned to the Hinnom Valley did nothing initially to dampen the satisfaction in the Temple over his death. But at some point priests reminded each other that Jesus had actually promised to return: early on, when the agents had first set out to trap him, Jesus had rounded on them and said just as Jonah had spent three days and nights in the belly of a whale, "so shall the Son of man be three days and three nights in the heart of the earth." While Caiaphas did not believe Jesus could possibly rise from the dead, he became steadily convinced that his disciples could remove the body and claim Jesus had fulfilled the greatest of all his prophecies.

Next morning, in spite of it being the sabbath, the high priest and the judges who had tried Jesus hurried to the Antonia Fortress. Ignoring the law of purity, they demanded to be taken to Pontius Pilate. He received them in his salon, surrounded by money chests. The high priest explained that any belief in Jesus' resurrection would be an even greater threat than he had posed in life as the promised Messiah. The procurator finally agreed to provide a detachment of centurions to guard the tomb. Joseph Caiaphas took great care in positioning the soldiers so that no one could possibly approach the sepulchre. The high priest finally left the burial ground, no doubt satisfied, and certainly unaware that what he had done would help to provide the most striking proof of the divinity of Jesus. Between them the high priest of the Jews and the imperial procurator of Rome had helped the world to enter shortly into a new relationship with God through the resurrection of Jesus which would make Christianity possible. No death, since or before, would achieve more. His had, indeed, been an inevitable crucifixion.

EXPLANATIONS

Be not curious in unnecessary matters; for more things are shewed unto thee than men understand.

Ecclesiasticus 3:23

AFTERWORD

> Now that you know all this, happiness will be yours, if you behave accordingly.
>
> John 13:16–17

In the preparation for the reprinting of this book, I said to a friend that I could not have written it today; that so much had changed. He replied, "You don't have to write it; you already have. The text is still meaningful."

Others have, however, quite properly drawn attention to the absence of any attempt to state my position on the resurrection. I do so now. I firmly believe as a Christian that Jesus is the Son of God and all things are therefore possible for him. For me the resurrection is Christ's vindication. It reveals his triumph over sin and death; that he had not been pointlessly murdered, but laid down his life for the world. The risen Christ provides the purpose we need for our life on earth, guarantees us a place in the life to come.

You either believe that or you do not. I believe. That, for me, is the end of the matter.

Yet I recognize that, since I first wrote this book, of all the claims made in the name of what is called a "new" approach to religion, none is more persistent than the argument that the resurrection did not happen. The exponents for this truly staggering claim are not heretics, but often important figures in various Christian institutions. They present their case as impartial conclusions of careful research and scholarship that seems to be dauntingly impressive.

A closer examination reveals otherwise. Each claimant to disproving the resurrection has his own story. One theory cancels out the other. One claim presents "irrefutable proof" that Jesus' body remained in the tomb. Another, with the same lofty confidence in how the research can be interpreted, argues his body was secretly removed. And so on.

I find it strange that all this contradictory "evidence" is aimed at coming to the same conclusion—that there was no resurrection. Surely the ground rule of historical evaluation demands that the essential facts must be the same? Either Jesus' body remained in the tomb, or it did not.

Can it simply be that those scholars who deny the resurrection and the evidence of the New Testament, do so because each one of them is trying to dispose of the overwhelming evidence that it occurred? That they came to a predetermined conclusion long before they had examined all the evidence—and that which they did study was through the prism of scientific materialism which teaches that miracles do not happen and that everything has a rational explanation? And that includes the impossibility of the dead rising after three days.

For those scholars, the words of Matthew—whom it now turns out may have been an eyewitness to the words set down in his Gospel—are not enough. Yet, when I read them again, they hold a truth that is far more believable than the frantic efforts of those who wish to gainsay the miracle of the resurrection as recorded in Matthew.

> Now the next day, that followed the day of the preparation, the chief priests and Pharisees came together unto Pilate, saying, Sir, we remember what that deceiver said, while he was yet alive, After three days I will rise again. Command therefore that the sepulchre be made safe until the third day, lest his disciples come by night and steal him away, and say unto the people, he is risen from the dead: so the last error shall be worse than the first. Pilate said unto them, Ye have a watch: go your way, make it as sure as ye can. So they went, and made the sepulchre sure, sealing the stone, and setting a watch.
>
> Matthew 27:62–66

> And, behold, there was a great earthquake: for the angel of the Lord descended from heaven, and came and rolled back the stone from the door, and sat upon it. His countenance was like lightning, and his raiment white as snow: and for fear of him the keepers did shake, and became as dead men . . . Some of the watch came into the city, and shewed unto the chief priests all the things that were done. And when they were assembled with the elders, and had taken counsel, they gave large money unto the soldiers, saying, Say ye, his disciples came by night, and stole him away while we slept. And if this come to the governor's ears, we will persuade him, and secure you. So they took the money, and did as they were taught: and this saying is commonly reported among the Jews until this day.
>
> Matthew 28:2–4, 11–15

Jesus foresaw his death as the principal reason why he was on earth. Once he had completed that, why wait any longer? As he said to Judas: "What you are going to do, do quickly" (John 13:27).

In all he did on earth, Jesus lived with the expectation of his death with almost little theological elaboration. For him such justification was not necessary to give a meaning to his earthly death. For Jesus it was the final acceptance of a mysterious plan.

All the revisionism cannot take away that one unassailable fact. We can only begin to comprehend the true meaning of that plan when we view it from the standpoint that, for his people, Jesus was the totality of their undying hope. He amplified their every yearning. He urged them to look constantly beyond their immediate world, one in which the Roman occupiers held their life or death at the point of their swords; where their other leaders appeared to be entangled within a set of circumstances that all too readily showed their human frailty.

To his people, the Jews, Jesus was the precursor of the God who comes. He was their hope of a better life. It was there in the way he breathed new life into old prophecies, the way he made clear that the long-awaited hour was upon them.

For Jews that promise has still to be fulfilled. It is rooted in their belief in the failure of Jesus to reconcile his vision with their existing world.

Yet today there is within Israel itself, a sense that it is a time for reappraisal. It is difficult to define, for it is not the consequence of change, but rather the fact of change itself. Much of this has come about through collaborative scholarship. The faiths of Judaism and Christianity still follow paths which do not finally mesh. But they are coming closer.

I have returned to Israel many times since this book was written, keeping in touch with current thinking. Increasingly I have seen that one of the more intriguing aspects is how the personalities of scholars interact with their inquiries. In his book, *Cynic, Sage or Son of God*, Gregory Boyd, Professor of Theology at Bethel College in St. Paul, Minnesota, writes, "the control belief of a scholar determines what kind of Jesus he or she is looking for by defining what kind of Jesus is and is not possible."

That is worth remembering when assessing the many claims of those who seem intent on reducing the Christ of Christianity to a figure linked to a mere chronology of sayings and deeds. It is also worth repeating again the judgment of Luke Timothy Johnson, Professor of New Testament and Christian Origins, at Emory University in Atlanta: "religious knowledge is not the same as historical knowledge."

To which should be added that the Gospels are works of commitment, written with missionary intention. Thus John tells us he is "writing that you may believe that Jesus is the Messiah, the Son of God, and that believing you may have life in his name" (John 20:31). The concern of the Gospels is to advance a spiritual belief rather than a material truth, even though the material existence of Jesus is the means by which that spiritual truth is given expression.

Shortly after I had begun my research I had the good fortune to meet that renowned Anglican theologian, Dr John A. T. Robinson, Dean of Trinity College, Cambridge. When he heard that I intended setting out on a rigorous personal search for answers as to why Jesus had to die—he diffidently suggested I could do worse than take as a starting point the question that had preoccupied him throughout his ministry: can we trust the New Testament?

We sat in his room in Trinity on a damp autumn day in 1975 discussing the daunting mass of conflicting material about his death. Dr. Robinson leaned forward and, in that careful and considered way that none of his students will surely ever forget, he passed a hand over a great dome of a brow.

> What you must write is a book which is an invitation to trust. Don't get side-tracked by the confusion of voices. Just remember that you can trust the New Testament when you approach it as providing a portrait of the human face of God. But a portrait is *not* a photograph. A portrait is an interpretation of the sitter by the artist, or in the case of Jesus, by many artists. And also remember that any book about Jesus, while depending on historical inquiry, will in the end require faith; that, in a purely historical sense, none of the answers will be more than extremely probable. What you must do is write a book that is rooted in proper Bible criticism—and by that I mean using your critical faculties *on* the Bible. Then what you write will be totally positive, confirming rather than denying. It will be a book which is an invitation to trust.

I have tried to keep such wisdom to the fore. The more I read and the wider grew my circle of distinguished interviewees and correspondents, a number of clearly-stated and opposing positions emerged about the life and death of Jesus. What forcibly struck me was that considerable scholars in other fields were quite prepared to play fast-and-loose with the truth when they entered the Christian arena. Controversial claims were often buttressed by extensive references and quotations. Purely as an exercise I decided to run the normal checks and balances on one such work. To my astonishment it was largely based on a book published some eighty years earlier and long discredited. But its claims had become subsequently respectable because a professor had attached *his* name, *his* university and *his* degrees of academic distinction to them. A historian achieved considerable fame with his thesis that Jesus probably never existed. What I found as remarkable as that claim was his book carried an endorsement from a professor of modern history whom I knew from previous contacts to be the epitome of caution. Yet he had allowed his name to promote the idea that Jesus was a creation of the early Christians.

Nor was I encouraged by my contacts with the exponents of religious fundamentalism. Its very conservatism seemed to have grown more entrenched in the face of the wilder excesses of some radical scholars. The problem of so much fundamentalism was neatly explained in the course of a pleasurable summer afternoon I spent with that formidable Catholic scholar, the late Franz Koenig, cardinal-archbishop of Vienna. In his view the classic dilemma of fundamentalism was Jesus' reported prediction about the end of the world coming in his generation.

> If that is what he said, and if we are to take his words literally, then clearly Jesus was wrong. On the other hand, I would not need much convincing that his words, at least on this matter, have been adapted and interpreted by the Early Church for a perfectly understandable purpose, the propagation of faith. Of course that means that what Jesus said or meant is not exactly reflected in our Bibles.

Around a year or so into the research I came across a judgment by the Oxford Classical historian, Professor A. N. Sherwin-White who, in his study of the Roman law as applied to the New Testament, made the point that so many Bible scholars fail to realize the excellent sources at their disposal. Sherwin-White's argument not only held a profound scholarship, but seemed to depend on where the emphasis for proof was placed. For instance, if the question is put: is there any reason why Jesus should *not* have fed the five thousand, then very likely the answer would be: no, there is none. If the emphasis is reversed, for example, is there any reason why Jesus *should* have attacked the Temple money changers, it is possible to argue plausibly that there is no good reason. Depending therefore on the approach, whether a matter is initially perceived as positive or negative, the end conclusion must be very different. It was a valuable lesson to remember in trying to make sense of his life.

I began to grasp others. Among them was to view with some caution what may properly be called the *Dissimilar Test*. This relies upon a challenge: is a particular point or statement one that can be traced to Judaism, Jesus' first contact with faith, or to the early Church, which was founded on his faith? If so can it be attributed to Jesus? Useful though such a yardstick is, to make it the prime, or even the only way to try and establish a truth about him, is a mistake: it narrows the field and distorts any view of Jesus by virtually removing Jesus from his times.

To try and set him *in situ*—to place Jesus against the sacred places, the walls and gates, the mountains and valleys, springs and rivers, rocks and caves—would have been that much harder without studying the lucid and scholarly accounts by the great French rabbi-scholars, Shelmo Izhaki and David Kimche. Their commentaries set down some six hundred years ago remain to this day as essential reading. So does the work of the historian, Josephus. Born in Jerusalem shortly after Jesus died, his various treatises on the Jews have survived, including the indispensable *Antiquities of the Jews* and *Wars of the Jews Against the Romans.*

More recently there is the work of Zev Vilney, lecturer in military history and cartography at the Military Academy of Israel. He has made what must probably be an unsurpassed study of the land that Jesus would have known, drawing from the Hebrew Bible, Talmudic and medieval literature. His work made it possible for me to understand the life and traditions of Galilee at the time of Jesus and to evaluate the cultural conflicts of the Jews and the political position of Jerusalem, the actual layout of the city and its focal point, the Temple, and many of the major events in Jesus' ministry, the sites where he healed and preached, where the raising of Lazarus took place and, of course, the place of his passion, Gethsemane and Golgotha.

While indeed it must still be said that every precise word and action of Jesus is probably irrecoverable by even the most exacting analysis, and that all we can speak of with total confidence is the Christ of faith, there can be no denying that a study of Gospel parallels can be invaluable. There are a number of such studies available. I drew upon the version prepared by the American Standard Bible Committee; it offers not only a full account of the non-canonical parallels but also cites the main non-Christian manuscript support. These extant sources were a further aid in establishing the probability of something Jesus said or did.

Those sources included the *Gospel of the Ebionites*, written around the middle of the second century, or perhaps slightly after, by the Ebionites, Jewish-Christians who believed that Jesus so fulfilled the Jewish law that God chose him to be the Messiah; the *Gospel According to the Hebrews*, known as the "Jewish Gospel," probably written around A.D. 120 in Egypt; the *Gospel According to the Egyptians*, written in Greek around A.D. 130–40 and circulated among Gentile-Christians in Egypt and not regarded as heretical at first in spite of its strong ascetic quality; the *Gospel of Peter*, written probably in Syria around A.D. 130; *Acts of Philip*, a fourth-century Gnostic work; the *Gospel of Thomas*, probably written around A.D. 140 and discovered in 1945 near the village of Nag Hammadi on the Upper Nile;

written in Sahidic Coptic it is a collection of the sayings of Jesus, many showing a strong Gnostic influence.

The material led me down some extraordinary byways, not least the search for an answer to a question that has begun to intrigue many scholars: was Judas Iscariot the first and greatest villain of Christianity or has history misjudged Jesus' treasurer? In the popular mind he remains an infamous betrayer driven to a remorseful suicide. However, I encountered a growing body of respectable opinion that questioned whether the apostle Matthew was right to say: "It had been good for that man if he had not been born."

In the spring of 1986 I traveled once more to Israel, this time to speak, among others, to Dr Robert Fleming. He is a Bible scholar, a social scientist who argues that any portrait of Judas as a mere reprobate is incomplete. At the time Fleming was the director of the Tantur Ecumenical Institute, housed on the road between Bethlehem and Jerusalem. Students come from all over the world to be exposed to Fleming's ideas. Shortly before I arrived he had sent a ripple through conservative religious circles with his claim that Jesus was most likely older than his traditional thirty-three years. Fleming based his findings on a lengthy study of Syrian scripts dating from a census held in Judea in 12 B.C.—and in a closely-argued case concluded that was the year Jesus was born, making him forty-two years old when he went to the cross, an elderly man in those times.

> He was probably not entirely a fit man. In human terms Jesus could have been over his physical peak. There are no theological implications in revising his age. But it does help to explain why Jesus died so quickly.

Such claims placed Fleming among the *wunderkinder* of biblical revisionists. He is very much in the mold of a new kind of religious scholar, taking his students through the Wilderness, lecturing as he goes: inviting them to sit down and partake in what he insists is a faithful reproduction of the Last Supper in a replica of the original upper room. The Tantur Institute is a remarkably active and productive place in which a number of disciplines—theology, history and active ministry—coexist under one roof. Some of Fleming's conclusions, such as the layout of the original upper room, along with the social customs of Jesus' time, have found a place in this book—as indeed has Fleming's argument that Judas was not merely a money-grabber, motivated purely by the shallowest of motives.

Fleming's point is that Jesus would never have given Judas such an important post as treasurer if Judas had been totally evil. In Fleming's portrait, Judas emerges as the outsider in a group of clannish Galilean-born apostles—a man alone, driven in the end to betray Jesus because Judas actually thought that was the only way to bring about the kingdom.

In Jerusalem, not far from Christ's final walk to Golgotha, I found support for Fleming's views from one of the most astute legal minds in Israel: Haim Cohn, then a judge of the supreme court of Israel. The author of an influential legal study of the trial of Jesus—a work which he cheerfully admitted had attracted its share of criticism in Christian circles—included his assessment of Judas.

> The whole Gospel portrait of Judas is so unlikely, so incongruous that it merits no credence. If Judas wanted to betray Jesus all he had to do was to denounce him to the Romans as a rebel—and he would be certain of swift action. My own conclusion is that the prevailing portrait of Judas was included in the Gospels for purely theological reasons—a reminder that a Jew set in motion the death of Jesus.

Mr. Justice Cohn was a source of valuable guidance on the law and procedures—both Roman and Jewish—which operated at the time of Jesus, providing penetrating insights into the political and religious motivations of those involved in mounting and conducting the most famous law case in history. Through him it was possible to get a strong sense of the atmosphere in Annas' palace and the Antonia Fortress and, of course, obtaining that perspective of Judas.

The feeling that the treasurer may have been badly misjudged was echoed by the Reverend Dr. John Gosling, a noted Anglican theologian and adviser on Continuing Ministerial Education to the Diocese of Salisbury, England. He expressed the view that Judas' behavior could be seen as that of a man making a final desperate attempt to implement the kingdom by bringing Jesus into confrontation with the Roman and Jewish authorities. Dr. Gosling argued that Judas might well have believed that in such a confrontation Jesus would have emerged victorious. It was a possibility that I felt had to be reflected in my own assessment of Judas.

It would be a further ten years, in November 1995, before a panel of fifty biblical scholars would assemble in Santa Rosa, California, and conclude that it was highly unlikely that for thirty pieces of silver Judas kissed his master and thus betrayed him to the authorities to be crucified. Their verdict would make a cover story for *Time*.

What distinguished Judas from the other apostles is that final betrayal. Yet nowhere in the New Testament is a motivation for doing so ascribed to the treasurer. Both Jewish and Christian scholars continually reminded me that the Gospels, by themselves, do not allow, or indeed are meant to provide, a complete assessment of events. Extant to their testimony is a literature often forgotten or overlooked by Christians. The Vatican libraries alone have over 100,000 such volumes, many of them rarely consulted from one century to the next. Undoubtedly some of the most interesting include Jewish and pagan writing.

It was Duncan M. Derrett, Professor of Oriental Law at the University of London, who reminded me of the importance of that material. During my research he maintained a flow of challenging data. From it emerged the full horror of Roman and Jewish scourging and the precise manner of crucifixion. He also proved to be a brilliant scene-setter for the pretrial atmosphere in the Sanhedrin, the relationship between Sadducees and Pharisees, the intertension between the Roman and Jewish administrations, including some highly useful glimpses of Herod Antipas. Above all this distinguished lawyer provided a compelling assessment of why Jesus had to die.

> His doctrines were incomprehensible except in flashes to his contemporaries. Jesus was put to death by strangers for passing on a brand of wisdom which, if it had been popular at the time, would have stripped the powers that were of their authority and profits.

It was a logical research step from Professor Derrett to those Jewish scholars who see Jesus as a rallying figure for the Zealots. At the forefront is Hyam Maccoby. He has gone further than any revisionist with his claim that Jesus was at the actual center of the revolutionary movement in Judea. It is not always easy to follow, let alone accept, Maccoby's thesis, but his Jewish sources deserve to be studied by any Christian. Through Maccoby I spent several profitable months reading Jewish history, including a remarkable document by Travers A. Herford dealing with the Pharisees; published in 1924 as a monograph, it remains unequaled. Some of the great names of Jewish biblical scholarship—Israel Abrahams, Moses Aberbach and Herman L. Strack—became as familiar to me as their Christian counterparts. I am particularly indebted to Abraham's *Studies in Pharisaism and the Gospels*, Aberbach's magnificent account of *The Roman-Jewish War (A.D. 66–70)* and Strack's *Introduction to the Talmud and Midrash.* Through them I began to see it was possible to give flesh and blood to the behavior of Caiaphas and Herod Antipas.

Among my contemporary guides were Ze'ev Falk, Professor of Family Law and R. J. Werblowsky, Professor of Comparative Religion. At the time both were on the faculty of the Hebrew University in Jerusalem, whose libraries are a treasure trove that allows for a fuller and, hopefully, truer record of Jesus to emerge. These two gifted men guided me to the tractates; a full list appears at the end of the bibliography.

Modern Jewish scholarship has also produced a clearer picture of Herod Antipas and his background. In this wealth of writing I encountered the first important clues about Pilate and Claudia Procula. The Roman administration in Judea also came vividly to life in Suetonius' account *Tiberius* (XXX 11.2); Cicero's *In Verrem II* (12 and 11.2); Tacitus' *Histories* (IV.74.1) and Emil Schürer's masterful *The Jewish People in the Time of Jesus Christ*, translated into English in 1885 and still an indispensable source about Pilate and his wife and their lifestyle in Judea.

Inevitably, the research trail led to Professor S. G. F. Brandon. His scholarship—and I must add in my case his encouragement—made it not only possible for me to trace more easily the public career of Jesus from his baptism by John, but also to accept that though theologically necessary and politically convenient, a number of Christian versions of the trial of Jesus are misrepresentations of what actually happened. Brandon's work in this area of historical analysis is best seen in his *The Trial of Jesus of Nazareth.*

Brandon was the first to admit that there are theologians, philosophers and interpreters of the great legends and shibboleths of his life who want to crack the tough kernel of Jesus' "very starkness and to grind to dust the acceptable core of his life. They are the ones who would say, in answer to the question—'can we trust the New Testament?'—that, no, we cannot because the Gospels are only a record of faith."

One of the most sobering tasks I had to pursue was the work of those who are intent on stripping Jesus of anything which places him beyond all mortals. There are, for instance, those who argue that Christ had actually married Mary Magdalene at Cana. There is, like so much in their revisionist world, a certain spurious plausibility to the claim: the uncontestable fact remains that there is not a word in the New Testament to show that Jesus voluntarily renounced marriage. Therefore, runs the argument, why should Jesus' marital position be different from any other devout Jew of his time, that after all, God's first commandment in the Torah is "be fruitful and multiply." Indeed, the Old Testament, upon which Jesus had been nurtured, accentuated the importance of marriage—to the point where a Talmudic commentary of his days argued that failure to wed was a crime akin to murder; that from Genesis onwards it was written that "it is not good that man should be alone"; "any man who has no wife is no proper man"; "he who is not married is, as it were, guilty of bloodshed; he caused the image of God to be diminished and the divine presence to be withdrawn from Israel."

Again, the Jesus-was-married school point out that the apostle Luke confirmed that Jesus, on the threshold of manhood, was still an obedient son of Joseph and that within the prevailing Jewish culture betrothals were usually arranged by fathers. Joseph had made such arrangements, as the book of Corinthians indicated, for the brothers of Jesus. Is it not possible, runs the argument, that Jesus shared the same Jewish belief in marriage as a sacred duty for himself as well as others? If not wed to Mary Magdalene, could not his wife have died during those years before his public life began? Is it not significant that, when questioned about marriage, Christ endorsed the view in Genesis—"for this cause shall a man leave his father and mother, and shall cleave to his wife and twain shall be one flesh"—instead of offering a new teaching? Is it really, in the end, conclude the insidious persuaders, fantastic to accept that Jesus had been wed and widowed?

There are those who even argue that the climax of Holy Week, Good Friday, is really an elaborate sham: that Jesus arranged his own death; that the Romans and the Temple authorities connived in the plot; that the centurion had not pierced his side; that Joseph of Arimathea, another of the plotters, with the help of the women in Jesus' life, cut him down—still alive—from the cross at dusk and placed him in the tomb; that later, under cover of darkness, he was taken away, his wounds tended and that he lived for a further forty days before finally succumbing.

A demented intellectualism—last seen over a century ago in Europe—seems to be on the increase. The Vatican today regularly receives solutions to the birth and life of Jesus. He was the product of an affair between Mary and a handsome Arab prince. She had been seduced by Joseph of Arimathea, which would explain his role after the crucifixion. Joseph was Mary's uncle; their son the offspring of an incestuous union. There are claims, often supported by detailed genealogical charts, that Jesus had been a Tibetan, a Hindu, a Mongolian or a Mead. Some even insist he came from darkest Africa and was a Bushman. Zoologists and biologists write that the Virgin Birth is a scientific impossibility: parthenogenesis, as they prefer to rationalize it, is only seen in aphids and crustaceans.

If I was asked to put a name and date when this revisionist onslaught began, I would answer without hesitation, Ernest Renan, 1862. That was the year the French theologian published his *Life of Jesus*; a volume that not only became one of the greatest religious best sellers of the nineteenth century, but the springboard from which, in the next hundred years, others would follow with their arguments that references to angels announcing his birth, and accounts of his miraculous curing of the sick, are no more than fables; that events which bear out the Old Testament predictions, such as Jesus being born in Bethlehem, entering Jerusalem on a donkey, and his betrayal, should be rejected as wishful thinking, purely designed to bolster the myth that his life had been foretold. These statements coolly and dispassionately argued, have opened a floodgate which still threatens to engulf traditional belief, sweeping away the Jesus of convention.

There are supposedly Christian scholars who account for Jesus' periodic bouts of fasting as proof he had a pathological fear of food, making him the prototype for male anorexia. Others argue he is the original model for the Oedipus Complex, actually taking his mother to heaven so they could be together eternally. Some claim that while in her womb he had experienced neurophysical trauma brought about by Mary having to explain to Joseph how she had become pregnant. Jesus is accused of suffering from dromomania, tuberculosis and theomania, the sadly misguided belief he actually was God.

Emerging from this numbing morass of speculation, I began to see that my investigations must focus upon Jesus the Jew; that any assessment must be made within the framework of the faith Christ was born into and grew up with. Jesus had been raised in a circumambient world, already two thousand years old when he arrived, one where the Jewish identity was clear-cut and sharply divided from paganism. Jesus had existed, like any Jew, in a compartmentalized historicism. He, and all those around him, were regarded by their fellow Jews as no more than part of a particular epoch, each charged for the moment as sole architects of Jewish destiny. For his fellow Jews, that had been the world he, like them, had been expected to live in, and when their time came, to die from. It was one in which there was no possible resurrection, and no possible hope of eternal life beyond the grave.

Almost a full hundred years after his death, the first description of Jesus was discovered. It had been set down by a Roman officer called Lentulas stationed in Caesarea in the year A.D. 30:

> Nut-brown hair smooth down to the ears and from the ears downwards formed soft curls and flowed to the shoulders in luxuriant locks with a parting in the center of the head after the fashion of the Nazarenes; a smooth clean brow and reddish face without spots or wrinkles; nose and mouth flawless; a full luxuriant beard parted in the middle. Eyes with an unusually varied capacity for expression.

Two hundred years after Lentulas, another Roman, Origen, represented Jesus as a short, ungraceful figure with a lame right leg, a limp. A century later Epiphanius had created a towering Jesus, well over six feet tall, with a burnished complexion, aquiline nose, coal-black eyes and reddish hair. From then on it became open-season for the length of his hair, the colour of his eyes, the shape of his lips and the prominence of his cheekbones. His would become the original facial melting pot: from it would come all the others: face resolute; face calm; face compelling; face compassionate and face tortured—all to be painted, sculpted and carved. There would be no scholars who would insist it was deliberate that he had no discernible features and was virtually without biography; that he was meant to remain a figure physically and emotionally beyond human description—to ensure that the importance of his message would not be diminished by irrelevant detail.

Yet there is much in the literature of such writings that is worthwhile studying. For instance, in the Prologue to the *Gospel of Nicodemus*—the Pharisee judge twice mentioned by John as a friend of Jesus—there is a graphic account of one of the pretrial Sanhedrin debates, with Caiaphas, Annas and Gamaliel clearly identified.

Through *The First Gospel of the Infancy of Jesus Christ*, translated in 1697 from Syriac, yet largely ignored because it had been part of Gnostic belief since the second century, a much clearer picture emerges of Christ's childhood and adulthood—the so-called "unknown years." There are details in this gospel of Jesus disputing with his schoolteacher, and later, Christ performing his first miracle, lengthening a plank of wood that Joseph had cut too short; there, too, is the account of Jesus learning the craft of a dyer, which is why even today Iranian dyers honor him as their patron. While it is clear there will always be a great divergence of opinion as to the place and importance of this and other writings, they do provide detail about rites and ceremonies Jesus would have participated in.

The skeptics, of course, distrust all such sources. Yet, where it is possible to check them against data on contemporary background of Roman and Jewish society, the material is rooted in fact. In his *New Testament Theology*, Jeremias argues that it is the "inauthenticity and not the authenticity that must be demonstrated." Dr. Robinson, who set me off all those years ago on my investigation, went further. "A Christian has nothing to fear in the truth. For to him the truth is Christ. It is large—larger than the world—and shall prevail. It is also a living and a growing reality. And therefore he is free, or should be free, to follow the truth wherever it leads."

That seemed to me to be a very worthwhile *leitmotiv* in pursuing my research.

In 1995, Robert Smalhout, Professor of Anaesthesiology at University Hospital, Utrecht, and a distinguished Dutch biblical scholar, brought a doctor's viewpoint on the crucifixion of Jesus.

He pointed out that Christ's crucifixion, as such, was unexceptional. By the time Jesus was taken to Golgotha, death by the cross was already close to a thousand years old. It was the Romans who developed the idea from the Phoenicians and turned it into a technique guaranteed to produce the maximum pain and agony of adjustable duration. In the hands of a skilled practitioner, it was possible to decide how much hurt should be administered before a person finally succumbed. Crucifixion was the usual punishment for all serious crimes, including sedition against the state. Thousands of war captives and slaves were executed in this way. After the defeat of Spartacus in 71 B.C., almost 7,000 crosses lined the Appian Way. From each one hung a rebellious slave.

Smalhout makes the valid point that so common was crucifixion that the authors of the Gospels did not waste time to describe the process in detail. Everyone in the Roman empire knew only too well what was involved.

The cross used for Christ's execution, says Smalhout, was the *crux commisa*, and shaped like the letter T. The crosspiece that Christ carried through the streets of Jerusalem would have weighed the equivalent of a bag of cement. But for a man who had undergone the extra punishment of being flayed, the weight would have been excruciating. It would be nothing compared with what was to follow.

> The nails securing Christ's arms to the cross were driven through the wrists, not his palms. The palms could not withstand the weight of the body. Instead the eight-inch nails were driven precisely into the space between the wristbones. These were displaced but not shattered. That in itself is painful enough, as anyone who has even sprained a wrist will know. (Smalhout)

From there he uses his medical knowledge to offer a clinical view of what Jesus suffered. How an important nerve, the median, would have come into contact with the nails, causing severe cramp in the thumb, so agonizing that the thumbnail embedded itself in the flesh.

Next Christ would have to be hoisted, so that the crosspiece slotted on to the vertical stem, or *stipes* of the cross. Once the crossbeam had been positioned, Jesus' knees were bent until the sole of one foot would be pressed flat against the *stipes*. Then another eight-inch nail was driven through the flesh—precisely in the middle between the second and third metatarsal bones. As soon as the nail emerged through the sole, the other leg was bent into position, so that the same nail could be hammered through the second foot and into the wood. The victim was then left to hang from the three nails. Blood loss was slight but the pain was unbearable. The death struggle had begun.

Smalhout continues with the precision of his profession:

> A body suspended by the wrists will sag downwards, pulled by gravity. This produces enormous tension in the muscles of the arms, shoulders and chest wall. The ribs are drawn upwards so that the chest

> is fixed in position as if the victim has just drawn a large breath—but cannot breathe out. The severely strained arm, shoulder and chest muscles develop agonizing cramp. The metabolic rate is raised but the oxygen supply is reduced. One result of this is the production of large amounts of lactic acid in the bloodstream leading to what is known as "metabolic acidosis," often seen in athletes driven to exhaustion and severe cramp. This is aggravated by the difficulty in breathing and in ridding the body of carbon dioxide, leading to respiratory acidosis. Unrelieved, the victim finally dies of suffocation. This can occur within half an hour.

The Romans wished to prolong the death agony. So they would have arranged Jesus on the cross so that he could continue to live by forcing himself up on the nails in his feet. By this stretching of his legs, Jesus could relieve the stress on his arms and chest, allowing him to temporarily breathe a little easier. Soon Jesus would have realized that this new position—with his full weight being borne by the nail driven through his feet—intensified his pain. To combat that Jesus would have let his legs once more sag, so that he was once more hanging from his wrists.

In that way Christ would have lowered and raised himself in a desperate struggle to find some escape from the suffocating and rending pain. The slow, deadly and inevitable course would continue for six hours. Sweat would have run down his body. His temperature would have soared. Both would have contributed to his great thirst. Deduces Smalhout:

> Blood loss and oedema caused by flogging reduced the circulation volume, blood pressure would have fallen, and his heart pounded faster. The severely acidic condition of the blood, combined with the excessive loss of salt through sweat was barely compatible with life. The heart began to fail and the lungs fill with fluid. The beginnings of the death rattle croaked in each failing, painful breath as his heart began to give out.

Finally Jesus called out, "I thirst."

One of the Roman soldiers lifted a sponge soaked in a soldier's potion of wine, vinegar, water and beaten eggs.

When Jesus had drunk from it, he cried, "It is finished."

Then, in the words of the apostle John, "he bowed his head and gave up the ghost."

The historical background came into that much sharper focus by personal research. It is one thing to read about Mary Magdalene; quite another to come across her tomb in a field where Magdala once stood; to stand in the synagogue where Jesus began his ministry in Capernaum; to follow the shore of Galilee as he once did; to walk the path where he was betrayed on the Mount of Olives; to retrace his steps through Jerusalem; to hear sounds and see sights that have not changed greatly from the time of Jesus.

There are many ways to see his land but probably the best is by air—in my case from the open door of an Israeli helicopter rushing in from the sea south of Haifa to pass over a stretch of long sandy coast where Joshua, at the end of the exodus, had led his people. They had found little peace as, from the sea, came the Philistines, pirates and booty-hunters, rapacious adventurers who spearheaded the Aryan invasion of this land in the twelfth century before Christ. They had been finally overcome by the Israelites. Some four hundred years before Rome was founded, the Pharaoh Rameses III had claimed all this land.

Once more the sons of Israel, among them the mighty Samson and the wise kings, Saul and David, rallied their people, just as Abraham, Jacob and Joseph had done under earlier tyrannies—driving the enemy beyond the Land of Edom, a virtual Wilderness to which the red-haired Esau had retreated to conquer his anger after Jacob had taken away his birthright. The helicopter passed over the peak from which Moses, close to death, had looked down on the Promised Land he would never reach. Then came the craggy hill called Machaerus, upon which Herod the Great had built a massive stronghold where later the king's son, the malevolent Herod Antipas, watched while his wanton stepdaughter, Salome, danced and had rewarded her with the head of John the Baptist.

The river in the middle distance: that was perhaps where Jacob had wrestled throughout an entire night with an angel. And beside the river, that winding track: it had been the road which had led from Alexandria to Damascus, a journey of months, a caravan route whose stopping places included Nazareth.

Tens of thousands of years before Christ had walked this ground, nature had folded in on itself, crushing the limestone and other rock strata into new formations, while at the same time creating two fissures so deep that the Ancients believed they were the anterooms to hell. Between these gigantic openings the earth collapsed, an inversion that over aeons gave it distinctive natural regions: Samaria, Galilee, Idumae, Judea, all occupied by the legions of Pompey. Rome, for easier administration, called it Judea; a country they reckoned to be from north to south, no more in length than a hundred and sixty miles, about the distance from Florence to Rome, and at its greatest width to be eighty-seven miles, less than three days march for a legion even over the roughest of ground.

Running the length of the country is a plateau ridge along which Jesus must have walked many times, the ground at the southern end still pitted with hollows of red silt, the residue from its creation. This is the Wilderness, a forbidding tawny colored vista, its shading suggesting the hide of a lion. It had been the first citadel of faith, where Abraham had settled, where great Jewish kings had later ruled, where the true God was acclaimed—and which would be forever remembered as the scene of Christ's confrontation with Satan.

In the distance a glimpse of Jerusalem, its Herodian and Crusader walls clearly discernible and the gold dome of the Mosque of Omar offering a modest substitute for the Temple. The shimmering heat makes the sun-baked limestone buildings appear dun-colored. Abruptly, below was the ancient plain where Barak, another of Israel's great warriors, responding to the plea of the prophetess Deborah, had defeated Sisera and his heathen army.

This plain had all been part of the original Land of Canaan, a name chosen long before it was called the Holy Land or Palestine, let alone Israel. Canaan: from the Phoenician, *kinella*, the red-purple dye that was an important commodity for trading in the decisive time when the Israelites finally won this ground, and which, after their victory, they also named the Promised Land, a permanent reminder for them of the covenant between Abraham and Yahweh, confirming them as Chosen People and their right to live here in peace.

Then: the only true river in the country, mentioned more than two hundred times in Holy Scripture and about whose banks the psalmist had sung—the Jordan. From its source in the north, it passes through wooded country once the home of the most industrious of all the tribes of Israel, the tribe of Dan. A few miles beyond, at one of the massive rock outfaces, Jesus had paused, and said to his devoted Simon "Thou are Peter, and it is upon this rock that I will build my Church."

Then the Sea of Galilee, no doubt even more breathtaking in the time of Jesus, when the trees had been more plentiful and a score, or more, white-walled villages and towns had rimmed the lake's harplike shape.

In Christ's time the land to the south was to be avoided, an area of dark and deep valleys and canyons pockmarked with caves. In one such cavern David had bided his time to challenge and defeat Goliath near the Dead Sea. The lake is close to the Ghor, a fearful gash on the face of the planet, running two thousand further miles beyond this point. On ground near this rift stood the cities of Sodom and Gomorrah. And, somewhere nearby was a village where Judas Iscariot was born and from which he had made his way to that most pleasant of all the regions, Galilee. There he had met Jesus and through his actions remained inexorably bound to him.

They both may well have looked like any of the men who today worship before the last fragment of the Temple of Jerusalem—that towering edifice of stones Christians call the Wailing Wall, where devout Jews stand and pray, rocking back and forth, remembering Moses and the miraculous crossing of the Red Sea, and the manna from heaven which had kept the Israelites alive in the desert and how, when they were safely delivered, God had told them that they alone could henceforth know him as Yahweh, "He who is."

In Nazareth, the women's faces are mostly veiled, only the dark and darting eyes indicating awareness as they cross the main square—where in his day the local rabbis had pronounced punishments for infringements of the law not serious enough to be referred to the Temple in Jerusalem. Mary, his mother, had almost certainly come this way, barefooted, perhaps to purchase new wicks for oil lamps or replacement straw mats which served as both seats and mattresses, spread over a floor of compacted earth. I still wondered in 1996 whether without their veils, any of the women moving slowly across the square, burdened with panniers and pitchers resembled the Madonna of popular mythology.

Central to that question is the one that Dr. Robinson had put to me: can we trust the New Testament?

I believe we can not only trust it, but by also going back to all the other discarded literature, our understanding and perception of why Jesus had to die becomes clearer.

The bibliography which follows shows the road I traveled. My reading will almost certainly not be quite the same preference as anyone else's. I may have chosen books which are more radical over some matters and more conservative on others. But then, there is nothing fixed or final in any account of his life. Yet, all my years of research have only strengthened my trust in the primary documents of the Christian faith—all of them. The undoubted scholarship of many of the authors in my bibliography did not give me faith—they only encouraged me that it had not been misplaced. In the end a Christian goes through life trusting. This book has been an invitation to do so.

CHRONOLOGY

The most important happenings in the background and life of Jesus along with parallel events in general history. Compiled with the help of members of the faculty of the Hebrew University, Jerusalem; the Reubeni Foundation, Jerusalem; the Jerusalem Center for Biblical Studies and Research; the Archivio Segreto at the Vatican.

Date	Israel	Historical Parallel
c. 1900 B.C.	Abraham proclaimed new religion, so strict God must never be invoked by his name, Yahweh.	Hammurabi, king of Babylon, built new temple to moon god called Sin. Egypt's tenth pharaonic dynasty fell to Hyksos armies. Egyptian godhead contracted from nine to three—Ra, Horus and Osiris—but national faith still based on trinity concept of father, mother and son.
c. 1700 B.C.	Sodom and Gomorrah destroyed. Joseph died in Egypt.	Egypt liberated from Hyksos occupation. Pharaoh Akhnaton banned worship of all deities except Aten, the sun god.
1500 B.C.	Jerusalem, already 1,000 years old, established as one of the great walled cities of the world, owing to fortification techniques of its Canaanite builders.	Hinduism emerged in India as major religion after centuries of developing from sacrificial cults.
c. 1300 B.C.	Moses, adopted son of Queen of Egypt and former viceroy of Nubia, finally persuaded Pharaoh Merneptah to "let my people go." The exodus. Moses descended from Mount Sinai with Ten Commandments.	Assyria established itself as third-ranking power in world.
c. 1200 B.C.	Moses died after leading his people for forty years through the Wilderness.	Philistines invaded Gaza, Ashdod and Sidon. The Trojan War began.

Date	Israel	Historical Parallel
1180 B.C.	Joshua led Israelites into land of Canaan. Won major battle, defeating combined forces of five pagan kings.	Fall of Troy. Hector, brother of Paris, killed in single combat with Achilles.
1140 B.C.	Famine in Canaan. Bethlehem among worst hit of cities. Samuel became leader of all twelve tribes.	Tomb of Rameses II looted near Cairo. The influence of Egypt as ranking power on wane.
1130 B.C.	Israelites began new series of wars against Philistines and Midionites. Gideon refused to accept kingship over tribes. Samson latest Jewish folk hero.	New Assyrian legal code established. Many tenets bore close resemblance to Torah.
1026 B.C.	Saul became Israel's first king, crowned in small town of Silgal in eastern Benjamin. Israelites faced annihilation by Philistines. David-ben-Yishnai of Bethlehem slayed Goliath in War of Attrition.	Phoenician traders established business links with Europe.
1007 B.C.	Saul dead. David crowned. Foundations laid for sacred belief that expected Messiah will only come from royal house of David.	Brahmanism gained ground in India. Babylonia gripped by tribal warfare.
990 B.C.	David drove Philistines out of Promised Land. The holy ark of the covenant brought for first time into Jerusalem. The king's psalms written down.	Phoenician script introduced into Greece.
958 B.C.	Solomon king of Israel. First Temple dedicated. Queen of Sheba visited Jerusalem.	Hiram, king of Tyre.
933 B.C.	The Promised Land divided into two nations, Israel and Judah. Jerusalem remained loyal to dynasty of David.	Baalazar, king of Tyre. Greece completed domination of Aegean Sea.
900/ 800 B.C.	The prophets: Amos, Hosea, Isaiah.	Greek migration and expansion. Shalmaneser III launched new period of Syrian aggression. Rome founded.
753 B.C.	First supreme high court, Sanhedrin, established in Jerusalem; composed of priests, Levites and important laymen. High priest appointed president. Court's power included trying cases of blasphemy and sedition.	

Date	Israel	Historical Parallel
722 B.C.	Northern kingdom of Israel fell to Assyria. Judah remained intact, but tens of thousands gathered in Temple to mourn exile of 150,000 Jews from north.	Zoroaster in Persia.
700/ 600 B.C.	The prophets: Micah, Jeremiah.	Anarchy in Athens as Solon's constitutional reforms fail. Babylon invaded Egypt.
588 B.C.	The prophet Jeremiah arrested in Jerusalem on charge of treason.	Dorian ban on all the works of Homer. Buddhism flourished in India.
586 B.C.	Nebuchadnezzar captured Jerusalem. First Temple destroyed. Jews exiled to Babylon.	Delphi, home of the Oracle of Apollo, chosen as model for Pythian Olympiads.
538 B.C.	Jews returned to homeland.	Babylon fell to Cyrus.
448 B.C.	Rebuilding of Temple began. First Knesset opened in Jerusalem. The nation's leaders—120 in number—pledged new nation would obey Torah: intermarriage forbidden; work on sabbath banned; Temple offerings reinstituted.	Thirty-year-old peace pact between Athens and Sparta collapsed. Confucianism and Taoism continued to dominate Chinese spiritual thinking.
399 B.C.	Ezra completed compilation of the Bible.	Death of Socrates. Sparta overrun. Alexander the Great established Greek superiority in Mediterranean basin.
334 B.C.	Greek forces occupied Judea, Samaria and Galilee. Jews resisted introduction of Greek as equal language to Hebrew.	Rome established the social pyramid dominated by its small, warring, shifting ruling class, highly educated and motivated. Greek and Oriental scientists encouraged to come and share their knowledge.
332 B.C.	Temple expanded in Jerusalem.	Alexander dead. Greek Empire divided up, and weakened, by his generals.
300/ 200 B.C.	The Ptolemies occupy Israel before being ousted by the Seleucids.	First Punic War (264–241) claimed annexations for Roman empire. End of Second Punic War (218–201) saw large areas of Spain under Roman control.
165 B.C.	Judas Maccabee liberated Jerusalem from Syrian occupation.	Antiochus IV, Tyrant of Syria, dead. Decline of Carthage. Fall of Macedonia. Unprecedented corruption revealed among Roman senators and consuls.

Date	Israel	Historical Parallel
134 B.C.	Yocham Hyrcanus appointed high priest of Temple and Sanhedrin. Deep-seated differences surfaced between rival parties of Sadducees and Pharisees over matters of faith and tradition. Violent demonstrations in Jerusalem.	Greece a Roman province. Third Punic War saw destruction of Carthage.
76 B.C.	Queen Salome Alexandra first woman to rule nation. Sadducee influence to decline. The sect's leader, Diogenes, sentenced to death by Sanhedrin.	China added to its empire by occupying Korea. King Nicomedes III bequeathed his entire kingdom to Rome. Pompey defeated Mithridates.
63 B.C.	Pompey entered Jerusalem. Temple desecrated.	Sixteen-year-old Roman–Parthian peace treaty broken by surprise Roman attack. Cicero Rome's leading lawyer. The Spice Route from East and trading links with China flourished.
44 B.C.	Herod, the son of Antipater the Edomite, establishing reputation as leader Rome favored to rule its newly named Judea province.	Julius Caesar murdered on Ides of March.
40 B.C.	Hasmonean king Antigonius rejected Herod's ultimatum to abdicate. Herodian forces, supported by three Roman legions, occupy Galilee and lay siege to Jerusalem.	Treaty of Brindisi gave Octavian crucial hold in battle for control of Roman empire.
37/27 B.C.	Herod became king of all Judea. Ordered Second Temple to be built. Began an unprecedented rule of terror.	Elected divine emperor, Octavian changed his name to Augustus, one with ancient significance in pagan religion.
20 B.C.	Herod Antipas born—the son of his father's fifth wife, the Samaritan, Malthace.	Augustus appointed unfailingly competent Agrippa as virtual co-regent and the degenerate Maecebas to watch over the army and empire's finances.
12 B.C.	Census in Judea and Galilee as part of empire-wide check by Rome for tax-evaders. JESUS BORN(?) Celestial phenomenon to be known as Halley's Comet, and "Star of Bethlehem," seen from August to October. The Holy Child family fled to Egypt.	Augustus married off his witty, licentious daughter, Julia, for third time—to his stepson, Tiberius. Roman expansion placed its forces on River Elbe but empire's resources dangerously over stretched. Augustus faced rebel lion in Pannonia and had to abandon plan to conquer Bohemia.

Date	Israel	Historical Parallel
8 B.C.	Herod Antipas, like all sons of Herod the Great, sent to Rome to complete education and gain knowledge of imperial policies, essential grooming as a potential successor to his father's throne.	Roman forces strengthened in Gaul in preparation for cross-Channel invasion of Britannia.
5 B.C.	Herod Antipas returned home, romanized, to be with his dying father.	Augustus claimed Armenia conquered, but his puppet government unable to control population.
4 B.C.	Herod the Great dead. His kingdom divided between three sons. Herod Antipas made tetrarch of Galilee. Continued father's tyrannical rule. The Holy Family returns from Egypt to live in Nazareth.	Egypt main corn provider for Roman empire. Rioting in Spain during celebrations to mark another year of its incorporation into empire.
0	The Onset of the Christian Era Jesus challenged the doctors of law at the Temple.	Herod Antipas' brother, Archelaus, deposed. Rome appointed first procurator to Judea, Copenius.
A.D. 6	Jesus among the actors at - Sepphoris.	Annas appointed high priest.
A.D. 14	Jesus in Nazareth, eldest son of growing family of brothers and sisters.	Augustus dead. Accession of Tiberius.
A.D. 26	Joseph of Nazareth dead.	Pontius Pilate appointed procurator.
A.D. 27	Jesus' cousin, John the Baptist, began to baptize on banks of River Jordan in autumn.	Rome reported to have record number of slaves, estimated as from one quarter to one third of entire population.
A.D. 28		
March:	Jesus is baptized. Attends Cana wedding. In Capernaum.	Vast majority of Roman empire, including many of the most highly educated, reaffirm belief in astrology.
April:	In Jerusalem for Passover.	
May:	In Judea. John the Baptist arrested.	
June:	Jesus in Galilee.	
October:	Returned to Jerusalem for Feast of Tabernacles. Then resumed his ministry in Galilee.	
A.D. 29		
April:	John the Baptist beheaded. Jesus went from Jerusalem to Phoenicia and Iturea and back to Galilee.	Pilate informed Tiberius of execution. Emperor reminds his subjects of power of pagan "savior" deities who guaranteed life hereafter. Cults based upon magic rituals and sacramental banquets to purge human unworthiness flourished in empire.

Date	Israel	Historical Parallel
October:	Went to Jerusalem for Feast of Tabernacles.	
November:	Preached in Perea before returning to Jerusalem for Feast of Dedication.	
A.D. 30		
February:	Jesus ministered in area adjoining northern shores of Dead Sea.	
March:	In Ephraim.	
April:	Arrived in Bethany. Entered Jerusalem. Last Supper. Captured, tried, scourged and crucified upon the bare mound of Golgotha. Finally succumbed some time late in the afternoon—fifteenth day of Nisan (later known as Good Friday, 7 April in the year 30 of Our Lord).	In the daily life of Tiberius and his subjects the most important event in the history of the world passed by all accounts unnoticed.
A.D. 36	Pilate recalled to Rome by Tiberius. Caiaphas deposed on orders from Rome.	
A.D. 37	Caius (Caligula) becomes emperor.	
A.D. 39	Herod Antipas deposed. Agrippa becomes tetrarch of Galilee.	
A.D. 40	Agrippa made king of the Jews. Execution of James, son of Zebedee.	Caligula assassinated. Claudius becomes emperor.
A.D. 44	Agrippa dies.	
A.D. 45	Paul begins his first missionary journey.	
A.D. 49	Jews expelled from Rome. Paul's second missionary journey.	
A.D. 54	Paul arrested in Jerusalem, taken to Rome.	Death of Claudius. Nero becomes emperor.
A.D. 62	Death of James, "brother of the Lord."	
A.D. 64	Death of Paul in Rome. Fire of Rome.	
A.D. 66	Outbreak of Jewish revolt against Rome.	
A.D. 70	Destruction of Jerusalem.	
A.D. 71	Josephus writes The Jewish War.	Triumph of Emperor Titus in Rome.
A.D. 94	Josephus writes Antiquities. Possible date for Mark's Gospel, followed by those of Matthew and Luke.	

BIBLIOGRAPHY

Adam, K. *The Son of God*. New York: Sheed & Ward, 1934.

Akavia, A. A. *Calendar for Good Years: Comparative Calendar of All Chronological Tables from the Creation Until the End of the Sixth Millennium*. Jerusalem: Mossad Harav Kook, 1975.

Albright, W. F. *The Archaeology of Palestine*. London: Penguin Books, 1956.

Allegro, J. *The Dead Sea Scrolls*. London: Penguin Books, 1956.

———. *The Sacred Mushroom and the Cross*. London: Hodder & Stoughton, 1970.

Allen, Richard Hinckley. *Star Names: Their Lore and Meaning*. New York: Dover Publications, 1963.

Amos, S. *The History and Principles of the Civil Law of Rome*. London: Kegan Paul, 1883.

Aron, R. *The Jewish Jesus*. New York: Orbis Books, 1971.

Barclay, William. *Crucified and Crowned*. London: SCM Press, 1961.

———. *Jesus as They Saw Him*. London: SCM Press, 1962.

———. *The Master's Men*. London: SCM Press, 1970.

———. *The Mind of Jesus*. London: SCM Press, 1960.

Bell, H. I., and T. C. Skeat. *Fragments of an Unknown Gospel*. London: British Museum, 1935.

Bishko, Herbert. *This Is Jerusalem*. Tel Aviv: Heritage Publishing, 1971.

Blinzler, J. *The Trial of Jesus*. Translated from the 2nd revised, enlarged edition by McHugh, F. & I. Westminster, Md.: Newman Press, 1959.

Bornkamm, Günther. *Jesus of Nazareth*. London: Hodder & Stoughton, 1973.

Bouguet, A. C. *Everyday Life in New Testament Times*. London: B. T. Batsford, 1954.

Brandon, S. G. F. *The Trial of Jesus of Nazareth*. New York: Scarborough Books, 1979.

———. *Jesus and the Zealots*. Manchester: University Press, 1967.

Bultmann, R. *Jesus and the Word*. New York: Scribner, 1958.

———. *The History of the Synoptic Tradition*. Oxford: University Press, 1963.

Caillois, R. *Pontius Pilate*. New York: Macmillan, 1963.

Cohen, Boaz. *Jewish and Roman Law*. 2 vols. New York: Jewish Theological Seminary, 1966.

———. *Law and Tradition in Judaism*. New York: Ktav Publishing House, 1969.

Cohn, Haim. *The Trial and Death of Jesus.* London: Weidenfeld & Nicolson, 1972.

Craveri, M. *The Life of Jesus.* London: Panther Books, 1969.

Culican, W. *The Medes and Persians.* New York: Frederick A. Praeger, 1965.

Daniel-Rops, Henri. *Daily Life in the Time of Jesus.* London: Weidenfeld & Nicolson, 1962.

Daube, D. *Collaboration with Tyranny in Rabbinic Law.* Oxford: University Press, 1965.

Davies, W. D. *Christian Origins and Judaism.* Philadelphia: Westminster Press, 1962.

———. *The Setting of the Sermon on the Mount.* Cambridge: University Press, 1966.

Derrett, J., and M. Duncan. *Law and Society in Jesus's World.* Berlin/New York: Walter de Gruyter, 1982.

———. *An Oriental Lawyer Looks at the Trial of Jesus and the Doctrine of the Redemption.* London: School of Oriental and African Studies, 1966.

Dodd, C. H. *The Authority of the Bible.* New York: Harper Torchbooks, 1960.

———. *Historical Tradition in the Fourth Gospel.* Cambridge: University Press, 1963.

Douglas, J. D. *The Temple: Its Ministry and Services.* Grand Rapids: Eerdmans, 1958.

Driver, G. R. *The Judean Scrolls.* Oxford: Blackwell, 1965.

Endo, Shusaku. *Silence.* London: Peter Owen, 1976.

Falk, H. *Jesus the Pharisee—A New Look at the Jewishness of Jesus.* New York: Paulist Press, 1985.

Ferguson, John. *Jesus in the Tide of Time: An Historical Study.* London: Routledge & Kegan Paul, 1980.

Flannery, E. H. *The Anguish of the Jews.* New York: Macmillan, 1965.

Flusser, D. *Jesus.* New York: Herder & Herder, 1970.

Foerster, W. *Palestinian Judaism in New Testament Times.* Edinburgh: Oliver & Boyd, 1964.

Fosdick, H. E. *The Man from Nazareth.* London: SCM Press, 1950.

Freyne, S. *The World of the New Testament.* Dublin: Veritas Publications, 1980.

Gibbon, E. *The Decline and Fall of the Roman Empire (1776–88)* (quotations are from Modern Library Edition) London: Penguin Books (n.d.).

Goldstein, M. *Jesus in the Jewish Tradition.* New York: Macmillan, 1950.

Goodspeed, Edgar J. *The Twelve.* Philadelphia: The John C. Winston Co., 1967.

Grant, Michael. *The Jews in the Roman World.* London: Weidenfeld & Nicolson, 1973.

———. *The World of Rome.* New York: The New American Library, 1964.

Graves, R. *King Jesus.* London: Cassell, 1946.

Gross, W. J. *Herod the Great.* Baltimore/Dublin: Helicon Press, 1962.

Guignebert, Ch. *The Jewish World in the Time of Jesus.* London: Kegan Paul, 1939.

Guilding, A. *The Fourth Gospel and Jewish Worship.* Oxford: University Press, 1960.

Guitton, J. *The Problem of Jesus.* New York: P. J. Kenedy, 1955.

Hall, G. Stanley. *Jesus, the Christ, in the Light of Psychology.* Vols. 1 & 2. London: G. Allen & Unwin, 1921.

Harnack, A. von. *The Sayings of Jesus.* New York: Putnam, 1908.

Harvey, A. E. *Jesus and the Constraints of History*. The Bampton Lectures, 1980. London: Duckworth, 1982.

Hengel, M. *The Atonement*. London: SCM Press, 1981.

Herford, R. T. *Christianity in Talmud and Midrash*. London: Williams & Norgate, 1903.

———. *The Pharisees*. Boston: Beacon Press, 1962.

Hirsch, E. G. *The Crucifixion from the Jewish Point of View*. Chicago, 1892.

Hoenig, S. B. *The Great Sanhedrin*. Philadelphia: Dropsie College, 1953.

Hoever, Rev. Hugo. *Lives of the Saints*. New York: Catholic Book Publishing Co., 1967.

Hophan, Otto. *The Apostles*. London: Sands & Co., 1962.

Hunter, W. A. *Introduction to Roman Law*. London: Sweet & Maxwell, 1934.

Husband, R. W. *The Prosecution of Jesus*. Princeton, N.J.: University Press, 1916.

Innes, A. Taylor. *The Trial of Jesus Christ*. Edinburgh: Clark, 1899.

Jacobs, J. *Jesus as Others Saw Him*. Boston: Houghton, 1895.

Jennings, P. *Face to Face with the Turin Shroud*. Oxford: Mowbray, 1978.

Jeremias, Joachim. *Jerusalem in the Time of Jesus*. London: SCM Press, 1969.

Jewish Encyclopedia. 12 vols. New York: Funk & Wagnall, 1901–6.

Jolowicz, H. F. *Historical Introduction to the Study of Roman Law*. Cambridge: University Press, 1952.

Josephus. *The Jewish War*. Translated by G. A. Williamson, Rev. E. Mary Smallwood. Harmondsworth, England: Penguin, 1981.

Jowett, George F. *The Drama of the Lost Disciples*. London: Covenant Publishing, 1970.

Keller, Werner. *The Bible as History: Archaeology Confirms the Book of Books*. London: Hodder & Stoughton, 1956.

Kilpatrick, G. D. *The Trial of Jesus*. Oxford: University Press, 1953.

Klausner, J. *Jesus of Nazareth*. New York: Macmillan, 1925.

Lagerkvist, P. *Barabbas*. London: Chatto & Windus, 1952.

Loewe, H. M. J. *Render Unto Caesar: Religious and Political Loyalty in Palestine*. Cambridge: University Press, 1940.

Maccoby, H. *Revolution in Judea: Jesus and the Jewish Resistance*. London: Ocean Books, 1973.

———. *The Sacred Executioner: Human Sacrifice and the Legacy of Guilt*. London: Thames & Hudson, 1982.

Mackey, James P. *Jesus—the Man and the Myth—A Contemporary Christology*. London: SCM Press, 1979.

Martin, Ernest L. *The Birth of Christ Recalculated*. 2d ed. Pasadena, Calif.: Foundation for Biblical Research, 1980.

McArthur, H. K., ed. *In Search of the Historical Jesus*. London: SPCJ, 1970.

Morison, Frank. *Who Moved the Stone?* London: Faber & Faber, 1930.

Morrison, W. D. *The Jews Under Roman Rule*. New York: Putnam, 1893.

Neil, W. and S. H. Travis. *More Difficult Sayings of Jesus*. London/Oxford: Mowbray, 1981.

Nweeya, Samuel K. *Persia: The Land of the Magi*. 5th ed. Philadelphia: The John C. Winston Co., 1913.

O'Collins, Gerald. *Interpreting Jesus*. London: Geoffrey Chapman, 1983.

Olivier, E. *Mary Magdalen*. Edinburgh: University Press, 1934.

Olmstead, A. T. *Jesus in the Light of History*. New York: Scribner, 1942.

O'Rahilly, A. *The Crucified*. Edited by J. A. Gaughan. Dublin: Kingdom Books, 1985.

Oursler, Fulton. *The Greatest Story Ever Told*. Kingswood: The World's Work, 1949.

Parkes, J. *The Conflict of the Church and Synagogue*. New York: Meridian Books, 1964.

Radin, M. *The Trial of Jesus of Nazareth*. Chicago: University Press, 1931.

Ramsay, William M. *Was Christ Born at Bethlehem?* Minneapolis: James Family Publishing Co., 1978.

Reich, Wilhelm. *The Murder of Christ*. London: Souvenir Press, 1975.

Renan, Ernest. *The Life of Jesus*. New York: Modern Library, 1927.

Richards, H. J. *The Miracles of Jesus: What Really Happened*. London/Oxford: Mowbray, 1983.

Riddle, D. W. *Jesus and the Pharisees*. Chicago: University Press, 1928.

Rivkin, Ellis. *What Crucified Jesus?* Nashville: Abingdon Press, 1984.

Robinson, John A. T. *The Priority of John*. London: SCM Press, 1985.

Roth, C. *The Historical Background of the Dead Sea Scrolls*. Oxford: Blackwell, 1958.

Sandmel, S. *A Jewish Understanding of the New Testament*. Cincinnati: Hebrew Union College, 1957.

Schoen, M. *The Man Jesus Was*. New York: Alfred A. Knopf, 1950.

Schofield, J. N. *The Historical Background of the Bible*. London: Thomas Nelson, 1938.

Schonfield, H. J. *The Passover Plot*. New York: Bantam Books, 1967.

Schürer, Emil. *A History of the Jewish People in the Time of Jesus*. New York: Schocken Books, 1961.

———. *History of the Jewish People in the Age of Jesus Christ*. Revised edition with new material by G. Vermes and F. Millar. Edinburgh: R&R Clark, 1973.

———. *The History of the Jewish People in the Age of Jesus Christ*. Vols. I and II. Revised and edited by G. Vermes. Edinburgh: T&T Clark, 1973–9.

Schweitzer, A. *The Quest for the Historical Jesus*. New York: Macmillan Paperback, 1961.

———. *The Psychiatric Study of Jesus*. Boston: The Beacon Press, 1948.

Sheen, Fulton J. *Life of Christ*. New York: Image Books, 1977.

Sherwin-White, A. N. *Roman Society and Roman Law in the New Testament*. Oxford: Clarendon Press, 1963.

Smith, Asbury. *The Twelve Christ Chose*. New York: Harper & Brothers, 1958.

Sox, H. D. *The Image on the Shroud—Is the Turin Shroud a Forgery?* London: Unwin Paperbacks, 1981.

Strack, H. L. *Introduction to the Talmud and Midrash*. New York: Meridian Books, 1959.

Stevenson, G. H. *Roman Provincial Administration*. Oxford: Blackwell, 1949.

Suetonius. *The Twelve Caesars*. Translated by R. Graves. Harmondsworth, England: Penguin Books, 1957.

Tacitus. *The Annals of Imperial Rome.* Translated by M. Grant. Harmondsworth, England: Penguin Books, 1956.

Taylor, V. *The Life and Ministry of Jesus.* London: Macmillan, 1954.

Thurian, M. Brother of Taize. *Mary, Mother of the Lord, Figure of the Church.* London: Mowbray, 1985.

Toynbee, A. *The Crucible of Christianity.* London: Thames & Hudson, 1969.

Trevor-Roper, Hugh. *Tacitus: The Annals and the Histories.* London: The New English Library, 1966.

Trotter, F. T. *Jesus and the Historian.* Philadelphia: Westminster Press, 1968.

Van Paassen, P. *Why Jesus Died.* New York: Dial Press, 1949.

Vermes, Geza. *Jesus the Jew.* London: SCM Press, 1973.

———. *Jesus the Jew: A Historian's Reading of the Gospels.* London: Collins, 1973.

———. *Jesus and the World of Judaism.* London: SCM Press, 1983.

Vilney, Z. *Legends of Jerusalem: The Sacred Land.* Vol. 1. Philadelphia: The Jewish Publication Society of America, 1973.

———. *Legends of Judea and Samaria: The Sacred Land.* Vol. 2. Philadelphia: The Jewish Publication Society of America, 1975.

———. *Legends of Galilee, Jordan and Sinai: The Sacred Land.* Vol. 3. Philadelphia: The Jewish Publication Society of America, 1978.

Weber, M. *Ancient Judaism.* New York: Free Press, 1952.

Wells, G. A. *The Historical Evidence for Jesus.* New York: Prometheus Books, 1982.

Wight, Fred H. *Manners and Customs of Bible Lands.* Chicago: Moody Press, 1953.

Wilkinson, John. *Jerusalem as Jesus Knew It—Archaeology as Evidence.* London: Thames & Hudson, 1982.

Wilson, I. *The Turin Shroud.* London: Gollancz, 1978.

———. *Jesus: The Evidence.* London: Pan Books, 1985.

Wilson, W. R. *The Execution of Jesus.* New York: Scribners Sons, 1970.

Winter, P. *On the Trial of Jesus.* Berlin: de Gruyter, 1961. Second edition revised and edited by T. A. Burkill and Geza Vermes. New York: Walter de Gruyter, 1974.

Wolff, H. J. *Roman Law: A Historical Introduction.* Oklahoma: University Press, 1951.

Womack, David A. *12 Signs, 12 Sons: Astrology in the Bible.* New York: Harper & Row, 1978.

Zahrnt, H. *The Historical Jesus.* London: Collins, 1963.

Zeitlin, S. *Who Crucified Jesus?* New York: Bloch Publishing, 1947.

Zugibe, F. *The Cross and the Shroud.* New York: Angelus Books, 1982.

THE TRACTATES

Abodah Zarah
Aboth
Arakhin
Baba Bathra
Baba Kamma
Baba Metzia
Bekhoroth
Berakhoth
Betzah (or Yom Tob)
Bikkurim
Demai
Eduyoth
Erubin
Gittin
Hagigah
Hallah
Horayoth
Hullin
Kelim
Kerithoth
Ketuboth
Kiddushin
Kilaim
Kinnim
Maaser Sheni
Maaseroth
Makkoth
Makshirin
Megillah
Meilah
Menahoth
Middoth
Mikwaoth
Moed Katan
Nazir
Negaim
Nedarim
Niddah
Oholoth
Orlah
Parah
Peah
Pesahim
Rosh ha-Shanah
Sanhedrin
Shabbath
Shebiith
Shebuoth
Shekalim
Sotah
Sukkah
Taanith
Tamid
Tebul Yom
Temurah
Terumoth
Tohoroth
Uktzin
Yadaim
Yebamoth
Yoma
Zabim
Zebahim

OTHER GOSPELS AND WRITINGS

(in the order they were originally set down)

The Gospel of the Birth of Mary
The Protevangelion of the Birth of Jesus Christ by James the Less
Thomas' Gospel of the Infancy of Jesus Christ
The Gospel of Nicodemus
The Epistle of Paul the Apostle to the Laodiceans
The Acts of Paul andThecca
The First Epistle of Clement to the Corinthians
The Epistle of Barnabas
The Epistle of Ignatius to the Ephesians
The Epistle of Ignatius to the Magnesians
The Epistle of Ignatius to the Trallians
The Epistle of Ignatius to the Romans
The Epistle of Ignatius to the Philadelphians
The Epistle of Ignatius to the Smyrnaeans
The Epistle of Ignatius to Polycarp
The Epistle of Polycarp to the Philippians
The First Book of Hermas
The Second Book of Hermas
The Third Book of Hermas
Letters of Herod and Pilate
The Gospel According to Peter
The Acts of Andrew
The Gospel of Andrew
The Gospel of Barnabas
The Writings of Bartholomew the Apostle
The Gospel of Bartholomew
The Gospel According to the Egyptians
A Gospel Under the Name of Judas Iscariot
The Gospel of Philip
The Gospel of Thaddaeus
The Gospel of Thomas

Gordon Thomas is a highly successful British investigative journalist and best-selling author of more than forty fiction and nonfiction books. He grew up in Palestine, and after schooling in England he returned to the Middle East as a foreign correspondent. His life experiences in the Holy Land gave birth to his interest in the life of Jesus. Begun as a screenplay over thirty years ago, *The Jesus Conspiracy* is the result of a lifetime of research.